INCIDENTS OF TRAVEL
ON THE ROAD TO SANTIAGO

With the History,

the Myths and Legends, the Monuments,

a New Translation of the Medieval

Pilgrim's Guide to Santiago de Compostela

and Everything Else You Ever Wanted to Know

About This Legendary Pilgrimage Route

Brooklyn, 4 April 2002

To my student Michael
Fricano, Fellow lover of
chess & of Spain.
Best regards,

INCIDENTS OF TRAVEL ON THE ROAD TO SANTIAGO

With the History,
the Myths and Legends, the Monuments,
a New Translation of the Medieval
Pilgrim's Guide to Santiago de Compostela
and Everything Else You Ever Wanted to Know
About This Legendary Pilgrimage Route

Alfonso J. García Osuna

with illustrations by
Manel Lledós

The McGraw-Hill Companies, Inc.

New York   St. Louis   San Francisco   Auckland   Bogotá
Caracas   Lisbon   London   Madrid   Mexico   Milan   Montreal
New Delhi   Paris   San Juan   Singapore   Sydney   Tokyo   Toronto

McGraw-Hill

A Division of *The McGraw-Hill Companies*

Incidents of Travel on the Road to Santiago

1 2 3 4 5 6 7 8 9 0 BKM BKM 9 0 9 8

ISBN 0-07-014354-4

Editor: M. A. Hollander
Printer/Binder: Book-mart Press
Cover photographs by Alfonso J. García Osuna

Perhaps the man who never wanders away from the place of his birth may pass all his life without knowing ghosts; but the nomad is more than likely to make their acquaintance. I refer to the civilized nomad, whose wanderings are not prompted by hope of gain, nor determined by pleasure, but simply controlled by certain necessities of his being, - the man whose inner secret nature is totally at variance with the stable conditions of a society to which he belongs only by accident.

Lafcadio Hearn, 1889.

Preface

Seen from the summits of the Pyrenees in the prodigious Spanish sunset, the trail we call the Road to Santiago is a little white line, winding its way through the green Navarran countryside like an unassuming byway that was forgotten long ago, an insignificant artery in a larger-than-life environment of lofty mountains and majestic forests.

Perhaps the image of the Road to Santiago as an artery is the most appropriate, for that small path was for many centuries Spain's "Main Street," the route taken by the many thousands from every corner of Europe who traveled its length, hoping to reach Santiago de Compostela in faraway Galicia. With them came their customs, traditions, technology and beliefs, all of which enriched and strengthened Spain at the time when it most needed it, when it stood alone in defiance of the great Moslem onslaught that once threatened to overtake Europe. These pilgrims were the lifeblood, the Road to Santiago the artery through which it flowed to that vibrant and prismatic body we call Spain.

Over a thousand years separate us from the era which saw the first pilgrims to Santiago blaze the trail westward towards one of the holiest shrines in Christendom. Over this period the resources of mankind have changed beyond all imagining, affording us the subjection of our environment and creating completely new conditions of life on this planet. And yet in spite of the changes to the face of the world over the centuries, we still build bridges toward that past, mythical Santiago which is at once so remote and so near, so alien and so familiar. Perhaps because some of us perceive our existence as somewhat prosaic, we strive to give it a meaningful image in the pattern of history and gratefully subscribe to the tokens left us by those courageous and venturesome early pilgrims; contemplating their feat with admiration, we labor to emulate them so that we may return to our routines moved and enriched by the experience.

This road that carried countless generations of pilgrims and travelers west -from the Pyrenees to the Atlantic- became a relic of calmer, slower times with the advent of the modern, technologically advanced society. When a national highway first took people speedily from Navarra to Galicia in a matter of hours, something precious was lost to all of us: the romance and serendipity of traveling on a rugged trail and of sharing the adventure with the thousands of souls that came before us. How can we even dream of those early times of risk and effort if we're traveling at 120 kilometers per hour, looking at the sights through a windshield while listening to some favorite rock group on the radio?

For me, my companions, and the many other wanderers whose imaginations are held captive by the lure of ancient paths and time-worn traditions, the Road to Santiago de Compostela is as alluring as it was to that first dauntless fellow who trekked to the Apostle's shrine in Galicia many centuries ago. The ribbon of dirt and stones that since prehistoric times bonded Spain with the rest of Europe will always live on in our dreams of a time when travel was an adventure, when arriving was not the only experience of a journey, when evenings on the trail were lit by a campfire and serenaded by the melancholy songs of the night creatures, and when every step you took was punctuated by the exhilarating uncertainty of what lay up ahead.

I first traveled this legendary Road in the 1960's when, as a child, I was steeped in its history and its traditions in the classrooms of a Spanish school. This first, imaginary trip filled me with longing for the real thing, and in my mind's eye I pictured every village, every mountain and every river crossing. Coming at last to the Road of Stars more than 30 years later I feel as though I've returned to the embrace of my first love, to a place where many of my youthful dreams were forged, to a time in my existence when I could only think of life as being forever and everything and anything was possible.

Yet the real Road had some surprises for which my imaginary travels had not prepared me. Most of them came on the first day when, rolling out of Roncesvalles with our credentials safely stowed away in our saddlebags and feeling for all the world like a million bucks, we noticed that the temperature was hovering around 50 degrees F

(Fahrenheit) and a chilly drizzle seemed to penetrate to our bones. I had not been so uncomfortable in my imagined journeys. The first uphill climb had us down for the count and taking pulses to measure heart rates. The mountains, in their anonymous majesty, were completely oblivious to our feeble human designs to cross them. But we gradually became aware that overcoming setbacks and our own weakness was what would make the journey memorable, worthwhile, and would ultimately make our arrival an achievement.

It was also on that first day, with the wet wind blowing and the trees swaying to its capricious rhythms, that I began to think about the local people that from time to time would cross our path carrying agricultural tools or leading a herd of sheep: for these gritty people, surely, there isn't much romance here. This is a road of survival, a tough, lonesome, wind-blown and humid environment that charges in sweat and tears for every loaf of bread a farmer puts on the family table. Perhaps what was important in my childhood wanderings was not the Road itself but the idea and the poetry of the journey: it was my route of escape, the road where a little boy growing up in Franco's Spain could travel in search of the knights and heroes that shaped his race's history. For this reason, this ancient road that for centuries was "Spain's Main Street" lingers in the imagination as the symbol of my enduring love affair with the country of my forebears, people not unlike those crossing my path on the Road to Santiago.

It follows that when asked the reason why I decided to make the pilgrimage to Santiago, I invariably answer that it is for the same reason that I return to Spain as often as I can. I am drawn to the place as by some mysterious cosmic strings which operate beyond my power to resist them. Perhaps the best answer can be offered by paraphrasing what Nathaniel Hawthorne said about his native Salem, turning it to fit my own situation: And yet, though invariably happiest elsewhere, there is within me a feeling for Spain, which, in the lack of a better phrase, I must be content to call affection. The sentiment is probably assignable to the deep and aged roots which my family has struck into the soil of Spain. There, countless generations of my people have been born and died, and have mingled their earthly substance with the soil, until no small portion of it must necessarily be akin to the mortal frame with which I walk the streets. In part, therefore, the attachment which I speak of is the mere sensuous sympathy of dust for dust.

ह**ल** The idea of making the actual pilgrimage to Santiago was reborn in the 1970's while I was still an undergraduate at Queens College, in New York. There, amid one of the many long discussions I had with my good friend Rodolfo González, I proposed making the journey on horseback. Although Rodolfo usually signs on immediately to my most harebrained projects, most of the time he brings in an element of common sense that makes them practicable: rather than depending on horses to get us across northern Spain, bicycles might prove less costly and by far less demanding of time and care. So it was that more than twenty years later we bought the bikes, studied the maps and set off on the journey, joined by a third traveler, Silvio Corona, an old friend and accomplished handyman who can fix a bicycle with one hand tied behind his back.

One of the most difficult elements of making a journey like this has little to do with the actual trip: we would be gone for the greater part of a month, lost to the world and virtually unreachable by the families we left behind. We assured everyone that we would be calling home as much as possible, that at no point would we be more than twenty-four hours away from them in case of an emergency. Besides which, the women we left back home are more than capable of handling any situation in our absence.

ह**ल** This book is based on the diary of my journey to Compostela. Looking back over the annotations contained therein for the purpose of writing it has been a sobering as well as instructive experience. I see now, in retrospective, that certain words or phrases that struck me -sitting perhaps under a tree at a high mountain pass- as beautiful or apt, I find nearly incomprehensible or out of place, while others seem excessive or over-rhetorical. Yet I hesitate to prune, amend or rewrite, even where it would certainly prove profitable to the clear understanding of the text, for what is in these pages is an unadulterated reflection of what I was feeling and experiencing during my sixteen-day journey to Santiago. Obviously, I often wrote in an altered state: I was at times tired, frustrated or upset; at others I was ecstatic. All this shows in what I wrote down on paper. Reading over the diary, I have been pleased to discover that I have managed to register through my particular sensibility what it's like to travel on the Road to Santiago. I hasten to add, however, that the two friends with whom I made the trip do not regard me as their appointed mouthpiece, but rather, I suspect, as a presumptuous apostle to the gentiles. They too have their story to tell.

    ह   Realizing that the Road to Santiago is not very well known among the English-speaking public, I have broken down the text into

separate sections, the first of which gives a brief history of the Road; the second gives an idea of how people have lived for many centuries along the Road; the third is the diary of our journey: the incidents of travel followed by a detailed explanation of the route, the monuments, historical events, in short, everything that is to be seen and experienced at every turn; next comes a translation of the medieval *Pilgrim's Guide to Santiago de Compostela*, a very telling and interesting text composed by early enthusiasts of the Road; and the last section is a glossary that gives a terminology of architectural words that are used in my description of the monuments along the Road. This should give the reader a more complete feel for the adventure.

ਟ੍ਰ   I should like to express my deepest appreciation to the people that made the trip and the book possible. Encarna and Alfonso, my parents, always supportive and encouraging; my children Elvira and Xavier, ultimate destination of all my journeys; Ángela my wife; Raúl my brother; and Rodolfo González and Silvio Corona, my traveling companions. I am also grateful to my colleagues at Kingsborough, professors Julio Hernández-Miyares, Ronald Schwartz, Frantz Leconte, Gloria Pollack, Eduardo Lolo, Joyce Miller and Liliana Soto-Fernández for their interest and help. I should also like to thank my colleague and friend Manel Lledós, who graced the pages of the book with his talented artistic drawings of medieval scenes.

With these people in my life, I never travel alone.

CONTENTS

APPENDIX II

APPENDIX III

I. A Brief History of the Road to Santiago.

A. Why the Road to Santiago?

Since neolithic times, Celtic klans and tribes from central Europe had been going to ancient Galicia, in northwestern Spain, on a pilgrimage that followed the road illuminated by the Milky Way, which pointed the East-West direction perfectly. Ancient stone monuments, strewn all over northern Spain, point to the fact that the Celts came to this, the end of the known world, where the sun sets over the wide expanses of the Atlantic, in order to help the souls of their dead on their way to the nether regions, believed to be somewhere near the place where the sun also dies each day. The culture associated with the traditions of that pre-historical pilgrimage may have remained latent in western European peoples, for that same Road of Stars was revived under the new banner of militant Christianity in the ninth century, with the "discovery" of Santiago's tomb in Galicia. Even the mysterious floral motif that recurs in medieval churches all along the Road may not be a flower at all, but an ancient sun-symbol of Celtic origin which, incorporated into the symbolic repertoire of the Jacobean pilgrimage, reminds us of the importance of the route long before Christ was born.

Thus, for over a thousand years, the image of the pilgrim crossing all of northern Spain on his way to Santiago has been a part of the landscape. During that time, a whole culture has grown up around the Road, with its legends, stories, anecdotes, etc., the physical evidence of which is apparent throughout the monasteries, churches, refuges and cathedrals you find there.

What force urges these people on through high mountain passes where the cold wind howls in the tree tops, through the unbearable heat of the high steppes, through the physical pain and mental anguish? If you asked a thousand pilgrims, chances are you would get a thousand different answers. Some go it alone, staring straight ahead as if with eyes fixed on a target. Others go in groups, keeping each other company through the trials and tribulations of the trip. Some go on foot, some on a bike, some even ride a horse. In those ten centuries, reality and myth have intermingled to form a rich, tangled web that traps the pilgrim's imagination and endows the Road with a larger-than-life spiritual environment. On it, we tread through mythical space.

It would be impractical and meaningless to attempt to separate myth from reality here, for the Road to Santiago offers real-life historical characters and events which are more incredible and improbable than any myth: one of these characters is the Leonese knight Suero de Quiñones, who, beginning on 10 July 1434 and for a whole month challenged and defeated a large number of contenders, on a bridge on the Road to Santiago, for the love of a beautiful lady.

This is the stuff the Road is made of: it is physical, with rocks, steep climbs, heat and cold, but also spiritual, emotional, historical and mythical. Any one of the rocks you step on might have also been tread upon by Suero de Quiñones or, for that matter, by any other of the myriad of improbable characters that have given this trail its very special place in history and in the hearts of wanderers and dreamers.

Because this Road was made by them.

B. Origins

Who was this man, Santiago, that has become the object of such adoration, whose tomb has been the goal of millions of pilgrims for over one thousand years?

Historical Santiago, the first Apostle to die for the Christian faith, was Jacob, James, Jaime, Diego or Yago, as he has been known in different lands. James the Elder, as he is known in the Bible, was the son of Zebedee and Mary Salome and was born on the shores of Lake Genesaret, his father being a fisherman there. He and his brother John were among the favorite disciples of Jesus, Simon Peter being the third. James was also one of the witnesses to Christ's Transfiguration and His Agony in the Garden of Olives in Getsemani. He was well known for his short fuse and hot temper, conditions which earned him the name "Boanerges," or "Son of Thunder."

As anyone familiar with the legend will tell you, at the death of Jesus on the Cross, Saint Peter asked James to go preach the Word of God to the ends of the earth, which in those times meant Spain, Finisterrae, the westernmost piece of land known to mankind. Crossing the Mediterranean, he disembarked in Cartagena, where he began his preaching. After stints at Granada, Jaén, Córdoba, Mérida, Braga and other places where he would leave behind small groups of new Christians, he eventually reached Galicia, in the extreme northwest of Spain. There, he spent much time with the locals, spreading the Word and attracting disciples. When he left Galicia he did not leave alone: several young Galicians left with him to help with the work of converting their fellow Spaniards.

Frustrated by the fun-loving Spaniards, set in their ways with their pagan festivals and indulgence in wine, James became desperate. Near Zaragoza it is said the Virgin appeared to him on a pillar, urged him to go on with his work, and requested he build a church in her name on that very spot. This is the origin of the Cathedral of El Pilar in Zaragoza and the reason so many Spanish girls bear the name "Pilar". This is also the first church in the world to be consecrated by one of the twelve Apostles.

When his work was finished in Zaragoza, he continued on to Tarragona, where he embarked to go back home to Palestine. After arriving there he must have rubbed its Roman governor the wrong way, for in 42 A.D. Herod Agripa had him beheaded and had his body thrown outside the city gates, there to be eaten by wild animals.

Tradition has it that his Galician disciples picked up the body under the cover of night and transported it to the port of Haifa, where a stone boat, without rudder, sails or crew was waiting to take them all back to Galicia. It was a very fast trip, during which even the Virgin stood on the stern in order to guide the improvised vessel out of harm's way. In a little hamlet in western Galicia, the locals will eagerly show you a large rock with two indentations on it which they claim is the part of the boat where the Virgin actually stood: there are her footprints to prove it.

The boat came into a fjord called Ría Flavia and sailed up it until it reached the river Sar. Upstream they finally made landfall at Iria Flavia, where they disembarked James's body. Lo and behold, after laying it on a large stone, it gave way, melting around the body and making a perfect sarcophagus. Thus weighed down by their ever-heavier master, the disciples headed east hoping to find one of the small communities of Christians that James had left behind, product of his preaching.

But their luck did not hold out, for they walked straight into the lands of a powerful woman the locals called "Queen Lupa", a no-nonsense strongwoman in the area who kept a tight control over her subjects. When James's disciples showed up at her doorstep requesting a suitable place to bury their master, Lupa smelled trouble and immediately set out to throw a wrench in their plans. "Go to my subject, up in that castle" -she told them- "he will help you." The subject in question was named Filotro, probably the Roman authority in the region. On her orders, when they arrived at Filotro's they were thrown into the darkest, dampest dungeon available. An angel intervened and opened their cell at night, but their escape was soon noticed and armed knights were sent in pursuit. But upon crossing a bridge, it miraculously gave way, sending the knights to their doom.

Again at Queen Lupa's doorstep, she must have marveled at the unlikely set of circumstances that allowed these fellows to survive their ordeal unscathed. Unimpressed, she again sent the unsuspecting bunch on a wild goose chase: "To make it easier to move your master, go to a field beyond those hills" -she said- "and harness my oxen, which you will find there." The supposed oxen were actually wild bulls, accomplished killers that should have done away with Lupa's unwanted guests. Yet what actually happened took everyone completely by surprise: the young men had harnessed the bulls and were quietly leading them back to Lupa's, this after having slain a dragon in their spare time by making the sign of the Cross.

Putting their master's heavy body on a cart, it was pulled by the bulls to a place where they stopped and refused to go any further. This place was Compostela, the Field of Stars. Lupa, witness to such portents, decided to repent all her sins and, mending her ways, spent the rest of her life doing God's work.

James was buried on that spot, which at first became known as "Liberum Donum," the Latin for "Free Gift." With time the place came to be known as Sant'Yago, Saint Jacob as Galician pronunciation would have it. James's disciples were granted the land on which to build a suitable sepulcher for their master by queen Lupa, who also bankrolled the building of a chapel to house it in (it was a gift, therefore the name "Liberum Donum"). Two disciples cared for the chapel, Atanasio and Teodoro, and they were buried right there with their master when they died. The chapel was frequented by groups of faithful Christians up to the year 257, when Roman emperor Vespesian prohibited the reunions that used to take place there. The site was eventually forgotten and the dust of centuries settled over it. Over centuries a succession of people like the Sueves, Vandals, Arrian Visigoths and Moors persecuted the Christians, contributing thus to that historical dust that ultimately buried Santiago. So much for the legend, but how much truth is it based on?

The first historical documents that talk of Saint James as having preached in Spain are from the seventh century: these are Saint Isidore's *De ortu et obitu Patrum*, and the Visigothic religious text *Libro de los Oficios*. Nothing older than that has been found. Furthermore, the first document that mentions the transport of Saint James's body from Palestine to Spain is from the twelfth century, and only in the thirteenth century does one come across any mention of the appearance of the Virgin Mary to James in Zaragoza. So the "production" of the legend is recent, relatively speaking.

It appears, then, that the cult of Saint James in Galicia is a Christianization of an earlier pagan cult, possibly the Jupiter cult that was so popular among the Romans. This theory is based on a number of interesting finds, among them a stone tablet that is dedicated to that god, unearthed right where James's body was supposedly found in 813 A.D.

Having said this, I must now add that the fundamental arguments against the legend's historicity can easily be refuted. The first of these is based on the fact that Apolonius, a second century writer, says that the martyr Trasea preached that Jesus ordered the Apostles not to leave Jerusalem until twelve years had passed after His death. Remembering that Jesus died in 33 A.D., that would mean that the Apostles didn't go forth until 45 A.D. at the earliest. James was decapitated in 42 A.D., making it improbable that he ever left Jerusalem. But since the chronology of Jesus's life is tenuous at best and was not set until the sixth century, this argument is inherently weak.

The second argument rests on Saint Paul's *Letter to the Romans*, written from Corinth around February of the year 58 A.D. In that document he states that he has "gone to preach where Christ's name was not uttered." If Paul preached in Spain and states that Christ's Name was not uttered (i.e. unknown) there, this must mean -the argument goes- that James had not been there before. But it is historically accepted that Paul preached in Spain between the years 64 and 66 A.D., years after writing the famous *Letter*, making it entirely possible that by "where Christ's Name was not uttered" he did not mean Spain, since he had not gone there yet.

The third argument is based on the fact that no document exists before the seventh century that even mentions James's coming to Spain, an event of such import that written testimony of it should be extant. But we must remember that countless documents from that era have been lost, and that among them might be one that documented James's legendary voyage.

The truth of the matter is that early in the ninth century a group of devout Christians thought they had discovered the remains of the Apostle James in a remote area of Galicia. How it was that they decided that the bones they had dug up in that mysterious place were that of one of Christ's favorite followers can only be the subject of speculation. Perhaps a partial or faulty reading of unearthed stone tablets that mentioned Jupiter, the ancient "god of thunder," made them think that here was the final resting place of James, "Boanerges," the "Son of Thunder." If so, this was the most fortunate mistake in the history of Spain.

C. Santiago: Legends, Important Events and the "Reconquest" of Spain.

The beginning of the IX Century was a trying time for Spanish Christians. Ever since the battle of Guadalete, in the year 711 A.D., the armies of Islam had overrun most of Spain; the Moslems then built a great civilization centered around cities like Córdoba, Seville and Granada. The small Christian kingdom of Asturias, nestled in the mountains of the north, managed to hold out and even beat back the Islamic onslaught, beginning what is called the "Reconquest" of Spain. But it needed an ideal around which to gather the disparate and antagonistic peoples of the north against the Moslems. Northern Spaniards were an independent-minded, freedom-loving bunch who did not care to be held under the yoke of any king. Once the Moslem threat was gone from their back yard, they did not see a reason to keep fighting for the very abstract project of a free, united, Christian Spain. Spain, to these simple mountain folk, was not a nation in the strict sense of the word, but a geographic entity in which their particular village, town or region happened to be located. This is where Santiago comes in.

The myth of Santiago is very closely tied to the building of Spain as a nation, for it provided the ideal and the rallying point around which all Spaniards could gather; the battle cry "Santiago!" could be used by all Spanish warriors in their struggle against the "infidels" and their "Allah". The myth united and gave direction to a previously disunited and contentious people. But how was the myth born?

Legend has it that, in the year 813 A.D., a strange rumor began circulating among the people of the Sar river basin, in Galicia. Apparently many had witnessed lights in the sky, accompanied by melodious chants. The lights seemed to be shooting stars that fell into a wooded area next to the little church of San Fiz de Solobio, and among these was one star, larger than the rest, that seemed to hover, pointing to a specific spot.

Having heard the rumors, a hermit named Pelayo went to the site personally to check out the story. After observing the phenomena for himself, he soon made the connection between the lights and the old legend of Saint James. He immediately contacted a higher authority, Teodomiro, bishop of Iria. Teodomiro himself was witness to the strange occurrences and had the area cleared of trees, expecting to find an answer to the spooky happenings. And an answer he found, for in the cleared forest there appeared the ruins of an ancient and long-forgotten building, and within it an object that would change Spain forever: a tomb. Remembering the ancient legend of Christ's Apostle who came to Galicia, Teodomiro immediately declared that this was the spot where Saint James had been buried.

A delegation was sent to Cangas de Onís, then the capital of Asturias, to inform the king of the portents and the discovery that they had brought about. Alfonso II (The Chaste) at once saw the importance of what was happening in Galicia and went there himself, along with all his court, to pay homage to the Apostle. Upon seeing the ancient ruins, he became even more convinced that this was, in fact, Saint James's final resting place, so he ordered a basilica built on the site, one that would do justice to such an important place and would also accommodate the pilgrims that were beginning to come there.

A city, Santiago de Compostela, soon began growing where the forest had been. The pace of its development was extremely fast, by medieval standards, with convents, palaces, inns and stores springing up everywhere. More and more pilgrims started to make the trip to the sacred sepulcher of the Apostle, and in a short time Santiago came to rival Rome as one of Christianity's most important places.

Money flowed in Santiago, it was a vibrant and prosperous city of busy shops and inns. A new basilica was built at the end of the IX Century where the old one had been, and everywhere the fruits of prosperity were flaunted by its proud citizens; the downside to this was the considerable number of raids to which it was subjected by Normans and Moors, hoping to take a piece of the action. Yet no armed incursion, including that of the great Moorish leader Almanzor in 997, could destroy the spirit of the city, which built itself up from its ashes like an indestructible Phoenix.

Almanzor's raid is also the object of another legend. Having taken the city and burned it, Almanzor's warriors did not profane or otherwise disturb the Apostle's remains. A number of reasons might be offered to explain this fact: the priests, faced with the imminent fall of the city, might have hidden the remains in a safe place, or Almanzor himself, known to be superstitious, might have given the order not to disturb the remains, lest a terrible fate befall him. But popular tradition has it that, when Almanzor entered the basilica at the head of his warriors, he found an old priest defending the sepulcher with a little knife in his hand. As the rough and weathered soldiers surrounded the old fellow, they found that he would not budge, holding his ground courageously and with great resolve. Almanzor was so impressed by him, that he ordered his troops to withdraw from the place and not harm the valiant priest.

But fate would catch up with Almanzor anyway, as he was soundly defeated by Christian armies shortly after the Santiago raid, dying in relative obscurity a couple of years later.

Meanwhile, Santiago rose from the ashes, its streets full of people from all over Europe and beyond, its inns filled with the sounds of dozens of languages, its squares a mingle of cultures and customs. The significance of this for medieval Spain cannot be over stressed.

This prosperity and importance was recognized by both religious and political leaders: king Alfonso VI walled the city, while bishop Diego Peláez began the construction of a new church to house Saint James's remains. But bishop Gelmírez was the person who gave the city its definitive impulse, in the early XII Century, ordering the construction of many public and private buildings and refurbishing the basilica - now cathedral - of Santiago.

Santiago's importance quickly spread outside of Spain. William the Conqueror, for example, rode into the Battle of Hastings, in 1066, on a horse brought to him from Spain by a knight who had been a pilgrim to Santiago. Henry I of England founded the Abbey of Reading to house a relic of the hand of Saint James, brought over from Germany by his daughter Matilda. He conceded to the Abbey the privilege of placing Santiago shells on its coat of arms. How James's supposed hand got to Germany is still a mystery, but Matilda herself seems to have been a pilgrim to Santiago in 1125. Back in Spain, the famous El Cid may have worn the symbol of Santiago: one of the oldest paintings of that forger of Spanish nationhood show him wearing a shell on his girdle.

The city of Santiago also became a magnet of sorts when it came to depositing stolen relics in worthy places. In the Middle Ages, pieces of the bodies of saints, - relics - were much esteemed, and as such were the object of what is called the *furta sacra*, the theft of relics. Among the relics obtained by Santiago in that way, those of Saint Susana are worthy of mention. The *Historia Compostelana*, written in the early twelfth century, at the time of Gelmírez, describes how Mauricio, Archbishop of Braga, secretly took from a church in Jerusalem the head of Saint James the Less, fist Archbishop of that city, and brought it to Carrión de los Condes, where he presented it to Queen Urraca. She in turn gave it to Gelmírez, to be deposited in the cathedral of Compostela.

The might and power of this city rubbed off on its inhabitants. Book I, chapter 23 of the same *Historia Compostelana* states that in 1105 the citizens of Santiago were given a new charter in which all residents of the city were declared free men under the bishop of Santiago. Furthermore, they did not have to pay the inheritance tax, did not have to pay fines when they did not answer the call to military service, and were exempt from dowry and marriage annulment taxes. They were also exempt from the lord's exclusive right to stamp and seal documents and from military service, unless posted within a day's walk from Santiago. They were also authorized to pursue criminals and were exempt from answering for crimes committed in the city. They were, in effect, subject only to God, Saint James, and the clergy.

But every move in the way of granting freedoms to the residents of Santiago encouraged them to press for more and more. Being subject to a resident clergy actually decreased their opportunities for self-government, and many felt that being governed by a distant king would give them more opportunities to develop their enterprises; the clerics were too close at hand and too conservative in their economic and political philosophies. So, at the time of its greatest flourishing, Santiago was the stage for a number of tragic confrontations between its citizens and the clergy. The bloodiest occurred in 1117, when the city violently challenged the authority, not only of bishop Gelmírez, but of queen Urraca herself. During the uprising, the cathedral - as well as many other public buildings - was burned and the Bishop, trapped in his also blazing tower, managed to escape dressed as a regular citizen (some say as a woman). The queen was not so lucky. Having been left behind in the tower by the fleeing Gelmírez, she was arrested while trying to escape, was beaten and unclothed, but was finally left in a puddle of mud, as the citizens' rage was mainly directed at the clergy and not the monarchy. Gelmírez's ultimate escape is the stuff of secret-agent movies. Hiding in the church of Santa María, he was able to fool his pursuers into thinking he was not there, hiding under the main altar. There, he was joined by the Queen, who had been told by an informant that the Bishop was in hiding at that church. Climbing roofs and garden walls he was able to reach the house of a friend, Maurino, where he hid under tables and behind curtains, again dodging the rage of the bloodthirsty mob who ransacked the dwelling. Having heard that the mob was wise to the whereabouts of the Bishop and was returning, Gelmírez fled through a hole made in the wall of the house, which led him to the next-door house, and from there through another hole to the next, and so on until he reached the house of one Froilán Rosende, whose wife began screaming, thinking robbers were breaking in through the wall. Upon the arrival of Froilán, the master of the house, the Bishop was hidden in a dark basement storeroom, while two Frenchmen, friends of the Bishop, prepared fast horses for his escape. Not being able to make good his escape from Froilán's, he again dressed as a common man, walked through the mob, climbed walls, and crawled over roof-tiles until he reached the dormitory of the cathedral canons, where he rested until he was able to move again, this time to the house of Cardinal Pedro Gudesíndez. After resting there, the Bishop left in the middle of the night accompanied by two of the Cardinal's men. After a couple of close calls, they reached the outskirts of the city, where they joined the army of King Alfonso, Urraca's son, which was already besieging the city. The rampaging citizens, faced with the prospect of doing battle against the formidable army of the King, surrendered.

A city with so much history had to be endowed with the noblest of legends to go with it. One of the most powerful has to do with Charlemagne, King of the Franks. History tells us how, spurred on by the Caliph of Damascus, Charlemagne crossed into Spain in 777 A.D. at the head of a large army on a punitive expedition against the Moors of Spain, who had recently declared their independence from Damascus. He also hoped to gain from the fabulous wealth Moslem Spain was known for. But everything went wrong: unable to take Zaragoza, his main objective, he retreated through Navarra, sacking the town of Pamplona on his way. This irked the Navarrans, who attacked and wiped out his rearguard, killing Charlemagne's nephew Roland and the flower of French knighthood at the battle of Roncesvalles. The fact that all of this happened decades before Santiago's tomb was ever "discovered" did not prevent a legend from growing around Charlemagne; according to it, the French king saw a vision of Saint James urging him to come to Spain and clear the land of the infidel Moslems. If he followed the road lighted by the Milky Way, he would eventually reach the place where his body lay. Legend has it that he fought his way clear through to Galicia and, once there, endowed Santiago with the great riches he had come by through all his military campaigns.

In the sixteenth century Santiago was the object of an aborted raid by the pirate Drake which caused the loss of the Apostle's remains. Drake had disembarked English troops at La Coruña with the intention of sacking the Apostle's city. To safeguard the Apostle's remains, archbishop Juan de Sanclemente ordered them hidden. Lost, and for centuries supposed to be under the High Altar, they were eventually found in 1879 when cardinal Payá y Rico and canon López Ferreiro rediscovered the relics under a part of the pavement marked by a Cross. In 1884 pope Leon XIII, through a Papal Bull, declared that the remains that were found 5 years before by the two clerics were those of Saint James.

But the vast majority of pilgrimages were not as glamorous or as epic as Charlemagne's, or even Drake's. Northern Spain was essentially a battleground where Spanish Christians and Spanish Moslems fought each other in order to impose their particular world-view on the people of the country. Roads were either bad or non-existent, and in places where there was one, pilgrims often avoided it for fear of highwaymen and Moslem raids. With time, the myriad of trails which they blazed became consolidated and, with the Christian advance and the subsiding Moslem threat, became formalized into a definite network of roads, of which the so-called "French Road," crossing through Pamplona, Burgos and León, became the most important.

D. The Road Network and the Trip.

Upon the consolidation and formalization of the network of roads pilgrims used to get to Santiago, names were given to the different routes. Recognizing the social, cultural and economic significance of having thousands of people come through the Road every year, the Christian kingdoms of northern Spain, Navarra, Aragón and Castile-León, undertook a program of construction of bridges and refuges in an effort to create a suitable infrastructure that would ensure a relatively safe trip for the pilgrims. To this end, the order of the Knights of Santiago was created in the twelfth century; it was essentially a contingent of rough-and-ready warriors that policed the Road, but which at times were known to fight each other for preeminence. The Knights Templar also policed the Road up to 1312, when their order was disbanded.

If one is to point to a specific period in which the Road became consolidated, one would have to look on the eleventh century as that period. Beginning in 1071, for example, the monks of the French monastery of Cluny were invited to Spain in order to man the refuges and hospitals that were being built along the Road. The Cluny monks did this and also occupied the monasteries, such that by the end of the eleventh century every bishop in Spain was of the Cluny Order. Yet what is most important about the predominance of Cluny in Spain is the fact that the Order was a major Europeanizing influence. It was one of the major factors in establishing the Romanesque style of architecture in Spain, as well as the Gregorian chant. Furthermore, the Order's libraries were the best in the land and its priests were avid copiers; more reasons to think of Cluny as a major player in directing the cultural destiny of the Hispanic nation.

Construction of Road-based buildings also flourished in this century, with the Romanesque San Antolín Chapel in Palencia (1034), Santa María Church in Nájera (1052), San Salvador in Leire (1057), San Isidoro in León (1063), Santa María in Frómista (1066), the old hub in Santiago (1076) and the Jaca Cathedral (1077). Bridge construction was also at an all-time high along the Road during the XI Century: between 1076 and 1085 bridges were built at Logroño, Santo Domingo de la Calzada, Ponferrada, Puente la Reina and many other places. From this period we also find hospitals and inns, like that of Santo Domingo de la Calzada, the two at Burgos (San Juan and Emperador), Sahagún and Villafranca del Bierzo, all of them built at around the year 1085, the busiest year for construction on the Road.

It was also around this time (1095) that ecclesiastical authorities, recognizing the importance of the Road and of the cult of Saint James, decide to transfer the Bishops of Iria to Santiago.

By this time, four major routes to Santiago had been consolidated, named for the most important cities they traversed: Arles, crossing the Pyrenees at Somport; Le Puy; Vézelay and Tours, this last one being the westernmost, crossing into Spain at Valcarlos and heading south towards Pamplona and Puente la Reina, where it joined the other two routes and they all consolidated into one.

In order to direct the pilgrims on the Road, what is perhaps the first tourist guide in history was written: Book V of the *Codex Calixtinus*. This document, called the *Pilgrim's Guide to Santiago de Compostela*, gives a detailed explanation of the places which the traveler would see, the things needed for the trip, and it even gave some words in Euskera, the language of the Basques of northeastern Spain. Besides tips on how to avoid highwaymen, tricksters and unscrupulous businessmen on the Road, it gave a working idea of the culinary merits of the places through which the pilgrim would travel, the drinkability of the water, and the number of days in which to divide the trip, although some of the information, probably based on hearsay, is quite flawed. Its author/compiler, Aymeri Picaud, was a monk from Poitou who was the treasurer of the Santiago Cathedral in the twelfth century. His *Guide*, a translation of which I include in this book, gives a good idea of the mind-set of the era and the general *ambiance* of the Road, as traversed by pilgrims many centuries ago.

Although the main artery of the Road is the so-called "French Road," which leads from Roncesvalles to Pamplona, Logroño, Burgos, León and from there to Santiago, many other routes were taken by travelers to get to the Apostle's tomb. One of these was the Northern French Road, which entered Spain through San Juan de Luz and advanced through Fuenterrabía, San Sebastián, Bilbao, Santander, Ribadesella, Ribadeo, La Coruña and from there to Santiago. This route is thought by some to be the most ancient, being that it hugs the coastline and is the northernmost possible land route; as such it was the safest, being the farthest from the Moslem threat to the south.

The "Silver Road", starting at Seville and coming north through Mérida, Cáceres, Salamanca, Zamora, Orense and from there to Santiago, was used by Christians who lived under Moslem control in southern Spain.

Yet other routes began in Coimbra ("Portuguese Road"), Valencia, Barcelona and Tarragona, while many have been known to make the trip by sea, especially from Great Britain and Scandinavia.

Most of these routes could not be used year-round, as the high mountain passes were snowed-in for long periods of time during the winter, and the harsh conditions on the wind-swept high plains of Castile could make even the hardiest of pilgrims stop in his tracks. This is why pilgrims to Santiago usually left their homes in France, Germany, Italy or any other country at the first signs of spring; this would give them a good chance of getting back by September or October, in time to pick their crops and take them to market. If a group of pilgrims set out from a village, the townspeople would usually give them a send-off celebration, with food, wine and the expected blessing from the local priest. From the larger cities the pilgrims would assemble at a specific place, like Saint-Jacques Street in Paris, where they would be blessed and be given a send-off. They would then enter the special realm reserved for those with a higher calling: they were no longer the weaver, the farmer, the storekeeper or the candle-maker, they were now pilgrims, setting out on a spiritual journey that would take them to sacred ground at Compostela, the Field of Stars.

For people in medieval times, the Road was a ticket to a whole new world of cultures, languages and ways of looking at the universe. In their normal, day-to-day existence, they had a very limited exposure to new ideas, and the monotony of their lives was hardly ever broken. The Road, then, was the highpoint of many a life in the Middle Ages, an adventure many a grandfather would recount to his admiring grandchildren next to a warm fire on a cold winter night. When thus retelling a story, an elderly Scandinavian might recall the stretch of Road where he met up with a Lithuanian weaver, a Sicilian farmer, an Irish priest, an Ethiopian mule-driver, a Greek sailor or a Spanish nobleman.

He could tell of the snow-capped mountains he had to cross, the raging rivers that had to be forded, the sun-beaten plains, the quaint villages, the lofty knights in their war gear patrolling the route, the highwaymen from which he barely escaped, the twisted ankle that was healed almost miraculously by an expert fellow-pilgrim, the marvelous churches and cathedrals that dot the Road, and the brotherly bonds that developed among all the people on their way to Santiago.

These bonds might have brought together at a dinner table, on any inn on the Road, a priest and a prostitute, a soldier and a nobleman, a just man and a repentant criminal.

But not all was brotherly love on the Road. The frontier atmosphere along the route, caused by the constant state of war not only between Christians and Moslems, but among the Christians themselves, gave the vast region a Wild-West, free-for-all, anything goes character where anything and everything was possible. There were all types of bad guys, from the false priests who promised masses and forgave sins for a hefty price to a river boat ferryman who would drown his unsuspecting passengers and steal everything from the cadavers; from innkeepers who cleared the purses of sleeping pilgrims to unscrupulous businessmen who overcharged for their services. All individual crimes taking place over a background of armies on the move, wandering armed raiding parties and besieged cities.

But the Road to Santiago was ultimately made possible because the overwhelming majority of the people met by the pilgrim were kind, generous and respectful folk who helped the spiritual traveler as much as their means allowed. They are the main reason why, by the XII Century, some estimates put the figure of pilgrims going to Santiago at 250,000 to 500,000 per year. Although these estimates might sound a bit exaggerated, it is true that the Road to Santiago became a very heavily traveled route, so much so that the Santiago Cathedral itself was forced to institute regulations that controlled the flow of people through it, prohibiting animals from entering and not allowing pilgrims to come in with sleeping gear, as many who could not find overnight lodging would want to do. So the Santiago Cathedral was constantly overflowing with people, most of which had traveled a long way and had not bathed in a while. To counteract the stench with which the place was often endowed, the "Botafumeiro," a huge incense burner, was commissioned and placed in the cathedral; eight priests, the "Tiraboleiros," pulled on a contraption that made it swing to great heights from the ceiling across the church, filling it with sweet-smelling incense. The contraption, by the way, was far from perfect: it is recorded that in 1499, in the presence of a startled Princess Catherine of Aragón, the "Botafumeiro" broke lose from its chain and flew out of the "Platerías" portal, to the astonishment of all present. It is not known, however, if the *"Tirabolero magno,"* the fellow who gets to jump on the "Botafumeiro" to make it stop, had already hopped on when the mishap took place.

Among the countless and priceless objects that Napoleon's troops plundered from Spain in the early nineteenth century is the silver, 1544 "Botafumeiro," an invaluable artifact full of tradition whose loss did much injury to the national heritage. The present-day "Botafumeiro" dates from the eighteenth century, weighs 50 kilograms and stands one and a half meters tall. It is used only on solemn occasions nowadays.

E. Motives and Reasons for the Trip

It is an unwritten law of the Road to Santiago that the pilgrim must never be asked why he or she is making the trip.

The reasons for such a trip are, and were, as varied and different as the pilgrims themselves. Repentant sinners were always present on the Road, hoping to be forgiven for a sin, or host of sins, and thus save their eternal souls. There are legends which recount the story of noblemen who, in order to be forgiven for a terrible sin, would make the arduous trip and die at the main altar in Santiago Cathedral. Other legends tell of those whose sins were too horrible to confess; they wrote them on a piece of paper which they brought with them to Santiago. After sincerely repenting at the altar, they found to their surprise that the sins had been erased from the paper as a sign of forgiveness.

From U.S. history we know that, during the Civil War, some well-to-do citizens would pay others to fight in their stead, thus avoiding the trials and dangers of the battlefield. On the Road to Santiago it was not uncommon to find people who were being paid by others to make the trip for them; these pilgrims for hire would mingle with the other pilgrims: condemned men paying for their crimes by walking to Santiago (sometimes with chains on their arms and legs), repentant prostitutes and other individuals whom society not only wanted to punish, but also wanted to get rid of for some time by sending them to a far-off place. There were also those  who made the trip as an excuse to get to Spain, which, with its Arab, Jewish and Christian hodgepodge of culture and learning, was the most advanced civilization of its time.

I am sure that, among those early pilgrims, there were many like us who made the trip for enlightenment as well as enjoyment, to add a little transcendence to lives fraught with empirical practicalities.

Motives and Reasons for the Trip. ✠ 26

II. Daily Life Along the Road in the Middle Ages.

A. Political Structures.

The daily life of the people living along the Road to Santiago de Compostela was, in many ways, shaped by the political climate of the times. Although the highest authority was the king, his power was often compromised, if not curtailed, by other institutions that exercised considerable influence over his subjects. These were the Church, spiritual and political powerhouse of the Middle Ages, and the nobility, resident lords who, being close by, were the only real authority most people experienced first-hand.

In the Spanish leg of the Road alone the pilgrim would cross as many as five independent states: Aragón, Navarra, Castile, León and Galicia, each with its own laws, customs and even language, often at war with each other or mounting campaigns against the Moslems to the south.

Yet, in these small kingdoms the maximum authority, the king, was never far afield , and his subjects often saw him as a necessary entity, enforcer of laws intended for the common good and protection of the populace; recourse as well against nobles who overstepped the boundaries of their privileges and abused their rank.

So the foundations of government rested on contracts between the sovereign and the nobles who were his vassals; these would, in turn, have their own vassals, the people living in their particular region. The lords swore loyalty to the king and assumed the obligation of performing military service for him; the king reciprocated by providing for his nobles; protection and for their maintenance, which normally consisted of an estate or public office given to him and his heirs. As landlord, the noble was entitled to receive rent from the peasants who lived and worked on his land and was also charged with the administration of justice in his dominion. During lean times, some of these nobles were not beyond aiding and abetting those of their vassals who, risking terrible punishment, strong-armed pilgrims to Santiago in order to get the extra coins at border crossings and river fords (as we can see in the medieval *Pilgrims' Guide to Santiago de Compostela)*.

If a pilgrim to Santiago were invited to come to the king's palace (as some who were of high rank presumably were), he would get a good glimpse of the formal organization that surrounded the monarch at his court.   This organization was the king's council, or *aula regia*, composed of those individuals who accompanied the king in his travels and helped him in the business of government. Perhaps the pilgrim would be surprised at the uncomplicated nature of government administration in these small northern kingdoms, for the council consisted of  members of the royal family, important men who were friends and counselors of the king (*consilarii regis*), royal vassals (*milites regis*) and officials (*armiger*). Also important in the royal household was the royal standard-bearer and commander of troops (*alférez*), a man who was also charged with holding the the king's battle-sword before the monarch as he walked in and out of official functions as the symbol of authority; the *alférez* also received the royal oath when a new king was crowned. There was also the accountant for the king's house, (*maiordomus*), supervisor of the household who administered the royal domain, including the collection of the royal rents. The notary (*notarius*) was always busy drafting royal documents and keeping the archives up to date; the stable master (*strator*)

was a very important character in medieval courts; the treasurer (*thesaurarius*) was the custodian of the king's treasure; the chamberlains (*cubicularii*) were responsible for the upkeep of the king's quarters and clothing, and finally the chaplains administered to the king's spiritual needs.

More often than not, these people lived in the palace compound and saw each other daily, making for an atmosphere of familiarity which gave the place the feel of a household rather than a government center.

B. The Law.

The *Liber Iudiciorum*, the law of the land in the old Visigothic Kingdom of Spain, had very little application after the disappearance of that kingdom in the second decade of the eighth century. In the states along the Road to Santiago, the chief source of law was custom, unwritten law that was sanctioned by usage. These laws were at times written down in the charters (*fueros*) given by the king to the settlers of specific areas, specially those recently conquered from the Moslems. The city of León, for example, was given its *fueros* in 1017 by king Alfonso V.

Administering justice based on charters which were far form comprehensive was not easy. Following the Germanic customs of the Visigoths, litigation was thought of as the private concern of the parties involved, unless a violation of the king's peace was involved. It was precisely the king's peace that protected the pilgrims to Santiago, as well as the Road on which they traveled, the markets at which they bought provisions and the places where they assembled and took refuge. A crime against a pilgrim was considered a breach of the king's peace; a person committing such a crime was deemed guilty of an offense against the monarch himself.

Judges appointed by the king usually sat in judgement at courts, but only determined the form of proof. The accused would commonly give a solemn oath of purgation, before a Cross or another symbol of the faith: that would stand up as proof of his innocence. Of course, if the defendant expressed doubts as to the validity of the oath, an "ordeal" would be ordered by the judge. The ordeal took the form of a physical test which supposedly would harm the accused if he was guilty, but if innocent God would somehow spare him and he would remain unharmed. One of the most common was the hot water ordeal (*pena caldaria*), where the accused had to grab red-hot stones from inside a pot full of scalding water and throw them out. Trial by battle, where the litigants got a chance to hack each other to pieces, was also considered a viable way to get at the truth, for God would surely protect the righteous party.

Private vengeance was also a right that was recognized by custom. The family of a murdered man defied the murderer either in the town square, outside the church after Sunday Mass, or at any other public gathering, after which they would seek to kill him. Thus, a pilgrim reaching a town on the Road on a sunny Sunday morning might witness the son, brother or father of a murdered man openly and publicly challenge the murderer. The tension in the town square would be almost palpable, with the neighbors talking about the details of the crime, its causes and probable outcomes.

To avoid blood feuds that would at times alter the normal daily activities of the towns, the family of the murdered person could opt for monetary compensation. According to the rank of the person killed, the amount could vary from 500 *solidi* for a noble to 300 for a freeman. These were rather considerable sums.

C. The Military.

Because the Moslems were a threat to the small Christian kingdoms along the Road, all adult males were required to perform military duty when called upon. Not all military activity was defensive, however, and the men were required to participate in major expeditions (*fonsado*) to acquire territories or punish and terrorize the Moslems to the south, raids (*cabalgata*), garrison duty (*vigilia*) and, of course, the defense of a fortress (*apellido*). It would not be terribly unusual for a pilgrim to enter a town that was devoid of able-bodied  men, since they might all be involved in a raid into Moslem territory or be participating in the defense of a fortress being besieged. Upon receiving the king's call, the men of a town would join others at an appointed assembly place where they would form under the command of the king's *alférez*. The army would then march to engage the enemy.

Along with it would go the king's guards and champions, the elite units of the host, all, of course, mounted on horseback. Also present were the nobles (on horseback as well) and their vassals, flying the colors of their family along with those of the kingdom. Lesser nobles would also join for pay (*solidata*), their services underwritten by a great lord whose good name would certainly benefit from their successes on the field of battle. Not to be forgotten are the peasants from our typical town: they would be the infantry force. The simple freemen of the town also participated; those who could afford it would fight on horseback (*caballeros villanos*).

Beginning in the tenth century a policy was instituted whereby, in poor villages, three men could team up in order to send one to war: pooling their resources, they would be able to buy a horse and other necessary tools of war. The two that stayed behind bore the brunt of the expenses and often tended to the other's household and crops, while the returning warrior would divide his booty into five parts: the first for the king (*quinto real*), one for each of his partners and two for himself.

For the beleaguered Christian kingdoms of Spain, war was a way of life from which not even the clergy was spared. Being, in its way, a religious affair, war was to be conducted properly. As such, the king would often ask the local bishop not only to bless the assembled troops before a battle, but to march into battle with a Cross held high over his head. Indeed, this was not an enviable task, for the opposing archers had, in the conspicuous bishop, a very obvious and important target.

All the conventional wisdom about medieval battles being akin to meat-grinders is true. The opposing armies, assembled in the field, would begin by shouting insults at each other concerning their religion, their king, or even the women they left back home. A rain of arrows would often follow that would fell a good number on each side, after which the heavily-armored, mounted knights of both armies would rush into the field where a loud clash of metal announced that the contest had begun in earnest. Each of the knights would be followed into the field by a diverse number of peons on foot, armed with lances, bows and arrows and long knives. The peons had a secondary, although important role: they had to incorporate their knight should he fall from his horse, or finish off an opposing fallen knight. Being heavily armored, the medieval knight on his also armored horse was the equivalent of the modern tank, but once dismounted, his armor would prevent him from mounting his horse again or even from standing up should he land on his back. Peons, then, ran back and forth around the battlefield tending to their knight, shooting arrows at every chance, engaging opposing peons and even dragging wounded opponents off the field in the hope of cashing in on any reward offered by his vassals for his return.

If the knights on one side had no mounted opposition or had succeeded in routing it, they attacked the infantry directly. This may sound easier than it actually was, since the infantry would normally be waiting for them in tight, compact units holding long staffs with pointed metal tips. These were five meters long and were placed very near each other, so that the knight essentially charged a wall of spikes in which he and his horse could be impaled. The first line of the charge usually took very heavy casualties.

But the event became truly ugly when the bulk of the infantry engaged on the field. These were, for the most part, lightly armored peasants and freemen, owners of a sword, a lance and a makeshift shield but full of religious and nationalistic zeal. An infantryman would set his sights on one opponent and engage him in personal combat, but since in the chaos of battle opposing numbers are seldom equal, he might have to deal with two or three enemies at a time for a while, or suddenly find himself fighting with six or seven of his own people against two or three opponents. In the turbulence of combat, things are not as antiseptic as portrayed in Hollywood movies: battles would rage for many hours, sometimes days, the field littered with the bodies of the dead, severed body parts, the wounded crawling about in the muck, their yells and screams an eery background for the ongoing struggle. Warriors returning to camp would be splattered with blood from head to toe, but their feet would be specially drenched in blood merely from having to tread upon the battlefield, generously watered with the bodily fluids of the combatants. Back in camp, the scene was truly hellish, with the field-surgeons unable to help in most cases, in an era when antibiotics were unheard of, when soldiers with severed arms at times survived but others with flesh wounds might die a tortured death of infection.

The fighting was fierce because the stakes were high. A successful battle might win over a rich region for a kingdom, which would then settle it with its own citizens: these settlers became landowners overnight, changing their lot and that of their heirs forever. Soldiers excelling in battle would often be given lands in the newly acquired territories. A successful battle might also make the threat of armed Moslem raids disappear, making it safe for people to live normal lives; it could also make returning warriors considerably wealthy from acquired booty.

Not all the battles were fought in a field. In their expansion south, Christian kingdoms had to take fortresses and walled cities. To do this, they had to employ the latest tools available in the military technology of the times. One of these was the "trabuco," a large stone encased in the skin of a cow. The "trabuco" would be swung back and forth in a contraption with roughly the dynamics of a child's swing set. Once the heavy stone achieved sufficient speed, it would actually swing around over the top in a complete circle. As it swung around again, the soldier working the contraption would pull on a rope, freeing the rock to fly into the enemy walls, or towers, or buildings (its ultimate destination was not known with absolute accuracy, only its general direction). The importance of the fellow working the "trabuco" cannot be understated, since an inexperienced or uncoordinated individual could cause his own people considerable headaches.

Another way to tackle the problem presented by a castle or walled city was to mine the walls. To do this, a contingent of soldiers would dig a tunnel reaching under the walls of the castle or city; once there, they placed wooden beams under the walls before extracting the dirt and rocks. The beams would be pasted with grease, which would be set on fire. When the beams burned up, they would no longer support the weight of the walls, which would collapse, allowing the besieging army a point of entry. But there were a number of problems attending this procedure. First, soldiers from inside the castle could foray to the mouth of the tunnel and make a fire there that would suffocate the diggers.

Second, people inside the castle could dig their own tunnel and meet up with the diggers, overwhelming them in the underground combat or even collapsing their exit.

Towers were a popular way to breach walled defenses. A tall, wooden structure on wheels would be pulled right up to the wall, at which point the soldiers inside the wheeled tower would rush the defenders. The main problem here was that the defenders could mass at the point where the tower was approaching, meeting the attackers with overwhelming force.

Some commanders would actually order their troops to climb ladders at many points along the wall to try to storm a castle. These troopers would be subjected to some rough treatment by the defenders, which included showers with boiling oil, stoning and arrows. Long staffs also pushed the ladders away from the walls, sending the soldiers on top to almost certain death. The trick here was to use so many ladders that the defenders would not be able to repel them all successfully. The ram was used to break down the gates of a castle, but this point of entry was usually the most dangerous, since it was set up with cauldrons of boiling oil, walls from which a rain of arrows would come through small holes, multiple gates that trapped the attackers, false floors that would give, dropping the attackers into another level whose floor was made of sharp metal spikes, as well as a number of other niceties, products of medieval ingenuity.

Later in the Middle Ages gunpowder would change things considerably, but the carnage would not subside.

For those maimed or otherwise hurt in battle, the Crown instituted a system of annual compensation intended to alleviate the economic disadvantage at which injury placed them. King Alfonso X had it thus:

	Maravedis
I. Injuries to the head.	
Without the loss of bone	5

With loss of bone	10
Injury cannot be covered w/ hair	12

II. Injuries to the body.
If the body has been run through	10

III. Injuries to arms and legs.
To arm or leg, but not run through	2.50
If run through	5
Broken arm or leg w/o permanent handicap	12

IV. Mutilations.
Loss of four teeth, upper or lower	40
Loss of an ear	40
Loss of a thumb	50
Loss of other fingers, in descending order	50-10
Loss of pinky	10
Loss of four fingers in one hand	80
Loss of an eye, nose, hand or foot	100
Injuries causing mutilation	100
Loss of arm, to elbow, or leg to the knee	120

V. Death.
Mounted soldier killed in line of duty	150
Peon	75

Although a *maravedí* is valued at less than one $ U.S., the fact is that a *maravedí* could buy you a lot more things than one dollar can today. The 120 yearly *maravedís* given for the loss of an arm, for example, were reasonably expected to make up for much of the loss in wages or productivity that the condition would cause.

D. The Lower Classes.

A pilgrim traveling on the Road to Santiago would meet people working the fields close to the Road. These would be either freemen, working their own soil or working as tenants, or peasants, working the lands of their lord. Under the law, both freemen and peasants had the same rights, except that the peasant was deprived of freedom of movement. The peasant's relationship with his lord was two-fold: he worked the land and gave the lord a share of the crop; the lord, in turn, protected the peasant and his family by force of arms against the raids and invasions to which  they were often subjected. As the Christian kingdoms expanded south and the threat of Moslem raids gradually subsided, the lord's protection lost more and more of its practical value. The peasants dreamed of fleeing south, to the newly acquired territories, where they might be granted land on which to work and grow their own crops. Many did.

The freemen who moved to the new territories were hardy adventurers who prized their liberty above all things. They were known for defending their individual freedoms with fierce determination against all comers, be they Moslem raiders or lords encroaching on their property. The mounted freemen of Castrojeriz, for example, fought with such courage against the Moslems that count García Fernández granted every one of them the privileges of an *infanzón* in 974 A.D. Giving them the status of minor nobility was akin to giving all of the adult male citizens of a modern U.S. city the Congressional Medal of Honor.

Peasants always dreamed of being freemen. The problem of escaping peasants was so widespread that in the year 1017 king Alfonso V had to sanction the practice. He thus allowed peasants to leave their lords' estates and settle somewhere else, this after giving their lord half of their movable property.

A medieval pilgrim moving west towards Santiago de Compostela might meet a peasant family crossing his path on their way south, their heads full of dreams and hope for the future. They would speak to him about their plans and expectations, about the marvelous new lands being opened up, about the myriad of possibilities, expressing themselves in basically the same terms a family of settlers from New England might have employed as they moved west on a wagon train in nineteenth century America.

The bottom rung of the Spanish social ladder was occupied by the slaves. Although scholars disagree as to their numbers, there were probably not many of them, and in their social and economic condition they were most likely indistinguishable from the peasants. Slavery was one of the most fluid of medieval social institutions in Spain: at any point a slave's deeds might win him his freedom, while a criminal or a man who had not paid his debts for a long period could be enslaved, as well as a Moslem soldier or farmer taken prisoner after a battle or raid. On the other hand, a Christian farmer peacefully working his fields one day could find himself being sold at a slave market in the Moslem south two days later, having been captured in a raid.

Normally, the individual would be enslaved until he paid his debts (many slaves earned wages), completed his sentence (in the case of criminals), or was ransomed by his family (in the case of prisoners of war), but as long as his condition of slave continued, he could not appear in court and was considered a mere object in the juridical sense, subject to being bought and sold.

A pilgrim sitting for lunch at an inn on the Road could find himself being served by an enslaved Moslem from Córdoba. Engaging him in conversation, he would learn of the marvels of Al-Ándalus, the great mosques, the public baths, the outdoor public lighting, the art, literature and architecture of his people. A bit incredulous, it would be difficult for the pilgrim to believe that such an advanced civilization existed to the south, and, moreover, that it was being defeated by these little, backwards Christian kingdoms through which he was crossing.

E. The Food.

When the tired pilgrim arrived at an inn or refuge and sat down to dinner, what did he eat? How did he eat it?

The folks along the Road to Santiago ate wheat bread, lots of it, along with roasts, fowl and rabbit. These they ate using an knife and bare hands; a small water cup called "lavadedos," (literally a "finger washer") was kept close by to help wash food remnants off their hands before starting the next course. Tablecloths were used not necessarily for aesthetic effects, but because of the need to keep the mess contained on the cloth.

Should a pilgrim on the early Road be invited to dine at the house of a nobleman, he would be assigned a *triclinium* (a sort of bed) on which to eat; resting in a horizontal position on his side with his trunk propped up with pillows, he would consume his meal from a dish placed directly in front of him. At some time during the tenth century the nobles decided that it was more comfortable to use chairs and tables like the common people and abandoned horizontal dining altogether.

The poorest peasants consumed a simple menu. If given shelter in the house of a peasant, the pilgrim would sit at a table where he would find rye bread, onions, cheese, garden vegetables, turnips and fruits like melons, pears, figs and apples.

Common to the noble and the peasant table were two items no Spaniard could do without: wine and bread. There were three basic types of wine: red, white and muscatel, which, due to the abundance of vineyards, were accessible to most folk. Apple cider was also popular.

Saltwater fish and seafood, except in Galicia, were not very common sights on that long stretch of the Road that crosses Castile and León. Here the Road is separated from the sea by imposing mountain ranges. Getting over them, a traveler coming from the coast would take a few days to reach any point along the Road. In medieval times, with refrigeration many centuries in the future, fresh seafood was a delicacy reserved for people living along the coast. Salted fish, the only option for folks along the Road, was expensive, although fresh river fish was prized and quite common.

On the other hand, potatoes, tomatoes and the other products that are native to the Americas would have to wait until the flag of Spain was planted on that continent in 1492 before they could be consumed (with reservations, at first) along the Road to Santiago.

Table side manners and customs were a little different from today's. Eggs, for example, were normally consumed raw, and therefore were a liquid meal to be drunk, not eaten. Many dishes, especially fruit, were placed between two diners who, after having their fill, would in turn place it between the next pair, and so on; this practice made medieval dining more of a communal experience, unlike the sort of dining we practice today, where one dish is placed in front of one individual who treats it like his personal parcel, to be consumed exclusively by him.

Excessive talk at the table was considered bad manners, and so was sneezing, an event that a diner should avoid at all costs. To keep from sneezing at the table, a pilgrim to Santiago might follow a rule of the times: "take two small pieces of bread, spread mustard on them, and stick them up your nose."

F. Town Government.

The villages through which the pilgrim passed on his way to Santiago had a form of government that was the result of the war of reconquest against the Moslems. In the first centuries after the discovery of the tomb of Santiago, these villages along the Road were settlements centered around a castle which protected them and served as refuge for their inhabitants. As the number of pilgrims crossing them steadily increased, their political, economic and military importance increased as well, to the point where some of them began to lose their rural character to become small urban centers, enjoying a flourishing mercantile and industrial activity based largely on the Road.

Because of their increasing importance, many of these once rural villages -now towns- obtained recognition from the king, who named them organs of territorial administration (*concejos*). These municipalities were largely autonomous, having their own laws, officials and local institutions. Some of the older settlements along the Road, for centuries dependent on feudal lords, looked with envy at the local freedoms enjoyed by the newer municipalities, which were subject only to the king. Things got to the point where Santiago de Compostela and Sahagún rebelled against their lords (Santiago against the bishop, and Sahagún against the abbots) in bloody attempts to gain power for their local citizens' assembly.

The *concejo* (concilium) was an assembly of neighbors (*boni homines*) who had to meet four requirements of membership: 1) be an adult; 2) be a male; 3) own property and 4) live within the municipality. This body was quite democratic for its time, with each member having the right to speak his mind and cast his vote; it was an assembly where the clergy and the nobility did not have a say and could not otherwise participate in its proceedings.

A pilgrim crossing one of these towns on Sunday after Mass might hear the sound of a horn. This was the call for the members of the *concejo* to gather at an appointed place, where they would discuss questions of taxes, upkeep of roads and bridges, the problems at the local market, military service and the election of officers, among other things.

So it was that in most of the towns along the Road to Santiago, the political and judicial leader (*juez*) was elected directly by the *concejo*, and usually for a one-year term. Each of the parishes (*colaciones*) that made up the town or municipality elected a man to assist the *juez* in the administration of justice; these were the alcaldes (*al-quadi*). Other officials elected by the local *concejos* were the police officers (*sayones*), the town accountants (*fideles*), the tax collectors (*merinos*), and even the public market inspector, called the *almotacén* (*al-muhtasib*), charged with keeping the weights, measures and prices of the vendors within specified parameters. *Concejos* also elected their own *alférez*, the man who headed all military affairs and carried the town's standard into battle. Some towns elected a special group of *sayones*, the *alguaciles* (*al-wazir*) to patrol those stretches of the Road to Santiago that fell within their municipal limits.

G. The Economy.

The boom in the construction of cathedrals, refuges, bridges, etc. along the Road to Santiago de Compostela in the eleventh century coincided with a remarkable economic expansion in the rest of Europe. The urban, commercial economy flourishing along the Road was now based upon the use of money as a medium of exchange. As Venice, Genoa and Pisa opened up the Mediterranean to trade, goods obtained in the Middle East and North Africa now made their way to central Europe along established trade routes. Northern Europe also experienced an economic awakening, with the establishment of strong commercial activity between Britain, Scandinavia and the Low Countries. The economic energy produced by all this activity in northern and southern Europe had a natural funnel that marshaled it westward: the Road to Santiago. The ever-growing class of merchants and artisans who in the beginning (ninth century) were largely itinerant, moving constantly to where their particular goods and crafts were needed, now began to settle in villages and towns. Because of the increasing volume of pilgrims and trade, these growing settlements could, by the eleventh century, afford them a steady supply of customers.

Urban activity in turn spurred the growth of the agricultural sector; the steady expansion of the urban settlements along the Road provided a reliable market for the agricultural products of the adjacent areas, which shared in the general economic well being generated by the Road. To meet the demands of the population, an ever increasing number of acres was cultivated, and, as a result, more hands were needed to work the fields. But as many people left the fields in order to find work and opportunities in the towns, farm workers became a scarce commodity, a situation that encouraged Spanish kings to repopulate many of the regions where the shortage was most keenly felt. The repopulation of the regions of El Bierzo and Montes de Oca with people from France, for example, gave birth to the towns of Villafranca Montes de Oca and Villafranca del Bierzo, as their names aptly imply.

As pilgrims, merchants, traders, artisans and others made their way west through the Road, many settled in villages along the way and, because they maintained personal and commercial contacts with people back home, they were able to initiate a whole new web of relations between their new country and their old homelands. The importance of the Road was recognized early on by the kings, who spent large amounts from the royal treasuries on its upkeep and on construction. During this very important eleventh century, as is reported by the *Crónica najerense* (III, 57), Alfonso VI of León built hospices, repaired long stretches of the Road, and "built all the bridges from Logroño to Sahagún." The extent of his commitment to the safety and comfort of the pilgrim must have been great, not only as far as construction and upkeep go, but also in his effort to have the Road patrolled and overseen by his knights and *alguaciles*. In this respect, the *Crónica najerense* is very clear: during Alfonso's reign, "merchants and pilgrims traveling through his entire realm had nothing to fear for themselves or for their goods." (III, 57).

Goods also reached the towns along the Road from the north. The Moslem geographer al-Idrisi named the Bay of Biscay the "English Sea," implying that there was regular contact with the British Isles by the eleventh century. British goods as well as goods from western France reached the northern Spanish ports of Santander, Laredo and Castro Urdiales; from there they would be brought across the Cantabrian range through places like the Escudo pass, south to Burgos, León, and other sites along the Road to Santiago de Compostela. By the early thirteenth century the seafaring trade had expanded to the extent that a new port had to be built and settled, named San Vicente de la Barquera (1210) and given the municipal rights (fueros) enjoyed by the other northern coast towns.

The constant expansion south gained important new markets for the Christian states in the eleventh century; Places like Toledo, Zaragoza, Talavera, Cuenca and Calatayud , with their long-established industries, came to enhance an already considerable commercial activity along the Road. Goods from the south now flowed north more freely than ever before.

Fairs were established along the Road to facilitate trade; of these perhaps the most important was that of Sahagún, authorized by Alfonso VII to be held for three weeks after Pentecost. Being under the protection of the monarch, all attending the fair could reasonably expect to be safe from harm. Fairs in the towns along the Road, like the rest of Spain, would be organized in and around the central public market or plaza. There, stalls would be set up where craftsmen and merchants offered their goods and services; these stalls might be grouped according to the particular trade or type of goods offered, and they could include, but not be limited to, vegetable vendors, spice merchants, fishmongers, wine merchants, builders, toolmakers, carpenters, stone masons, clothing merchants, tailors, dyers, tanners, horse traders, shoemakers and money changers.

Physicians, barbers and pharmacists would also set up shop at the fair, but their trade was difficult to regulate. While the town's *concejo* could basically determine the price of apples or wine, as well as their quality, establishing exact parameters for medical practice was another matter altogether. Formal credentials for those in the health care professions were tentative at best, and the town folk going to a physician to treat a persistent cough, to a barber to be bled (the prescribed treatment for many illnesses was to eliminate "excess" blood, a task usually performed by barbers), or to a pharmacist to obtain curative herbs, could be putting themselves in harm's way.

The most highly prized physicians of the time were Moslems and

Jews from the south of Spain. Christians from the north who had the means would usually travel south for the treatment of ailments. Among these was Sancho the Fat, king of Asturias-León, reputed to be so obese that it was impossible for him to ride a horse, let alone lead anyone into battle. Things got so bad for him that his hold on the throne was in jeopardy, so he decided to head down to Córdoba, where the Caliph's personal physician trimmed his weight dramatically. When Sancho showed up back at León, trim and fit, he was able to oust his rival Ordoño the Bad, who had all but installed himself on the throne.

Physicians from the Moslem south, then, would attract many patients when they came north, but a northerner would do well to beware of fakes and quacks, as many con men would dress themselves up as Moslems and try to pass for great physicians, extracting large sums from unsuspecting patients for sham treatment.

The general expansion in trade that began in the eleventh century in the towns along the Road necessitated a sizeable increment in the amount of money in circulation. The money used along the Road to Santiago de Compostela came in many shapes and forms: coins from the Moslem south such as the gold *dinar* were common, having found their way north thanks to trade, successful Christian raids into Moslem lands, or the payment of tribute by weaker Moslem rulers to stronger Christian kings. Christian states in the north also coined money, and in an event directly related to the Road's economic importance, king Alfonso VI allowed bishop Diego Gelmírez of Santiago to coin money in 1108 A.D. In 1172 king Alfonso VIII of Castile, in an effort to bring some semblance of uniformity to the circulation of money in his realm, began minting coins in imitation of the *dinars* produced by the Almoravids, rulers of the Moslem south; the name of the new coin, the *maravedí*, recalls its origin in the money used by the "Almorávides."

The Road crossed through a variety of agricultural zones on its way to Santiago. Its first portion, running through Navarra, came across pasture lands where sheep and dairy cattle were a common sight, with the odd vineyard here and there. Vineyards would fill the pilgrim's field of sight, from horizon to horizon, when he proceeded west to la Rioja. Past

La Rioja and into Castile, the pilgrim traveled through fields of wheat, barley, oats, and fruits and vegetables; on into León, the same type of agricultural products were cultivated. On the last leg of the journey, the one corresponding to Galicia, the humid, mountainous conditions propitiated the raising of dairy cattle and cool weather fruits like apples.

It is interesting to note that this same cattle industry, when moved south into the hot plains of southern Castile and Extremadura with the Christian reconquest of those areas, gave rise to a totally new type of activity where cattle free-ranged throughout immense grazing and pasture lands. In its essence, this is where cattle ranching was invented; it was later brought to North and South America by the Spanish settlers who began arriving there after 1492.

H. Village Life.

During the Middle Ages, villages along the Road to Santiago were little more than a conglomerate of small houses sharing a bare minimum of public utilities. There was no such thing as public transportation, hospitals were basically intended for pilgrims and were very simple, by today's standards. There was nothing like a sewer system and public lighting was unknown. If you needed to travel to the next village you'd prepare a sack with the things you required for the trip - including food and water- and walked the distance. A pain in your belly would be treated by a local woman who knew which herbs might make it go away. Toilets were a hole in the ground or a container that was emptied outside in the morning. Nights were pitch dark and eerily silent, and anyone venturing outside on a cloudy autumn night would carry a torch to avoid falling into a pothole or walking into a wall. The odd sound of a cricket or the rustling of a horse in a nearby barn were the only signs available to tell a nighttime traveler that he wasn't alone in the world. Prolonged rains could turn the streets in the town and outlying roads into mud streams, isolating its inhabitants from the outside world for weeks at a time.

As the towns grew, a more diverse group of people came to form the ranks of their inhabitants. In the larger towns some neighborhoods were occupied exclusively by the members of a particular trade, and thus even to this day the names of some of the streets (Weavers St., Stone Masons St., Silversmiths St., Leather Workers St., etc.) Designate the areas in town where these tradesmen lived and worked. All the members of each particular trade were grouped into a *gremio*, which functioned as an extended family, a syndicate, a training school and a credit union. To enter a *gremio* like the *Carpinteros* (carpenters), a young man would have to start off as the unpaid trainee (*aprendiz*) of a master carpenter. After years of training, he would have to pass a practical exam administered by a group of masters who, if satisfied, would proclaim him as an *oficial*, able to work for a master and receive a salary. After many years and another examination, he might become a master and open up his own shop. Each *gremio* had its own patron saint and could bankroll the construction and upkeep of a chapel dedicated to that saint in the local church.

But a pilgrim crossing any of the larger towns on the Road could readily see that not everyone was gainfully employed. Coming upon a town square in the early afternoon of a summer day, he would find paupers begging for money (some of them professional con men who claimed to be maimed or deformed in order to incite pity in the wayfarer), gamblers set up on makeshift tables, and roaming bands of young men who made fun of everyone and passed their time by insulting priests and women, peeping through windows and creating as much havoc as possible.

A very common form of gambling during the Middle Ages along the Road was that practiced by the "trileros." These people would put a little ball or chip with three upside down cups on a table. The ball or chip would be quickly transferred from under one cup to another, and the unwitting gambler would try to guess under which cup the ball or chip would end up. Anyone walking the streets of Manhattan today will see modern day "trileros" practicing their trade, called the "pasa-pasa" in medieval Spain.

But a pilgrim who wanted to try his luck could choose from a number of gambling options. Dice (*dados*) were very popular, but one should beware of weights and other tricks intended to part you from your money very quickly. There were also darts and a variety of ball games, including one similar to baseball, one to golf, one to soccer, one to hockey and one to tennis, all of which were the object of gambling. In a society where military pursuits were vital to its survival, many games and pastimes were derived from the art of war. Jousting, wrestling, javelin throwing, a crude form of boxing and archery were very popular.

Yet gambling was outlawed for long periods at a time, and the gambler should take note that there was legislation on the books that called for his punishment, from the simple imposition of a fine to lashing and the removal of up to "two fingers' length of tongue" from the culprit's mouth (king Alfonso X, *Partidas*).

Life was normally quiet in the villages, with the arrival of a group of pilgrims being a source of commotion and excitement for the townspeople. Often the pilgrim would bring news from the outside world, interesting objects, jewelry, strange clothing and stories to tell. From time to time a professional story teller (*juglar*) would come down the Road, and his arrival was an important and happy event. The *juglar* (from the Latin "jocularis," or "player") was one of the major sources of entertainment in the Middle Ages: he recounted the epic tales of the heroes who, like El Cid, helped to build the Spanish nation; he told of great battles recently fought, of marvelous feats of courage, of new laws enacted by the king and of the latest gossip from the court, many times in song and accompanied by musical instruments. The *juglares* were often followed by the *bufones*, who entertained the simple town folk with animal acts using monkeys, dogs and goats, but they were not considered as highly as the *juglares*, who often had access to the king's house.

Rounding off the contingent of professional entertainers were the musicians, traveling the length of the Road in order to play for the villagers during their town fairs and other celebrations; they brought a professional dancer with them to add color and life to the spectacle. The importance of *juglares* and musicians for the medieval Road is comparable to the importance of radio and television in the contemporary world. This importance is attested to by Master Mateo, who carved a whole range of musical instruments into the hands of the 24 elders of the Apocalypse in the portico of the Santiago de Compostela cathedral.

Prominent in the feasts and celebrations of the villages were the bullfights. In the Middle Ages, this spectacle was different from what we see today: the "torero" fought on horseback, and as such, he would normally be a "caballero," a nobleman, not a professional bullfighter. His horseless helpers, the peons, directed the bull his way with capes; dogs also participated, running around the bullring and biting the bull if it was disinclined to fight or confusing the animal if it proved overly aggressive.

Lastly, bored villagers in a lonely winter night, with the wind howling outside and the temperature falling well below freezing, might engage each other in a game of chess in front of the fireplace. Chess had been introduced in Spain in the eighth century by the Moors and it quickly became the rage; king Alfonso X commissioned a book on chess rules and strategy in the thirteenth century and it was played by nobles at court, warriors in camp and castle, and simple folk everywhere.

Such was the rhythm of life in the villages along the Road in the Middle Ages. By modern standards, it would seem boring, but we must remember that these villages were right on one of the busiest land routes in medieval Europe, and as far as excitement goes, there were plenty of wars, raids, rebellions, fairs and pilgrims from far-off places to keep ones attention in focus.

I. Relations Between the Sexes and Hygiene.

A pilgrim taking shelter in a house along the Road might find a common nuclear family consisting of father, mother, children and grandparents. Or he might find something else altogether. Until well into the Middle Ages, unions between men and women did not have the religious connotations with which they are formalized nowadays. Thus, following the old Germanic traditions of the Visigoths as legislated in the *Fuero Juzgo*, people could marry and divorce without the weight of religious dogma to sanction and direct their conduct. Many unions were not even formalized, and many men (including priests) elected to keep a woman to whom they were not married but whom they recognized as their legitimate companion. These women were called "barraganas," and they did not hide their relationships with their male companions as there was little or no stigma associated to their social station. In the case of priests, the *barraganas* were kept in the guise of housekeepers, nieces, etc., as the Church wanted to maintain at least a semblance of propriety within its ranks.

Formal relations between men and women underwent a major shakeup when Cluniac monasticism was introduced into Spain in the early eleventh century. Monks from the French monastery of Cluny (founded in 910 A.D. by the duke of Burgundy) were invited by Sancho el Mayor of Navarra (reg. 1000-1035) to come to Spain and reform the monasteries of Leyre, Oña and San Juan de la Peña, none far from the Road to Santiago. Alfonso VI of León (reg. 1065-1109) followed suit and invited the monks to man hospices, churches and monasteries along the Road to Santiago, making Sahagún a major
center of Cluniac reform. Cluny monks were followed in the twelfth century by Cistercian monks from the monastery of Cîteaux in Burgundy. Being as reform-minded as the Cluniacs, the Cistercians came to abbeys all over Spain, beginning with Fitero in Navarra and spreading west on the Road through Burgos (Las Huelgas) and León (Moreruela).

Wanting to recapture the primitive Benedictine spirit of sacrifice, poverty and simplicity, the monks imposed a strict new code of conduct on the society they encountered in Spain, making cohabitation a punishable crime and enforcing the Christian teachings concerning celibacy and marital behavior that were previously overlooked or loosely interpreted. Such was their influence that by the thirteenth century Alfonso X of León-Castile (reg. 1252-1284) was legislating stiff punishments for adultery and homosexuality in his *Partidas*. Prostitutes, however, managed to keep practicing their trade with relative impunity throughout the Middle Ages, and it is to be expected that the larger towns along the Road to Santiago had houses where the pilgrim, in a moment of weakness, could go to satisfy his natural inclination to be with a woman.

Hygiene and bathing, although not high on the list of things-to-do in the Middle Ages, were not as entirely lacking as some modern historians would have people believe. It is true that they bathed with much less frequency than most people normally do today. Some days they would wash their face in the morning. Once a week their feet might be washed, and once every few months they would go to the public baths (*baños*) run by the municipalities and clean the whole body. It is a fact that some of the municipalities (*concejos*) had to provide a public bath as part of the services to be offered to the populace. This public space had a strict schedule: 2 or 3 days per week only men had access to it; the same applied for women, and lastly, 1 or 2 days were reserved for the Jews, who in most municipalities were not allowed to bathe with the Christians.

Even in the summer, free-running water in northern Spain is ice cold, so there were probably no long lines waiting to use these few public utilities along the Road to Santiago; this is the reason some medieval Moslem historians claim they could smell a northern Christian from a great distance away.

J. The Dwellings in Villages Along the Road.

When gaining entrance to a house on the Road to Santiago, the medieval pilgrim would be entering a structure with walls made of mud reinforced with straw, its roof made of dried grass. There would typically be no interior walls, and the main, central part of the interior space would be occupied by the kitchen, with its wood-burning stove that served for cooking and for heating. The windows were square openings in the wall; these were covered with two wooden planks each that had latches in the middle. In a corner were the beds, made of wood and with a mattress on top. This mattress was usually made of a tough cloth and filled with straw; feathers were also a common mattress-fill. Different sections of the house might be separated by a curtain-like piece of cloth hanging from a beam, and the animals were sometimes kept inside, in their own part of the dwelling that resembled a stable and jutted out to the side of the structure, but was not separated from the rest of the house by any wall.

The walls were filled with agricultural and cooking utensils hanging from hooks, and the chairs were either all wooden, or had the seat and backrest made of leather, stretched between two pieces of wood and held to them by sturdy metal tacks. A simple candle lights the house at night, but only when absolutely necessary. The few valuables are kept in wooden boxes (*arcas*) that can also serve as seats.

The houses of the nobility and of well-to-do freemen were quite different, often made of stone and with richly appointed interiors: silver candle holders, oriental rugs, interior walls and individual quarters, large fireplaces and handsomely carved furniture, silverware, curtains, large kitchen with matching chimney; in short, these were places where even a modern tourist would feel quite comfortable.

This is the Spain a pilgrim would cross on his way to Santiago. For many centuries conditions remained basically the same, and even today there are many places along the Road where time has stood still, where only your bicycle and the watch on your wrist reassure you that you have not traveled back in time.

II. My Journey to Santiago.

DAY 1. 31 July 1996. Incidents.

From the standpoint of the pilgrim to Santiago, the world is one indivisible unit, that is to say, there are no identifiable separate parts to it. The Road seems to bring everything into a perfect harmony that transcends cultural, racial, national and religious categories, so that the traveler is all human beings coming from everywhere and moving in the one, common direction towards the place, the ideal, the sacred ground that will change us the moment we set foot on it.

But from the beginning comes the realization that it is the Road itself, the effort, the setbacks and the will to overcome them that effects the change, that puts pressures on the character which will ultimately make you a pilgrim and a new person. Arriving is only the one last step of the many taken. The Road to Santiago, then, extends without limits in time or space, for it is a road of the spirit, and the spirit has no boundaries. In a way, the Road is a spiritual microcosm of man's journey through life searching for meaning, his baggage the realization that he might never find it.

Our journey had an inauspicious start: the day we were to set out on our adventure, it rained so much in New York that we had to drive through very large pools of water, dodging stuck cars and trucks, to get to Rodolfo's house to pick him up. Once there, we secured the three mountain bikes that would take us in our journey and loaded them on the jeep. The way to Kennedy International Airport was a picture of watery doomsday: people who had abandoned their vehicles were wading through knee-deep water down the middle of the parkway. Making it to the airport through service roads, we soon found that the main airport roadway was closed due to flooding. I decided to walk the mile to the airline terminals to check in. I was soaked when I arrived, but I checked in without incident (although the security agent asked me several times why I was only carrying a small saddle-bag and had not checked-in any baggage). When Rodolfo finally arrived, he was told that his connection from Madrid to Pamplona, Navarra, had not been confirmed, so he and the three bikes (which were traveling with him) would be on stand-by in Madrid while Silvio (who was already in Madrid) and I had had our Pamplona flights confirmed. For me, the flight to Madrid from New York was accompanied by the uncertainty of maybe having to start for Navarra while leaving Rodolfo (and the three bikes) behind in Madrid for who knows how long.

DAY 2. 1 August 1996. Incidents.

After an overnight flight in which I was sleepless, Rodolfo and I arrived in Madrid and immediately put Rodolfo on the waiting list for the flight to Navarra's capital Pamplona (he would eventually get a seat, and in first class, no less). We then set out to meet Silvio at his Madrid hotel, the Agumar. There, we took a shower, went for tapas and basically hung around Madrid waiting for our 7:35 flight to Pamplona.

The flight was uneventful, and we found two cabs that took us to Casa García, the inn ("hostal") where we were to stay for two nights, right in the Medieval section of Pamplona. The one inconvenience was that we had to carry the boxed bicycles up four flights of steep and narrow stairs to our rooms. A good "cocido" and veal that night at the "Iruñazarra" restaurant made us recover from the busy day. So did a stout rosé wine from Navarra.

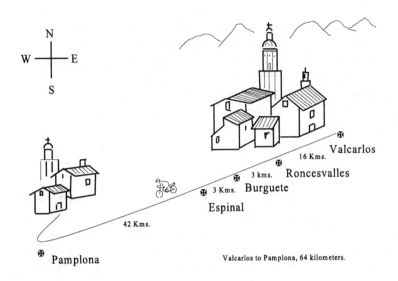

N
W —|— E
S

Valcarlos
16 Kms.
3 kms. Roncesvalles
3 Kms. Burguete
Espinal

42 Kms.

Pamplona   Valcarlos to Pamplona, 64 kilometers.

DAY 3. 2 August 1996. Valcarlos to Pamplona. Incidents.

After sleeping late, we assembled the bikes. After having a good breakfast of churros and chocolate, we made a few calls and found a company that rents vans that take you to Valcarlos, on the French border, where one can begin the Road. Agustín, our driver, was also a tour guide of sorts; he gave us many pointers and provided much information on the Road through Navarra.

The drive to Valcarlos gave us a good idea of what the Road was going to be like: tiny trails through the Navarran Pyrenees, skirting ravines, through forests and mountains the likes of which I had not seen before. The cold and the fog also made it seem like we were in Norway in March, not Spain in August. We asked Agustín to drop us off a bit down the road, in Roncesvalles.

After picking up our credentials in the small but historical town of Roncesvalles, we took to the trail, through green meadows, rolling hills and meandering streams, at times having to walk our bikes around herds of grazing cattle, nervous horses or sheep. The dreamlike atmosphere soon changed when we began the long, steep climb up to the Roldán Pass and the mind-boggling "Altos del Erro," the passes that take you from the north slopes of the Pyrenees across to the south. Most of the time is spent on foot pushing the bike up a rock-strewn trail covered with thick foliage that makes it seem as if it were night-time in the middle of the day. From time to time a steep descent, dodging rocks and crevasses at high speeds, punctuated with a hint of real danger the tedious, almost constant climb. I rejoice when I reach what I think is the summit, and yell back to my two companions telling them the good news. A little farther up we see the real summit, an imposing, challenging mountain pass several hundred meters ahead in a straight climb. Along the way the trail becomes a foot-wide path straddling a ravine with an impressive vertical drop. It is here that Rodolfo falls no less than four times from his bike, followed once by Silvio, with the good fortune that there always happened to be something to grab on the way down in Rodolfo's case (once even a rose bush), whereas Silvio dropped straight into a wide, fluffy bush that cushioned the fall quite nicely.

When we reached the top, it was already nightfall, almost pitch dark. Here, the trail parallels a highway all the way to Pamplona. Owing to the circumstances, we decided for the highway, a smooth drop of about four kilometers where our bicycles reached speeds of up to sixty kilometers per hour. On the way, we stopped at a small-town café for a refreshment of Pacharán (a strong Basque beverage), beer and water.

Arriving in Pamplona at midnight, we went straight to the Plaza del Castillo for a dinner of callos (tripe), squid, salads, potatoes and rosé wine, followed by a good, strong coffee. People milled in and out of this medieval square, and we watched the life of the city parade in front of us as we dined al fresco. Our conversation centered around the day's journey and the expectations for the days ahead, albeit from time to time the beautiful Pamplonese gentlewomen, taking their evening constitutionals, would take our minds off the trip and its incidents.

Naturally, we had a rough time bringing the bikes up the four floors of Casa García, where we again stayed for the night.

Although we had brought two cameras for the trip, Rodolfo's had faulty batteries and did not take any photographs that day, while Silvio pressed a wrong button on his and it re-wound, wiping out the pictures taken. We came away without any pictures of the Navarran Pyrenees, but it is impossible for a photograph to capture the majesty of the place, so not much was lost.

Valcarlos to Pamplona. Details.

Valcarlos is a small town on the Spanish side of the border between Spain and France, this first village on Spanish soil on the Road to Santiago. Fittingly, its church is called the Church of the Apostle Santiago, a nineteenth century construction that replaced the ancient church that was destroyed, along with most of Valcarlos, by French forces in the War of the Convention in 1793. The church contains a sixteenth century silver processional Cross in the Renaissance style, and it is the only Road-related construction in the town, although in early times there used to be a hospital for pilgrims called San Juan de Irauzqueta.

Valcarlos is situated in a deep valley in the Pyrenees, 64 kilometers from Pamplona, and it has 586 inhabitants. Legend tells us that Charlemagne and the traitor Ganelon, in their epic retreat from Spain in the year 777 A.D., were encamped in Valcarlos playing chess when they heard Roland's horn sound, calling out in desperation as his army was being wiped out by the Navarran Basques. Although Ganelon knew that his rival Roland and his forces were being slaughtered, he convinced Charlemagne that nothing was amiss, that the blowing of the horn was merely Roland hunting. For the horn to be heard in Valcarlos, the battle must have been raging in the deep valleys and ravines that lead from Valcarlos up to the Ibañeta Pass. The village's coat of arms shows a chess-board, recalling the event, and the supposed original board is kept in the Colegiata Museum in Roncesvalles. In Valcarlos the pilgrim crosses the neighborhoods of Pecocheta and Elizaldea; the tiny hamlets of La Reclusa and Gorostagaray are on its outskirts.

The heights around Valcarlos and the Cize Pass are the source of another Santiago legend: Thirty French knights on pilgrimage to Compostela are forced to abandon one in their number who has fallen ill. Only one other knight stays behind to care for the stricken companion, and they both trek up the Cize Pass hoping to make it into Spain and get some shelter. But the ill knight dies, and his faithful friend is terror-stricken by the loneliness of the heights, the prospect of meeting up with the barbarous Basques that inhabit the area, and the lifeless body of his friend. After praying to the Apostle, a Spanish knight appears on a battle charger, mounts both of them on his horse, and takes them to Compostela overnight. The dead Frenchman is buried and the other gets a revelation: it was Santiago that gave them the unexpected lift. Santiago charges him to go back and meet up with his other companions in León, where he will accuse them of bad faith and tell them that they must do penance if they are to continue on to Compostela.

Although **Valcarlos** is steeped in the symbols of the Charlemagne legend, as its name (Valley of Charles) and its coat of arms proclaim, there is also a profound sense of tradition that links it to the Road to Santiago. July 25, the traditional day of Santiago, is celebrated in Valcarlos with 6 straight days of dancing, religious processions and "pelota" matches. Always present in the revelry are the traditional dancers (*dantzaris*) called the *Bolantes*.

From Valcarlos, at 350 meters above sea level, there is a 14 kilometer climb that takes you to the Ibañeta pass, at 1,092 meters. Close to the summit, at Alto de Ibañeta (1,057 meters) there used to be a monastery called San Salvador de Ibañeta. At present there is only a chapel of the same name, whereas the hospital that was dependent on the monastery was moved to Roncesvalles.

Alto de Ibañeta is the precise spot where, according to legend, Roland and his men met their fate. This is also believed to be the place where Charlemagne, upon entering Spain, had a Cross erected; medieval pilgrims planted Crosses here to help them attain their goal of reaching Santiago de Compostela, kneeling towards Galicia and praying. There is a monolithic monument dedicated to the victory of the Spanish over Roland and the French, erected by the Navarran government in 1965 in commemoration of the jubilee year (Año Santo Compostelano), a holy year for the Road to Santiago. The chapel of San Salvador has an interesting stela that exhorts pilgrims in Basque, Castilian and French to pray for the Virgin of Roncesvalles. The 1.7 kilometers that stretch from the Ibañeta pass to Roncesvalles (952 meters above sea-level) is mostly downhill.

Roncesvalles, with its 27 inhabitants, is much more important than the numbers would indicate. It is the center of the Charlemagne legends and formal beginning of the Spanish leg of the Road to Santiago.. 47 kilometers away from Pamplona, most of its population consists of clerics and laymen that man the Church's installations there, including a hospice for pilgrims. Its name has several possible geneses, including the French "Roncevaux" (Valley of Thorns), the Basque "Ronzabals" (Valley of the Roses) or simply Erro-Zabalies, a combination of the names of the two valleys next to the town, Erro and Zaballes.

Roncesvalles has many places of interest, including the ruins of the monastery of San Salvador and the Great Hospital of Roncesvalles, founded by Sancho de Larrosa, bishop of Pamplona, in 1130. The *Colegiata de Nuestra Señora de Roncesvalles,* built mostly in the French Gothic style in the first half of the thirteenth century, is in reality a group of monuments of diverse stylistic elements. It houses the Virgin of Roncesvalles or Orreaga, a statue found in the area in the tenth century and whose hiding place was revealed to a group of shepherds by a deer with flaming antlers.

The general floor plan of the *Colegiata* consists of three naves that are not equal in size and a fortified tower built in the fourteenth century. Inside the *Colegiata,* carved from cedar wood, is the image of Our Lady of Roncesvalles, covered in silver, gold and precious stones. In its chapel of San Agustín, built in the fourteenth century, one finds the tomb of king Sancho VII el Fuerte (The Strong) of Navarra topped by a large sculpture of the king at rest. The tomb reproduces the king's true dimensions, and by the look of it he was a true giant. Some chain links that he brought back from the battle of Las Navas de Tolosa (1212) lie next to him. The *Colegiata's* chapel of Sancti Spiritus, also called *Silo de Carlomagno* (twelfth century, and thus the oldest structure in the *Colegiata*) is the place where Roland and his men, along with other heroes of the battle of Roncesvalles, are supposedly (and probably) buried. Pilgrims who died in Roncesvalles are also buried in its crypt.

The chapels of Santo Cristo and El Tesoro are also worthy of a visit.

The Museum of Roncesvalles, property of the *Colegiata*, has a number of interesting pieces, from gold and silver work objects to wood carvings, ancient coins and books, a Romanesque-style silver gospel from the year 1200 and even Charlemagne's famous chessboard, which on closer inspection turns out to be an enameled silver board, obviously Gothic and dating to the mid fourteenth century.

Also interesting in Roncesvalles are the church of Santiago, a Romanesque structure built in the thirteenth century, and the Pilgrims' Cross, on the road about one hundred meters south of town, dating from the fourteenth century.

Also in the Roncesvalles Museum is the Miramamolín Emerald, a trophy of war won by Sancho el Fuerte in the battle of Las Navas de Tolosa (1212), in which Spanish Christian armies dealt the decisive blow against the Moslems. The emerald's historical background is verified and thus clearer than that of Charlemagne's chessboard, which is perhaps the reason why it has been given a prominent place in Navarra's coat of arms.

3 kilometers from Roncesvalles is **Burguete**, a town of 350 inhabitants whose name is a diminutive of its ancient name Burgo de Roncesvalles. Burguete is in a valley nestled among mountains, at the foot of mount Menditxuri (1201 meters) and surrounded by forests of beech. The clear

waters of the river Urobi flow past, well known for their abundance of trout. A couple of kilometers southwest of Burguete is the forest of Irati, one of the largest in Europe.

Human habitation in the **Burguete** area goes back to prehistoric times, as shown by the large stone constructions (dolmens) of Urepel Ibañeta, of which the impressive dolmen of Lindux is the centerpiece. The old Roman highway that comes into Burguete from the Ibañeta pass is worth a look, as well as the Romanesque bridge of Arrobi; the church of San Nicolás de Bari is from the sixteenth century, although parts of it are medieval. The Burguete cemetery is interesting, as all the gravestones are of identical size.

Burguete's 350 inhabitants enjoy a number of feasts during the year, most important of which is that of St. John (*San Juan*), which lasts for five days. These events are enlivened by groups of folk-dancers that perform typical dances of the area, such as the "*Inguruxo*," the "*Ezquila fraile*" (the friar's cowbell), "*Ugal dantza*" (dance of the belt), and "*Priot'aren antatzea dantza*" (dance to choose the organizer of the feasts).

Out of Burguete the Road leads into the valley of the river Erro, with its forests of beech, oak and pine. The first village one comes to, 3 kilometers from Burguete, is **Espinal** (60 inhabitants), founded in the year 1269 by Thibault II (Teobaldo II), king of Navarra from 1253 to 1270. Always busy keeping Alfonso X's Castilians from attacking Navarra, and participating in enterprises like the botched 1269 crusade against the Moslems of northern Africa, Thibault founded Espinal just before leaving for Tunis with Louis IX of France, leader of the 1269 crusade. The town was to be a place to give the pilgrims to Santiago an overnight station before moving on to Pamplona, 40 kilometers away, but Thibault never saw it again, as he died in Sicily in 1270 on his way back from Tunis.

Espinal's houses have interesting decorated, dated lintels, and its parochial church, Saint Bartholomew (San Bartolomé) is a modern construction finished in 1961, with mosaics, artful stained-glass windows and a sixteenth century plateresque Cross that are good reasons to pay a visit. Lovers of prehistory might want to take a hike to the dolmens of Arriurdin and Auritz, less than half an hour away from town.

36 kilometers from Pamplona, 4 kilometers from Espinal, the Road bypasses **Mezkiritz**, with its large three storey houses and 101 inhabitants. Its Saint Christopher church (San Cristóbal) is a baroque style construction. Mezkiritz also has a stela, written in Basque, Castilian and French, that asks pilgrims to pray for the Virgin of Roncesvalles.

2 kilometers further on, at the foot of the Alduides mountains the Road crosses **Viscarret** (108 inhabitants), which used to have an inn for pilgrims; its church of Saint Bartholomew (San Bartolomé) has an interesting Romanesque portal, and the prehistoric tomb of Mugarri, on the road up to mount Tiratún, offers the traveler yet another glimpse into the remote past of the area. The palace of Ureta reminds one of this town's connections with the Road to Compostela, as its ornate Santiago's Cross proclaims from a portal. The Santiago feasts, on July 25, are an annual event.

2 kilometers from Viscarret the pilgrim enters **Lintzoáin** (65 inhabitants), at the foot of mount Tiratún (1,108 meters) and 32 kilometers from Pamplona. Two places stand out in Lintzoáin: first the church of San Saturnino, with its striking Romanesque portal; and second a curious long stone called "Los Pasos de Roldán," or "Roland's Steps," purporting to be an exact measurement of the distance covered by the hero every time he took a step. He must have been a very large fellow, if one is to judge by this stone.

From Lintzoáin there is a road, the C-135, that leads to Erro, a bulging metropolis of 118 inhabitants that is the capital of the Erro Valley district. The Road to Santiago does not go to Erro, but rather continues directly up to the Erro pass (Puerto de Erro, or Altos del Erro), at 810 meters altitude, through thick forests of beech, box, pine and oak. The Road then descends from the Erro pass to the town of **Zubiri**, which has 416 inhabitants and is only 526 meters above sea level. In Basque, Zubiri means "next to the bridge." The bridge in question, "Puente de Zubiri," also called "Puente de la Rabia," spans the Arga river and is built in the Gothic style. Old chronicles affirm that animals affected with rabies could be cured by crossing under the bridge. **Zubiri**'s hospital used to be a leper colony; it also had an important monastery which offered services to the pilgrims, but it no longer exists. Its church is dedicated to Saint Steven (San Estéban).

The Road now takes the pilgrim to **Urdániz**, a hamlet of 53 inhabitants 17 kilometers from Pamplona that has a modern church, San Miguel. **Larrasoaina**, 2.5 kilometers further on, was a very important stop on the Road to Santiago in the past, with three pilgrims' hospitals to care for the weary travelers and the sick. A medieval bridge spans the Arga river here, and the town's Gothic-style church of San Nicolás de Bari has modern additions that have not enhanced the beauty of its original forms.

3.5 kilometers further on one comes to the hamlet of **Zuriain**, with its church of Saint Steven; 2.5 kilometers past Zuriain is **Zabaldica**, where the Road to Santiago again meets up with highway C-135; 4 kilometers down the Road from Zabaldica is **Villava**, a town that is 5 kilometers from Pamplona and has a medieval bridge spanning the river Ulzama. On the southwestern side of the bridge is modern Villava, and on the northeastern side is **Arre**, an ensemble of buildings grouped around the twelfth century church of Santísima Trinidad, a Romanesque structure. At one time **Arre** had a hospital and an inn for pilgrims.

Not on the Road to Santiago, but 2 kilometers east of Arre is **Huarte**, a place where pilgrims who were ill with leprosy would go to be taken care of at the hospital of Santa María Magdalena. Huarte's church of San Juan Evangelista dates from the sixteenth century, and it has a plateresque style reredos and a Gothic style image of the Virgin Mary.

3 kilometers from Huarte one enters the city of **Pamplona**, Navarra's capital, with a population of 185,000.

Pamplona derives its name from Roman general Pompeius, who encamped his troops there in the years 75 and 74 B.C., on a hill where the ancient Basque hamlet of Iruña was located. The city owes much of its growth to the Road to Santiago. A small town in the early Middle Ages, it later began attracting a large number of foreigners, lured by the economic well-being that the pilgrims to Santiago were providing. Becoming a major stop on the Road, Pamplona grew by leaps and bounds, adding to the original Navarrería neighborhood two new ones, San Nicolás and San Cernín. While Navarrería was populated by native Navarrans (it is the neighborhood located around the cathedral), San Nicolás and San Cernín were the home of the newcomers: merchants and artisans from France and other European countries who made Pamplona their new home.

But **Pamplona** became, in effect, three cities in one, with each neighborhood or "burgo" having its own laws, courts, and even its own defensive walls to protect it in times of war. Fighting between these neighborhoods became commonplace, until king Charles II (the Noble) of Navarra decreed that the city was one indivisible unit and, in effect, destroyed the physical and legal barriers that divided it. The document that formalizes this union dates from 1423 and is called the "Privilegio de la Unión."

So, in truth, the discovery of an ancient lost tomb 700 kilometers away in Galicia determined much of the history and the physical realities of this Navarran city.

Coming to **Pamplona** from Villava the Road to Santiago enters the city through the "Portal de Francia," or "French gate," which is one of the main gates in the city's medieval walls. Once inside, the pilgrim is on Carmen street, proceeding by the cathedral and the churches of Santo Domingo and San Lorenzo. Through the areas of Bosquecillo and Vuelta del Castillo, around the citadel and out to Fuente de Hierro street, you now come to the campus of the University of Navarra. Across a stream called Sadar and the river Elorz over two stone bridges, you go up to an ancient crossroads called "San Juan de Jerusalén" and exit the city, on your way towards Cizur Menor.

Pamplona is full of monuments that remind the pilgrim of its intimate connection with the Road to Santiago. Upon entering the city on its eastern fringe, the pilgrim crosses the Magdalena bridge over the Arga river. This Romanesque-style bridge, traditional approach of the pilgrims to the city, has Jacobean reminiscences , such as the crucifer which was given to Pamplona by the city of Santiago in 1963 in commemoration of that jubilee year for the Road.

The **Pamplona** cathedral was begun in 1397 and the finishing touches were not given until 1530. The present neo-Gothic style edifice is built upon an earlier twelfth century Romanesque cathedral, and it has undergone a good number of changes and renovations in its long history; its façade, for example, was done in the eighteenth century and is the work of Ventura Rodríguez. The interior is laid out in the shape of a Latin Cross and has three naves. Its altar pieces are notable: San Juan Bautista and Santo Tomás are from the sixteenth century, Cristo de Caporroso from the fifteenth. The choir stalls are carved from English oak and were done in 1540 by Esteban de Obray; the tomb of bishop Sancho Sánchez de Oteiza is worth a look, as well as the mausoleum of Charles III and his wife, doña Leonor of Castile, situated in the central nave. The tombs show the king wrapped in a golden cope, and his draperies are edged with a galoon of French blue studded with golden fleurs de lis. The queen has her chestnut hair confined in a gold net and wears a crown; her head rests on a blue cushion. Almost in their entirety, the tombs are executed in alabaster from Sastago, a quarry near Zaragoza, and were carved by Johan Lomé of Tournay, commissioned by the king to prepare his tomb.

The pilgrim must not leave the **Pamplona** cathedral without visiting the cloisters and the kitchen. The cloisters are a marvel of design: the arcades and gables are delicately ornamented, and the capitals are striking. The cloisters were begun in the first years of the fourteenth century during the reign of Philip of Evreux, king of Navarra, a valiant warrior who would later die in Jerez (1343) while participating in the siege of Algeciras. At the time of their construction, Arnold de Barbazan was bishop, and we must presume that they were finished by the time the original Romanesque cathedral collapsed in 1390. The part of the cloisters that adjoined the original cathedral must have suffered extensive damage at the time, for it was reconstructed during the reign of Carlos III el Noble (reg. 1387-1425). The architect who built the cloisters was probably, like bishop Arnold, French; the sculptor definitely was, and we can still see his name above the Adoration of the Magi, a high relief on a plinth imbedded in the wall: *Jacques Pérut fit cet estoire*.

The **Pamplona** cathedral was famous among medieval pilgrims for the quality of the food that it dispensed daily to weary and hungry travelers. The kitchen used to prepare these meals was that of the abbey church of Pamplona, which was later incorporated into the cathedral. The kitchen is an almost square room covered with an octagonal hod on squinches at the angles; three truncated pyramids form it, fitting into each other and tapering as they rise. The Diocesan Museum, located in the refectory and the kitchen, has notable works of art.

The church of San Cernín, also called San Saturnino, was constructed in the thirteenth century and around it the San Cernín neighborhood grew. It was built in the Gothic style and its towers are very tall. Inside, two Gothic style statues greet the pilgrim, that of San Saturnino and that of Santiago Peregrino (Saint James as a pilgrim). There is also a famous bas-relief of a knight crusader which for centuries has sparked a discussion as to his true identity: is he Thibault II of Navarra, Louis of France or a certain local knight of the Cruzat family? A sign over the presbytery assures us that "Our Lady of the Road appeared here in 1487." Her image, (She is the local patroness Virgin) can be seen in the baroque chapel that adjoins the church. Outside, one can still see the famous "Pocico," the baptismal font where San Saturnino (San Cernín as he is called here) baptized the first Christians of Pamplona, and a stark image of Santiago on the portal.

Other churches in **Pamplona** that should not be overlooked by the traveler are San Nicolás, dating from the early twelfth century, which, due to successive reconstructions presents an aggregate of Romanesque, Gothic and baroque styles; Santo Domingo is a late Gothic style church that has a baroque façade built in the eighteenth century and an interesting Renaissance reredos (it was also used as a university in the seventeenth and eighteenth centuries); San Lorenzo dates from the nineteenth century, but it has a medieval tower and the chapel of San Fermín, with the famous image of that saint in whose honor the feasts and the running of the bulls take place from 12 noon, July 6, to 12 midnight,

July 14. The San Ignacio basilica is from the seventeenth century and was built very near the spot where Saint Ignatius Loyola was wounded in 1521.

Pamplona's "Casa Consistorial" was built in the fifteenth century as the first town hall of Pamplona and as a symbol of the new union of the city's three neighborhoods; outstanding in this edifice is the baroque eighteenth century façade. In the interior can be read the following statement which refers to the nature of Pamplona,: *Patet omnibus jauna, cor valde magis.* (Our door is open for all, but more so is our heart).

Outside **Pamplona**, where today one finds the University Clinic, is the site of a legendary battle: that between Charlemagne's army (104,000 warriors) and Aigolando's host. Meeting in even groups of twenty against twenty, forty against forty, one hundred, two hundred, a thousand and so on, the Christians win every combat except the very few times when they retreat (one must never retreat in one's fight for the Faith). The blood of the Moslems bathes the field and Charlemagne wins the day.

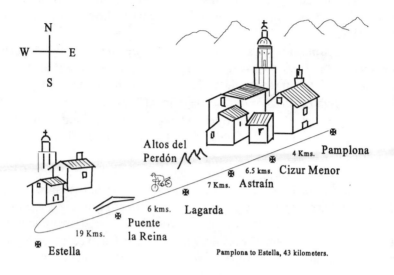

W —|— E (compass: N top, S bottom)

Altos del
Perdón

✠ Pamplona
4 Kms.

✠ 6.5 kms. Cizur Menor
✠ 7 Kms. Astraín

✠ 6 kms. Lagarda
✠ Puente
la Reina

19 Kms.

✠ Estella

Pamplona to Estella, 43 kilometers.

DAY 4. 3 August 1996. Pamplona to Estella. Incidents.

I was the only one in the group that was unable to sleep well, so I stayed in bed while my two companions went to get supplies for our lunch on the road and also to find out where to get our pilgrims' credentials stamped. When they returned, we set out on our day's trip after paying the housemaster at Casa García. We got our stamps at San Saturnino, where the image of San Cernín is kept along with one of Santiago. A quick breakfast at a bakery in front of San Saturnino and we were on our way out of Pamplona.

Outside Pamplona, we took a wrong turn and went south instead of west. Crossing the "Altos del Perdón" (which we had to get across anyway) was a task, walking most of the way and enjoying a thrilling high-speed descent on the other side.

After the "Altos del Perdón", at whose summit, I am sure, most of our sins were pardoned, it is breathtaking country into the medieval

Day 4   ✠   70

city of Puente la Reina, with rolling hills spotted with vineyards and olive groves, valleys washed by tranquil rivers and, at each side of the valleys, imposing mountains, usually crowned by castles and monasteries. As a pre-lunch snack, we stopped at an apple tree and partook of its sweet fruit.

Puente la Reina is an interesting place. It actually owes its existence to the Road to Santiago, like many other towns and villages along the way: needing a safe place where the pilgrims could cross the Arga river, the monarchs of Navarra built a bridge there in the XI Century, around which Puente la Reina grew.

At a beautiful, tree-lined avenue, we sat on a bench and had a lunch of bread, chorizo Pamplonica, ham cut fresh from a pork leg, raw onion, tomato and the ever-present Navarran rosé. Silvio put his camera on a hedge, on automatic, and it took our picture, stuffed and satisfied, whiling away the lazy mid-day hours.

Having thus regained our energy, we pedaled around town, crossed the famous bridge and began the long climb of the Mañeru-Cirauqui Range, at the summit of which we had a view of the Arga Valley and of several small white villages hugging the sides of the hills. The downward side was, again, a great thrill.

We arrived at Estella at nightfall to find that the city was in the midst of its yearly four-day feast in honor of its patron saint, Saint Andrew. We were indeed lucky to find a room immediately in the center of town. After a shower, we went into the streets and were carried away by the tide of merry-making, going from square to square and finding bands, orchestras, thousands dancing and drinking in the streets and inviting us to join them. At a nearby stand we bought two roasted chickens which we devoured in short order with beer and rosé; afterwards we walked through the ancient streets watching people have fun. The next morning, we were told, there would be a running of the bulls, Pamplona-style, at eight and nine (in Estella they run cows, which have proven much safer). We went to bed at three A.M.

We slept till ten.

Day 4. Pamplona to Estella. Details.

Out of Pamplona, at 449 meters above sea level, the pilgrim begins a steady climb. 4 kilometers from Pamplona is **Cizur Menor**, where one is greeted by the ruins of the church of San Juan de Jerusalén, which had an important hospital for pilgrims. Its Romanesque front, dating from the twelfth century, is still standing. **Cizur Menor** has other Romanesque churches: San Andrés (fourteenth century, restored), San Miguel Arcángel (thirteenth century), San Emeterio and San Celedonio, as well as a small palace (Palacio del Cabo de Armería) and the ancient hospital.

Six and a half kilometers from Cizur Menor one comes to **Astráin**, (yet another astral name) at 550 meters above sea level. Until the beginning of the twelfth century, **Astráin** had a hospital for pilgrims that no longer exists; presently one can visit the hermitage of Nuestra Señora del Perdón (at Alto del Perdón), and the church of San Cosme and San Damián, a Romanesque style structure.

Once having reached the Alto del Perdón, at 679 meters above sea level and 3 kilometers from Astráin, the pilgrim must be very careful, for on one of the trails leading to Puente la Reina there is a place called "Fuente de la Reniega," a legendary place due to the appearance there of the devil himself, who would offer thirsty pilgrims a drink from a fountain of clear, cool water for the price of renouncing God, the Virgin Mary and Santiago.

Descending into **Lagarda**, at 485 meters above sea level and 4 kilometers from Alto del Perdón, one can visit the church of La Asunción (Ascension), a Gothic style edifice from the fourteenth century, and the hermitages of San Salvador, Santa Ágata, Santa Bárbara, Santa Cecilia and San Francisco Javier de Basongáiz. **Lagarda** has 76 inhabitants.

Five and a half kilometers from Lagarda is **Puente la Reina**, where the Road coming from Roncesvalles and Pamplona meets up with the Road from Aragón. **Puente la Reina** has 2,165 inhabitants and its existence is closely linked to the Road to Santiago. It is here that, in the first half of the eleventh century, doña Mayor of Navarra, wife of king Sancho el Mayor, had a bridge built over the river Arga to facilitate the pilgrims' crossing. Due to the strategic importance of the spot, it is probable that an earlier, weaker bridge spanned the river at this precise place, but the Romanesque structure built at the queen's behest put a sturdy, reliable point of crossing over the unpredictable Arga.

The Road to Santiago enters **Puente la Reina** under the vault-like arch that joins the church of the Crucifix with the old pilgrims' hospital that was founded by Juan de Beaumont in 1469. It then follows the *Rúa Mayor*, a street that is flanked by houses with very interesting façades, as it was the original thoroughfare around which the town grew. The street is also flanked by two towers that were a part of the thirteenth century wall that protected the city.

The church of the Crucifix, at the entrance to **Puente la Reina**, is from the twelfth century and used to belong to the Knights Templar, a military-religious order that was invited to come to Puente la Reina by king García VI in 1142; the Templars defended the city and provided the pilgrims with food and shelter. The church has its original Romanesque doorway and two very interesting pieces in its interior: a Romanesque Virgin Mary and a Gothic style Crucifix of German origin from the fifteenth century whose "Y" shape reminds one of the foot of the mythical goose (*oca*). According to tradition, this Crucifix was being taken to Compostela from an unidentified German city as a sign of gratitude: Santiago's intercession had saved that city from a plague. But upon reaching Puente la Reina, the Crucifix became impossible to move, and there it has remained since the fourteenth century. Outside the church of the Crucifix the Road goes under arches formed by a vault that forms between it and the next-door convent. This situation is only repeated again when the Road proceeds under the arch of San Antón, in the province of Burgos.

Puente la Reina's church of Santiago is on the Rúa Mayor and dates from the twelfth century (Romanesque style), although it was extensively rebuilt in the fifteenth (Gothic style). On its lobe-shaped portico one can see Islamic influences, and inside it holds two Gothic style sculptures: Santiago (el Beltza) and Saint Bartholomew.

The church of Saint Peter the Apostle (San Pedro Apóstol) was built in the fifteenth century and has a Gothic style front. Inside is the Virgin of the Chori, which used to be located in the bridge tower. This Virgin (which is actually an image of the Virgin of Puy) is the source of another legend, a relatively recent one by Road standards. Our Lady's image was kept in a small tower chapel over the railing on the highest part of Puente la Reina's famous bridge, that is to say, in the middle. At some point around 1824 it began receiving the attentions of a little bird (*chori* is "bird" in Basque), who cleaned the image with its beak and kept it in tip top condition. The many feasts, processions and sundry revelry that occurred right on the bridge had no sway on the little bird, who kept doing its housekeeping with aplomb and dignity. During one of Spain's Carlist Wars (1834) a certain Count Viamanuel was the commander of the garrison that defended the city. Having taken the locals for buffoons and their legends as hogwash, he expressed utter contempt for the "chori" and its infatuation, to the point where he simulated an attack by the hostile forces of general Zumalacárregui only so that he could place his cannons right under the bird and fire salvoes to scare it. But the bird was unimpressed. Two weeks later Viamanuel was defeated and killed by the same forces that were the object of the ruse, and the locals could only interpret it as retribution for his contempt of the Virgin and her "Chori." In 1843 the Virgin was moved, in solemn procession, to Her birdless realm inside San Pedro Apóstol.

The most famous landmark in **Puente la Reina** is the bridge that gave it its name (Queensbridge). It is a Romanesque structure with six arches spanning the Arga river. The present bridge is, stone for stone, the same original eleventh century structure, except for the disappearance of a tower used to collect a toll from those crossing, and the chapel with the image of the Virgin of Chori on the railing.

Four and a half kilometers from Puente la Reina and 110 meters higher than that town is **Mañeru**, a village of 403 inhabitants. Mañeru has many seventeenth and eighteenth century houses and small palaces that show the owner's coat of arms engraved in the fronts. It has an eighteenth century Renaissance style church called San Pedro and a hermitage also built in the eighteenth century called Santa Bárbara. **Mañeru** was also given to the Knights Templar, and close by one finds the ruins of the Roman towns of Urbe and Aniz.

2.5 kilometers from Mañeru and still climbing one finds **Cirauqui**, a town of 489 souls that is 495 meters above sea level. Cirauqui is a typical medieval town, with interesting constructions like the church of San Román, built in the year 1200 with an impressive ogival front. The church of San Román still has its original semicircular Romanesque apse and its single-nave floor plan. Its front was rebuilt in the seventeenth century, and inside one can view a sixteenth century baroque reredos and a processional Cross from the same century. The early Gothic style church of Santa Catalina is also from the thirteenth century. Also of interest in **Cirauqui** are the Romanesque bridge over the Salado river, the Roman highway (*Calzada romana*), and the eighteenth century town hall, a neo-classic edifice.

5 kilometers further on the Road skirts by **Lorca** (from the Arabic "alaurque," meaning battle), a town of 156 inhabitants. Interesting in Lorca are the church of San Salvador (Romanesque apse, twelfth century), and a twelfth century bridge that spans the Salado river. Since the ancient Roman highway points toward that bridge, it is probable that there was an earlier, Roman-built bridge at that point that was used by early pilgrims.

4 kilometers on the Road comes to **Villatuerta**, a village of 790 inhabitants that at one time had six hermitages and a hospital for pilgrims on its outskirts. Villatuerta has a fourteenth century church, a Romanesque bridge and the ruins of a small Romanesque church, and one of its claims to fame is that San Veremundo de Irache, patron of the Road in Navarra, was born there.

In the year 1090, king Sancho Ramírez (Sancho V) of Navarra decided to divert this section of the Road, which previously went by the Irache monastery, at the foot of Montejurra mountain. As the old route was quite dangerous for pilgrims, the king founded a new town for the Road to traverse on the shores of the Ega river, populating it with French immigrants from Le Puy and its vicinity: **Estella**. To defend it, he had the castle of Zalatambor built.

From the beginning, **Estella** was supposedly the scene of strange occurrences that cemented its relationship with the Road to Santiago: first, a shepherd found an image of the Virgin of El Puy near the town, and second, a relic of Saint Andrew was discovered inside the tomb of a pilgrim to Santiago who had been buried in the cloister of the San Pedro de la Rúa church. These two events were interpreted by many as signs that celestial forces approved of the king's decision to alter the ancient route.

On the exact site where **Estella** was founded there existed an ancient Basque hamlet, later occupied by Romans, named Lizarra, which in the Basque language (Euskera) means "star." Many of the ancient place names all along the Road to Santiago bear the meaning of "star": names like Lizarra, Izarra. Estella, Estrella, Astráin and Aster. As most of the hamlets bearing those names are perhaps thousands of years older than Christianity and Santiago, and since in Spain the Road is entirely encompassed between 42 degrees 30 minutes and 42 degrees 50 minutes latitude, following two arms of the Milky Way, one can surmise that this route has been used since remote antiquity by peoples so ancient that history does not record them, who guided their steps by looking skyward at night as they dreamed of reaching some long-forgotten objective, which, for Christians, became associated with the tomb of one of Christ's Apostles.

With over 13,000 inhabitants, **Estella** is the most important town of this part of Navarra. Nature has endowed its surroundings with beauty, especially the area of Sierra de Urbasa, with its large forests of beech and mean altitude of 1,000 meters, where herds of cows, horses and sheep graze peacefully to the sound of clear water rivers that flow down from its heights.

Estella has many important monuments. The church of San Pedro de la Rúa is from the twelfth century, and parts of its original Romanesque cloister, containing impressive capitals, can be seen. San Pedro has a large staircase at the end of which one gains access to the church, and a tall tower of notable workmanship. San Pedro de la Rúa holds two important tombs in its serene cloister: First, that of Teobaldico, the nine-month-old Crown Prince of Navarra that died in September 1272 when he fell out of his nurse's arms into the void from the Atalaya castle ramparts, (the nurse herself also died; she may have jumped after him in a mad attempt to rescue him or may have committed suicide, precluding thus any punishment from the king). Teobaldico was the nephew of Thibault II and son of Enrique I, last monarch of the Champagne dynasty. Despite his youth, Teobaldico was already slated to be married to Violante, the daughter of Alfonso X of Castile, when he came of age. As he was the king's only male child, the dynasty was lost with him. The second tomb holds a legendary character: a Greek bishop who died in **Estella** while on his way to Compostela. As the legend has it, this pious man was bringing with him a marvelous gift for the Apostle James: the relic of Saint Andrew's back (the back of the torso, from neck to waist), which had been previously kept in Greece at the place where Andrew had been martyred. But the bishop died and was buried, and with him the relic. Yet such an object could not go peacefully into oblivion, and night after night wonderful shining light would come from the tomb, forcing the curious monks to open up the Greek bishop's resting place and find the back. The San Pedro church is located in front of the palace of the kings of Navarra, and its front is in a transition Romanesque style in which one can detect Moorish and Cistercian influences. The cloister of the church narrates in stone the martyrdom of the Apostle Saint Andrew, just as is done in the central nave and the sacristy of the Le Puy Cathedral, Estella's sister city in France.

The palace of the kings of Navarra is one of the few examples we have left of Romanesque civil architecture. Built by king Sancho el Sabio (Sancho the Sage) in the twelfth century, it contains windows of exceptional beauty and capitals of notable artistry. Nowadays it is home to the Gustavo de Maeztu museum and contains many of Maeztu's paintings (he was from Álava, but lived for much of his life in **Estella**).

The hermitage of Nuestra Señora de Rocamador is built in the Romanesque style and belonged to the convent of Rocamador, which was founded in the year 1201. Built by French immigrants, it was used as a refuge for pilgrims. In the interior, completely redone in 1961, one finds the image of the Virgin of Rocamador (twelfth century); the apse is Romanesque and contains interesting images of animals and human heads. This Virgin of Rocamador is the object of another legend. According to it, a Navarran princess was tied and thrown into the river in order to prove her guilt or innocence in an obscure matter for which she was being blamed. She invoked the Virgin of Rocamador and was saved. In a parallel occurrence, a Navarran knight who was surrounded by Juan II's Castilian soldiers threw himself fully clad in armor into the Aragón River, invoking the Virgin of Rocamador, and he too was saved. This is one of those events in which reality is stranger than fiction: it is recorded that the knight's name was actually Roque Amador.

Most of **Estella**'s church of Santo Sepulcro dates from the fourteenth century, although its ogival front is thirteenth century Romanesque; on it there is an image that seems to be that of Santiago. The front also has twelve archivolts flanked by two rows of Apostles.

The church of Santa María Jus del Castillo was in its inception the synagogue of **Estella**'s Jewish community. The original building was destroyed in 1328 and it subsequently became the headquarters of the religious order of Grandmond. The present building is Gothic and has a Romanesque apse and a baroque façade.

Among other interesting churches in **Estella** is San Miguel Arcángel (twelfth century Romanesque front, Gothic interior). San Miguel's north portal has a stone carving of the ancient Navarran Coat of Arms, the one that was used before the battle of Navas de Tolosa (1212). The old Coat of Arms has garnets instead of chains (the garnet, or ruby, was the favorite stone of the Navarran dynasty of Champagne); the ruby is also the stone out of which the mythical Basilisk's eyes are made, the symbol of the Archangel Michael, and a favorite stone among initiated alchemists. The church of San Juan Bautista has a Romanesque façade, sixteenth century reredos and a thirteenth century image of the "Virgen de las Antorchas." Nuestra Señora del Puy (founded in 1085, containing a Romanesque image of the Virgin that is completely covered in silver except for the hands and the face; the present building is new and was built over the ruins of the original by architect Víctor Eusa; it is on a hill overlooking **Estella**), the convent of Santo Domingo (founded in 1259 by Thibault II, Gothic church with a single nave that has three different levels due to the irregularity of the terrain, excellent cloisters), and San Pedro de Lizarra (Gothic style, believed to be on the site of the ancient original settlement of the hamlet, it has an interesting tower, *Torre de la Gallarda*).

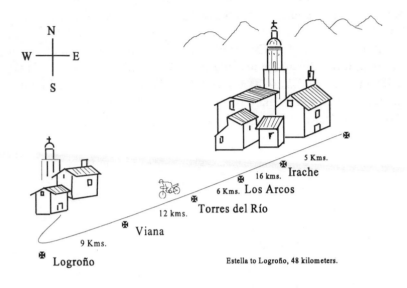

N
W —— E
S

5 Kms.
16 kms. Irache
6 Kms. Los Arcos
12 kms. Torres del Río
Viana
9 Kms.
Logroño

Estella to Logroño, 48 kilometers.

DAY 5. 4 August 1996. Estella to Logroño. Incidents.

After a breakfast of ham omelettes, bread and coffee in milk, we set out for Logroño, but were forced to make a stop of over one hour to fix a noise that Rodolfo's bike had developed in its pedal-gear. Up the trail to the monastery of Irache, we drank to our heart's content and filled up our water bottles with the wine that pours out of a wine fountain. From there we made a brief stop at the Irache Hotel, where I attempted to contact my family in New York from a phone that was either faulty or -most probably- I didn't know how to use. I managed to leave a message in my answering machine using the hotel's house phone, which the young lady at the front desk graciously offered me.

Upon leaving Irache, we had a problem. I usually went up ahead, attempting to set a good pace for the trip, while Silvio stayed in the middle and Rodolfo brought up the rear. Today, knowing we set out too late, I went unusually fast, and left my companions far behind. Realizing that this might cause us to loose contact with each other for a long period of time, I began pedaling back to where I thought the other two were coming. High on a hill, I waited for quite a while, until -great was my surprise- I saw Silvio come up the road, having left Rodolfo behind. We waited for him on that hill, which offered a very good view of the surroundings, but as the hours went by, Rodolfo did not show.

Concerned (Silvio was treating me to all types of possible disaster scenarios in which our friend could be involved), we started back to the last place Silvio had seen Rodolfo, a small town some seven kilometers away. Close to that town, we met a group of cyclists who assured us that they had seen nobody fitting Rodolfo's description come this way.

At this point, I assumed he had taken another route; this assumption was proven right when we detoured into the town of Los Arcos, where the man in charge of stamping credentials informed us that our friend had indeed passed that way some four hours before.

We started on the road at an even faster pace than before, trying to make up the four hour space that had opened between us.

Reaching Viana at around nine P.M., Silvio and I climbed to the top of the very large hill on which the oldest part of this ancient town is situated. Once on top, we recharged our systems, again "al fresco" on a narrow cobblestone street, with a pot of red beans and chorizos (Spanish sausage), mutton ribs, Irache wine and flan. Before us, in the sunset, now loomed the gray and imposing forms of the great Sierra de la Demanda, reminding us that in three days we must start that climb which will take us into the Central Plateau, the "Meseta Central," heart of Spain.

When we reached Logroño at 11:20 P.M., I was tired and had a bit of the chills. Rodolfo was nowhere to be found. We rolled around the center of the city until we reached an inn called "Pensión del Pilar," where we spoke to the owner about staying for the night. We got two comfortable rooms. The owner took a liking to us and began to relate his life story to us, whereupon Silvio began his own story in return. Not being in the mood for male bonding at this particular point, I said good night, washed up with the icy water offered in the bathroom, and collapsed in my bed.

Day 5, Estella to Logroño. Details.

3 kilometers out of Estella one comes to the town of **Ayegui**, with its 716 inhabitants. The town itself has a church (San Martín) and a hermitage (San Cipriano de Montejurra), but the greatest attraction in the area is the imposing Benedictine monastery of Santa María de Irache, where the oldest pilgrims' hospital in Navarra was located. The monastery was founded by king García Sánchez III (el de Nájera) in the mid eleventh century, shortly before he died at the battle of Atapuerta (1054) fighting against his own brothers for control of the kingdom. The monastery also served as a university from 1569-1824. It has a large Renaissance style (plateresque) cloister and a Romanesque church with a large tower adjoining it. The Irache monastery is where the abbot San Veremundo (1020-1099) lived; Veremundo was named the patron saint of the Road to Santiago in Navarra on 20 February 1969, and is one of the three great saints associated with the Road (the others are Santo Domingo and San Juan de Ortega).

4 kilometers from the Irache monastery the pilgrim goes through the hamlet of **Azqueta**, and from there, 2.5 kilometers further on is **Urbiola**, with its church of San Salvador (sixteenth century). Urbiola had (no longer) a pilgrims' hospital run by the knights of San Juan de Jerusalén.

Nine and a half kilometers from Urbiola is **Los Arcos**, a town of 1,401 inhabitants. **Los Arcos** came into being as a result of a repopulation effort in the Middle Ages, the reclaiming of a site that had been a Roman mining town. The town has two monuments that require a visit: the church of Santa María is a large structure that incorporated many different elements and period styles, ranging from the twelfth to the eighteenth centuries. Its front is from the Renaissance (plateresque) and the ogival cloister is Gothic (gótico flamígero). The image of the Black Madonna is on the high altar and dates from the sixteenth century, and there is lavish baroque decoration in the interior. High on the main portal, the stone image of the Madonna is shrouded in darkness except for a brief few minutes every June 15th, when a ray of sun touches upon the Virgin.

The other important monument in **Los Arcos** is the hermitage of San Blas, located right on the Road to Santiago. This Romanesque structure has an apse dating back to the seventh century, making it one of the oldest religious constructions on the Road

7 kilometers out of Los Arcos one crosses the village of **Sansol**, (San Zoilo); on the right is San Salvador de Penaba, where one leaves behind the basilica of San Gregorio Ostiense, where the tomb of this Italian saint is kept. This saint is the object of a strange veneration: his cranium, laminated in silver, is used as a water holder to bless the holy water that is taken to the fields, on Cruz de Mayo day, in order to bless and fertilize them. One more kilometer brings you to **Torres del Río**, a town of 238 inhabitants 477 meters above sea level.

The outstanding feature of **Torres del Río** is the church of the Holy Sepulcher (*Santo Sepulcro*), built in the twelfth century by the knights of the Order of the Holy Sepulcher in a regional Romanesque style called *románico navarro*. The layout of the building is a perfect octagon, crowned by a perfectly symmetrical star-ribbed Moorish dome. The capitals are lavishly decorated, and the Islamic influence is patent in their designs. Santo Sepulcro also has a notable Christ Crucified that dates from the thirteenth century.

The church of San Andrés, a Gothic-Renaissance building from the end of the sixteenth century, is also worth a visit.

11 kilometers from Torres del Río is the last town in Navarra on the Road to Santiago: **Viana**. With 3,470 inhabitants, it was founded in the year 1219 by king Sancho VII (el Fuerte) of Navarra (1194-1234) in order to safeguard that region of his kingdom from the always aggressive

Castile. Area place names suggest that the site had been populated in ancient times by Basques and later by Celts (Berones). Sancho VII ordered tax-breaks, exemptions and other incentives in order to lure people to come live in **Viana**, which many from twelve surrounding hamlets eventually did. Viana's condition of fortress-city can be readily seen even today in parts of the ramparts that still stand and in the fortified mansions that occupy the old part of town.

Places to visit in **Viana** are many. A first stop might be the collegiate church of Santa María, declared a national monument by the government. Its construction took place between 1250 and 1329, and its fortress aspect is in keeping with the primary purpose of the town. Santa María's tower was erected in the sixteenth century and so was one of its most important features: the front, built in the shape of a half-point vaulted niche. Close by is a flat, white, rectangular gravestone that indicates the place where the famous César Borgia, son of Pope Alexander VI, lies buried. Borgia came to Navarra in 1491 at age 16, when he was named bishop of Pamplona. At 19 he became Cardinal and at 22 was leading the armies of the Church. By 1507 he is Constable of Navarra, a job that gets him killed in the battle of Campo de la Verdad, right outside Viana, fighting the forces of Count Lerín. He was 32. His impious lifestyle led his detractors to have him buried in a place where everyone could tread on his grave, a place where one will find him to this day.

Santa María's interior has five naves. The apse aisle and the triforium are beautifully done, and also worthy of a visit are the small Magdalena chapel, the sacristy, the capitular and the chapel of San Juan del Ramo, with its decorations by Luis Paret.

Other places of interest in **Viana** are the church of San Pedro, originally erected in the thirteenth century but thoroughly reformed since. It has a baroque front with an image of Saint Peter. The convent of San Francisco is from the seventeenth century and it has a church and a baroque cloister. The old hospital of Nuestra Señora de Gracia is originally from the fourteenth century, although some parts were finished in the sixteenth. The town hall (*Casa consistorial*) is on the Plaza de los

Fueros and was built in the eighteenth century; its baroque façac
its monumental coat of arms is imposing, and so are its lateral towei.
The Balcony of the Bulls (*Balcón de los toros*) was built in the late
seventeenth century at the Plaza del Coso to serve as a sort of theater-box
from which dignitaries could observe the bullfights. Lastly, the city's
ramparts are worthy of a look.

Outside Viana is the monastery of San Francisco, or San Juan del
Ramo, a seventeenth century building that replaced the one built in 1440
by the Prince of Viana, who is said to have taken shelter on that spot
during a thunderstorm. The name "Ramo," meaning "branch," stems
from the fact that a bolt of lightning struck the tree under which the
Prince had sheltered, and one of the branches, according to tradition,
interposed itself between the Prince and and the bolt, saving his life. In
gratitude, he had the monastery built with that peculiar name. Between
Viana and Logroño one last stop is the hermitage of Cuevas, with its
fourteenth century Gothic image of the Virgen de las Cuevas. In its
proximity have been found the ruins of what may have been the most
important Celtic population center in this area of Spain, the ancient and
mythical Varea, capital of the great Celtic tribe of the Berones, said to
have been destroyed in 76 B.C. during the wars between Pompeius and
Sertorius. The large number of objects found, not only Celtic but Iberian
and Roman, tell of an important and busy population center, its coins
stamped with the word *Uarakos*, the Helenized name of the town. Close
to the Varea ruins there was a headquarters of the Order of Roncesvalles,
of Templar extraction, and many carved symbols of the "Tau" can still
be found in the area. The "Tau" is a mythical, mystical "T" associated
not only with the Templars and other orders, but with alchemy and Black
Arts. This is the place where the legend of the "Chicken that Lays the
Golden Eggs" is said to have originated, perhaps as a reference to the
alchemy that would have allowed for eggs to turn to gold. That there
were mysterious, strange occurrences in the place is attested to by the
fact that local tradition calls the warrior-monks who once lived there
"The Bad Friars." And they may never have altogether left: the nearby
Barragán fields would later be known for their concentration of warlocks,

Navarra, one can see on a hill to the left the famous forᴛ...   ᴏf Cantabria, where the locals that put up a terrible albeit doomed figᴎ. ᴢainst king Leovigildo (reg. 572-586) and his Visigothic army in the sixth century. The pilgrim now crosses into La Rioja and enters the city of **Logroño**, 10 kilometers from Viana and across the mighty Ebro river. This is the legendary Ebro, home to the goddess Lusina (Melusina), bearer of fertility, endowed with the webbed feet of a goose (Oca) and wife to the powerful Celtic god Lug. **Logroño** also owes its existence to the Road to Santiago and the famous stone bridge that was built there over the Ebro (in the eleventh century) to facilitate the pilgrims' crossing. The original bridge (*Puente de piedra de San Juan de Ortega*) was demolished in 1884 and a new one put in its place, with seven arches spanning 198 meters across.

    Logroño's Jacobean heritage is linked to San Gregorio Ostiense, the bishop of Ostia and abbot of San Cosme and San Damián in Rome. It is said that during the eleventh century a terrible locust plague was devastating much of Rioja and Navarra, so the locals contacted Pope Benedict IX, who, divinely inspired, sent Gregory to Spain to see what he could do. Arriving at Calahorra in 1039, he took the relics of Saints Emeterio and Celedonio on procession throughout the fields up to Logroño, followed by the populace. In the name of God he then ordered that the locusts leave the land, which they did by grouping in a tight formation and flying straight up into the skies. He stayed on in Logroño to care for the pilgrims to Santiago and better the Road. Here he met Santo Domingo de la Calzada and became his teacher. Upon his death in 1043 his coffin was placed on a donkey that was allowed to roam free; the animal came to a stop at the hermitage of San Salvador de Penaba, next to Sorlada, where he was buried. It is said that the water that passes through his skull has the power to repel locust plagues.

    In **Logroño** the original pilgrimage route crosses the bridge and advances through *Rúa Vieja* (Old Street), Barriocepo Street and *Rúa*

Mayor (Broadway). In this city the pilgrim might quench his thirst at the "Fountain of the Pilgrims" (*Fuente de los peregrinos*), and then enter the church of Santiago el Real, on whose front there is a large statue of the saint (sculpted in the seventeenth century) on horseback, sword in hand and slaying Moors (Santiago Matamoros). **Logroño**'s church of San Bartolomé is a Gothic building with some Romanesque elements; its tower dates from the eleventh century and is the oldest structure in the city. The front is Gothic, fourteenth century, and is decorated with sculptures by masters from the Navarran school of sculpture. The church of Santa María del Palacio has a pyramid-shaped tower with a pinnacle dome in a Romanesque-ogival style. It is said that Byzantine Emperor Constantine himself gave the funds to build this church, named del Palacio because the ancient palace of the kings of Navarra was on a lot right next door.

The church of Santa María la Redonda (cathedral since 1959) is a Gothic edifice built at the end of the fifteenth century, although it has undergone successive reforms since, especially in the eighteenth century. Santa María la Redonda was built over an earlier (tenth century) church, and it has two stylish towers (Las Gemelas). Because of successive transformations, the church also has baroque and rococo elements in its structure. The tomb of a Carlist War hero, the liberal general Espartero (who lived in Logroño from 1856 to 1879), can be seen inside.

In one of the few remaining parts of the medieval wall one can see the Charles V gate, the place where, traditionally, pilgrims exited the city on their way to Navarrete. The neo-Classical Palacio de Espartero (eighteenth century) is the seat of the provincial museum.

The **Logroño** area was protected in the Middle Ages by the military order of La Terraza, also called La Jarra, which made sure no harm came to the pilgrims to Santiago. In fact, the Virgin of La Jarra is said to have been discovered by don García, king of Navarra, in a cave where today stands the monastery of Santa María la Real de Nájera.

Not on the Road, but 17 kilometers south of Logroño, is a place worth visiting: **Clavijo**. It was in the plain of Clavijo that, on 23 May 848, the forces of Ramiro I of Asturias (reg. 842-850) met the army of

Abd-al-Rahman II, emir of Córdoba and powerful leader of Moslem Spain. As the story goes, the first day of battle went badly for the Asturians, whose army was badly mauled by the enemy. It was during the night that king Ramiro, after regarding his defeated and exhausted Asturian, Leonese and Galician troops, is said to have had a vision of Saint James, Santiago himself, appearing on a white charger while holding a white banner with a red Cross on it. Santiago told him that the fate of Christianity was in the hands of Spanish warriors, and that victory had to be won at all costs (he even told the king how to array his troops for battle on the following morning). Conveying this information to his men, the king found that their spirits soared, and a famous victory was won that day against the Moslem infidels (Santiago even appeared out of a cloud, sword in hand, making short work out of the astonished Moslems, whose dead bodies littered the field at the end of the contest).

Ramiro I was so grateful to Santiago for having helped win the battle of Clavijo, that he imposed a tax called "Voto de Santiago" over his subjects, monies that helped build, maintain and beautify first the primitive church and then the cathedral of Santiago de Compostela. After many centuries, the "Voto de Santiago" was abolished by the Spanish Congress (Cortes Españolas) in 1834.

What is so interesting about the battle of **Clavijo** is that it exists in that gray area between myth and reality, to the point where some historians doubt it ever took place. The possibility that the whole thing was a political ploy has not been lost to some few skeptics, who see it as the invention of some very sharp individuals who saw the need to create a national symbol for Spain at a time when it was most needed. It is true that after this battle (if it ever took place), the battle cry "Santiago y Cierra España!" became commonplace among all Spanish soldiers, who, no matter what region they were from, what language they spoke or who was their king, now had a common myth, a symbol that united them in their common cause against the Moslem enemy. I would add at this point that a battle of this magnitude, in this site and in this year would not be entirely inconsistent with the pattern of Christian expansion in this area.

It is in **Clavijo**, facing a hill on which an ancient castle keeps a stone-silent honor-guard on the hallowed plain, that the front of a little church proclaims, with unwavering resolve, the enduring relevance of the event with a beautiful stone sculpture of the armed and mounted "Santiago Matamoros."

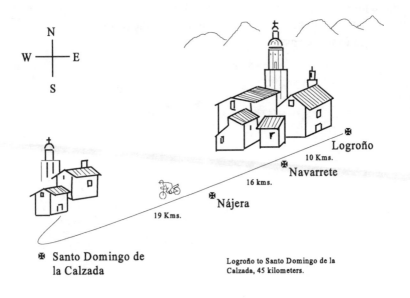

N
W —— E
S

Logroño
10 Kms.
Navarrete
16 kms.
Nájera
19 Kms.

✠ Santo Domingo de
la Calzada

Logroño to Santo Domingo de la
Calzada, 45 kilometers.

DAY 6. 5 August 1996. Logroño to Santo Domingo. Incidents.

We left Pensión del Pilar early in the morning and went straight to the local Pilgrim's Refuge, sealed our credentials and enquired about our missing companion, but nobody had seen him. We waited a couple of hours and, when he did not show, we had breakfast and left the city. Another steep climb.

For many years I have taught my college students that, after Switzerland, Spain is the most mountainous country in Europe. Now that I have experienced the physical reality that is responsible for that academic statement, I will be able to speak about Spain's geography with much more conviction in the future.

There is a stretch of the Road to Santiago outside Logroño that coincides with a national highway. When we traversed it, it was undergoing some heavy road repair, and we toiled very hard, weighed down with our ever-heavier saddlebags (panniers), to climb the many kilometers using a two-foot-wide road margin, with trucks speeding right by us at a very intimate and uncomfortable distance.

Back on the trail, it winds its way up and down hilly country, vineyards everywhere (this is, after all, La Rioja), and is full of smooth round stones which, if you hit one straight on, can make your bike come to a full and unexpected stop.

Pedaling into Nájera at around 1 P.M., we came upon a restaurant that had a number of trucks parked outside. I instantly remembered the old adage "eat where the truck drivers eat." The owner allowed us to put our bikes in a large garage that was part of the restaurant complex, and we then set about regaining our strength with a hefty lunch of tocino (heavy bacon), tripe stew, Spanish omelette, chorizos and beer. Stocking up with water, we went straight to the local Pilgrim's Refuge, but no sign of Rodolfo. We waited in the square outside the refuge, looking at workers set up for an outdoor concert in which the Bilbao Symphonic Orchestra, one of Spain's most esteemed, would perform that night. I called home from a nearby telephone cabin, and was informed from New York that Rodolfo was alright, pedaling on his own and hoping to meet us "up the road." But that could be anywhere, behind or in front of us. The long wait afforded me some time to look at the architecture that surrounded the square. Noting the evident age of the buildings and the cracks that some had developed on their walls, I asked one of the workers about the safety of buildings that had such cracks. "Some of those cracks," he replied, "could be nine hundred years old: don't worry, these buildings are safer than many of today's modern constructions."

We waited until 6:30 P.M., visited Santa María la Real, an XI Century monastery which gave us a special pilgrim's rate at the entrance, and left for Santo Domingo de la Calzada. On instinct, we decided to take a stretch of the highway that parallels the Road into the town. This way, we hoped to either find our companion or get news from him, perhaps from other cyclists on the Road. As it happened, as we were pedaling on the outskirts of the town, a young lady ran out of a lonely gas station and explained that a fellow named Rodolfo had left a message there for us, saying that he would be waiting for us at the "parador" in front of the cathedral. As we approached the place, a smiling Rodolfo was waiting, and he had found very suitable overnight accommodations for all three of us at a place run by nuns.

Santo Domingo de la Calzada was also having its yearly feasts, so we walked around and enjoyed the party atmosphere, had a dinner of salmon, veal, potatoes and "lechada" (a sort of yogurt), and made it back to our rooms before 12 midnight, the hour at which the nuns close the gates for the night. Our mounts spent the night tied to a tree in the garden.

The nunnery is quiet and calm. Traveling on this Road that is as ancient as humanity and as infinite as the imagination of a child, it is easy to feel like a child again, and it is a splendid sensation. It may be because the "Camino de Santiago" is a road that not only leads to a specific place on the map, but is a path so steeped in myth and legend that every step you take is more than the physical exertion required to move forward: you are treading here on another level of reality, where you are one with your surroundings and with every other traveler that has come this way hoping that, at the end of the journey, he would experience an epiphany that would give meaning to his life. In effect, the journey affords you the luxury of entering your own self and, with every step, becoming increasingly aware of the miracle of life; your own life, with all its joys and wonder. You breathe here a marvelous atmosphere of *quest* that endows you with a window into the infinite structures of the universe. Perhaps what makes human beings truly different from all other forms of life is that we are involved in an eternal quest to discover universal truths. A child experiences life in this way, every day a wonderful roller-coaster of discovery, free of the walls and closed doors with which adults "protect" themselves. On the many occasions when I found myself alone, perhaps kilometers away from my two friends, I sensed that the loneliness gave way to a slow, deliberate introspection that uncovered the many layers of fallacies and pretenses with which we clothe our daily lives in order to function within the rigid parameters of modern society. All alone at a high mountain pass, a small trail ahead, with the only sounds being the wind rustling in the trees and the faint cry of a hawk flying in the valley below, one tends to put one's spiritual house in order, taking account of the values by which one's life is lived and contemplating the perceived objective of existing on this planet. One comes to the conclusion here that, as with this "Road of Stars," what is important in life is not some abstract future objective, but the road itself, living the present moment to the fullest, taking one step at a time, looking at the valleys below and the mountains ahead and knowing that on this Road, at this moment, on this precise spot is where God intended you to be; the road is long, Santiago is far and you might never make it there, so breathe the fresh air coming from the pine grove around you and be sure that you are here for a reason.

Day 6, Logroño to Santo Domingo de la Calzada. Details.

11 kilometers from Logroño is **Navarrete**. Founded by Alfonso VIII on what was an ancient hamlet (probably Celtic), Navarrete has a typical medieval fortress-town layout of concentric streets on easily defensible high ground. In Navarrete one can still see parts of the medieval ramparts and a twelfth century castle, as well as the church of Asunción or Sagrario (sixteenth century), with its baroque (Churrigueresque) reredos, a triptych attributed to Rembrandt and three naves. **Navarrete**'s cemetery has an interesting Romanesque portal (thirteenth century) with Gothic elements that was brought here from the old hospital of the Order of the Holy Sepulcher. Outside the town there used to be the convent of San Francisco that it is said was founded by San Bernardino de Siena, who passed through Navarrete on his way to Compostela in 1427. It was in this town that the French mercenary general Bertrand du Guesclin was imprisoned after his defeat in the battle of Nájera (1366) at the hands of Pedro el Cruel. One of Navarrete's streets has the curious name of "Certijo," probably because it was a good place to watch the movements of enemy armies in the valley below ("acertijo" in Spanish is to keep a watch, to spy upon).

16 kilometers west of Navarrete is **Nájera**, the traditional capital of La Rioja (Logroño is the modern capital). Nájera grew from its humble origins as a Roman encampment after it was incorporated into the Road to Santiago by order of king Sancho III el Mayor (reg. 1000-1035) in the year 1030. The origin of its present name is most probably Arabic, from that language's words for "place among the stones." The town is built on the site of large rock formations that contain a myriad of caves and grottos that provide evidence of human habitation since prehistoric times.

The pilgrim enters **Nájera** by crossing a bridge on the Najerilla river that was originally built in the twelfth century by San Juan de Ortega, but was replaced in 1886 by a more modern structure. Close to the bridge was the old Hospital de Santiago, and inside the town itself was the Hospital del Emperador, both charged with taking care of the pilgrims.

Nájera is king García Sánchez III's favorite city. Here he founded the monastery of Santa María la Real and put his family's pantheon there. He also had many relics brought here: those of the martyr Saint Vincent, Saint Prudencio, bishop of Tarazona, Saint Vital and Saint Agrícola. He also gave the church a solid gold Cross that was inlaid with the teeth of Saint Steven, proto martyr.

It was also in **Nájera** that king García Sánchez III instituted Spain's first known military order, the Order of the Grail (Orden de la Terraza) in 1044. The story has it that the king had gone hunting with his hawk and was following a dove through a dark forest. He then saw the dove fly into a cave from which a strange light was coming, and it was followed in by his hawk. Entering the cave in pursuit of his hawk, the monarch saw the image of the Virgin on top of a primitive altar, and next to the Virgin a Grail ("Terraza" in old Castilian). To his surprise, the hawk and the dove are getting along like old friends. In an era when many kingdoms were expending great resources in their search for the Holy Grail, here was the king of Navarra with a Grail of his own, and in his favorite city. The cave, with its Grail and an image of the Virgin, is contained within the monastery; it is over this cave that Santa María la

Real was built.

So the most impressive structure in **Nájera** is the monastery of Santa María la Real, founded by Navarran king García Sánchez III el de Nájera (reg. 1035-1054) in the year 1052. Shortly thereafter a church was begun, being consecrated on 29 June 1056 by the archbishop of Narbonne, who was assisted by Gómez, bishop of Burgos, and Gómez, bishop of Nájera. Three kings were present at the consecration: Fernando I of Castile (reg. 1035-1065), Sancho IV Garcés, king of Navarra (reg. 1054-1076), and Ramiro I, king of Aragón (reg. 1035-1063). The church was destroyed in the fifteenth century, when the present church was built (1442-1453). In 1053, one year before his death, king García Sánchez III attempted to enhance the prestige of his newly founded monastery by sending for the body of San Millán, which was venerated at the upper church (Suso) of San Millán de la Cogolla at the time. Legend has it that after traveling for a short distance, the body became impossible to move: the saint had no desire to be moved. The body was then brought back to its original resting place.

But Santa María la Real already has many important bodies buried in its royal pantheon, including that of Doña Blanca de Navarra, great granddaughter of El Cid, who died giving birth to her son, the future Alfonso VIII of Castile, in 1156.

In 1079 the monastery was incorporated into the order of Cluny by Alfonso VI of León-Castile, hoping thus to promote the pilgrimage to Santiago. The present building is a fifteenth century Gothic structure that was built over the original Romanesque monastery. In it, one can see a mix of Gothic and Renaissance elements, the result of intensive rebuilding. Inside is the image of Santa María de Nájera and the royal pantheon where several kings of Navarra, Castile and León rest. Outstanding in the pantheon is the Romanesque sepulcher cover of queen Doña Blanca de Navarra. The choir stalls are a masterwork of the Isabelline style, with some backrests showing Jacobean (Road to Santiago) imagery. The monastery's cloisters (Claustro de los caballeros) is a mixture of Gothic and Isabelline styles. In the summer, a play based on the medieval chronicle called *"Crónica najerense"* is staged in the monastery, with scenes where actors dressed as pilgrims take part.

The plains between Navarrete and Nájera traversed by the Road to Santiago were the scene of the bloody encounter between the armies of Pedro (the Cruel), king of Castile (reg. 1350-1369) and those of his half brother Enrique of Trastámara, rivals for the throne of Castile. The troops were mostly Castilian on both sides, with the Black Prince Edward of Wales and his Englishmen fighting on Pedro's side, while general Bertrand du Guesclin and his Frenchmen, with some Aragonese troops, sided with Enrique. The battle was joined on 13 April 1367, and when the dust cleared Pedro had gained a resounding victory. Years earlier, Pedro had murdered the "Red King" of Granada and taken a priceless ruby that this Moslem ruler was fond of wearing in his turban. As a sign of gratitude, Pedro gave the ruby to the wife of Edward of Wales, who left for England shortly after the battle. Today the ruby embellishes the Imperial Crown of Britain that is kept in the Tower of London.

But the story doesn't end there: Enrique de Trastámara managed to escape from the battlefield, and two years later killed his brother in hand-to-hand combat inside a tent in Montiel, calling him "you Jew bastard" as he ran him through (Pedro's state administration apparatus was run virtually in its entirety by Jews, a situation that irked many, who blamed them for everything that went wrong in Castile).

On another note, it is also in the valley of Nájera that the legendary Roland is said to have slain the giant Farragut.

6 kilometers from Nájera is the village of **Azofra**, a very hospitable place with an ancient fountain where pilgrims had access to clean, cool water. A hospital for pilgrims was founded next to the fountain in the twelfth century, and it had a church dedicated to Saint Peter. The name "Azofra" comes from the Arabic "as-sufra," which means "the tax." After the area was conquered by the Christians, a community of Moslems remained behind in this town, and its members were forced to pay a tax just like the Moslems had forced a tax on the Christians centuries earlier.

Detouring south from Azofra, and not on the Road to Santiago, one comes first to the royal monastery of Santa María del Salvador de Cañas (twelfth century, recently restored), which has a noteworthy reredos. Then, fifteen kilometers south of the Road, is the town of **San Millán de la Cogolla**, where one finds the "upper church" (*Suso*), a tenth century monastery that is partially excavated out of the side of a mountain. Mozarabic in style, its church has horseshoe arches and is the place where the relics of San Millán were venerated; this is where the tombs of the celebrated "Infantes de Lara," of epic fame, and that of San Millán are located. The monastery of Suso is also the place where Gonzalo de Berceo (c. 1190-after 1264), the first known author in the Spanish language, lived and worked, serving as notary and legal and financial administrator.

A new monastery, the "lower church" (*Yuso*) was concluded at **San Millán de la Cogolla** in 1067 on the spot where San Millán's body is said to have become immobile. Extensively reconstructed in the period spanning the fifteenth through the eighteenth centuries, many of its dependent structures are done in the style called "Herreriano," while its church is of a late Gothic style (sixteenth century). The Yuso monastery has a library that contains books written as far back as the tenth century, and the cloisters offer an interesting mix of styles: a Gothic lower level and a neoclassic top level. The museum and the royal hall are also worth a visit.

Back on the Road to Santiago, and 13 kilometers from Azofra, the pilgrim comes to **Santo Domingo de la Calzada**. The saint whose name this town bears is one of the great characters of the Road to Santiago, having dedicated his life to assisting pilgrims and to creating the infrastructure that made the trip possible and less dangerous. **Santo Domingo de la Calzada** originated (1044) and grew around the paved highway (calzada), the bridge, the hospital and the church that the saint had built in the area for the pilgrims, and it became so important that defensive walls and ramparts were built around it (parts of which can still be seen).

Saint Domingo, was born in Viloria, in the province of Burgos. His parents, García and Orodulce were of the minor nobility (hidalgos).

As a young man, Domingo wanted to serve God, so he was taken to the monasteries of San Millán de la Cogolla and Valvanera, where he was rejected because of his ineptitude (he even failed at learning to read). Frustrated, he goes to live with a hermit in the forests next to the river Oja, until he meets San Gregorio Ostiense, who, by the simple act of pronouncing his name, makes him a wise man. Domingo now settles in a place called La Hayuela, or El Fagal, where he clears whole forests with the use of a sickle, dries bogs, reroutes rivers and builds a highway for the pilgrims. Becoming famous for his work, he now receives visits from people like Santo Domingo de Silos, recently exiled from Navarra for his pro-Castilian views, and takes a disciple, San Juan de Ortega, who would emulate his master as a great patron of the Road to Santiago.

Santo Domingo de la Calzada now builds a bridge over the river Oja and begins a series of miraculous cures and even resurrections, mostly of people involved in work-related accidents; he also turns wild bulls into humble, helpful farm animals.

His mother, Orodulce, died in 1088. In 1090, his city having passed into Castilian hands, he is charged by Alfonso VI of Castile to repair or build every bridge from Logroño to Compostela, a job that will take him 8 years, to 1098. In 1102 he had his sepulcher constructed outside the cathedral of Santo Domingo de la Calzada, an action intended to force his disciples to enlarge the cathedral in order to incorporate his tomb. Domingo died on 12 May 1109, being well over 90 years old. His miracles, according to his devotees, have never stopped. It is also maintained that in the refectory of the pilgrims' hospital he built no one has ever seen a fly. Santo Domingo is the patron saint of public works in Spain.

The cathedral of **Santo Domingo de la Calzada** is a Gothic structure that was built over an existing Romanesque church dating from 1106. It has a stylish baroque belfry and a twelfth century Romanesque apse; the saint's mausoleum has Romanesque sculptures from the twelfth century and an interesting Gothic canopy (gótico florido). The also Gothic chicken coup up high on a wall is home to a rooster and a chicken, kept there as a reminder of the miracle in which two chickens, which had been cooked and served, flew away from the plate. Also interesting in the cathedral are the chapel of La Magdalena and the chapel of Santa Teresa, with a Flemish-style reredos. The plateresque choir stalls and the main reredos are superb.

Two other notable buildings in **Santo Domingo de la Calzada** are the palace of the bishop, a Gothic structure, and the convent of San Francisco, with its large sixteenth century church and the tomb of fray Bernardo de Fresneda, confessor to the great Philip II.

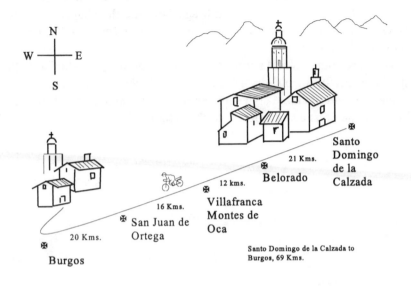

DAY 7. 6 August 1996. Santo Domingo to Burgos. Incidents.

We say our goodbyes to Santo Domingo de la Calzada by visiting the cathedral, where two chickens are kept in order to commemorate a miracle reported to have occurred here a long time ago. According to the residents, a local woman fell madly in love with a young pilgrim from Santu, a place near Wesel and Res, in Germany, who was traveling to Santiago with his parents. The pilgrim scorned her and she, furious and resentful, put a piece of silver tableware inside the unsuspecting traveler's bag. When she accused him of robbery and the loot was discovered, the young man was sentenced and was promptly hanged. His distraught parents continued on to Santiago, where they received a sign from the Blessed Apostle himself that, on their return to Santo Domingo de la Calzada, their son would live again. Back in Santo Domingo, they went to the unyielding judge, who declared that if their son was innocent, the two chickens he was now in the process of eating would get up from his dinner-plate and fly off. Which they promptly did. Upon returning to the place where their son had been hanged, they found him to be alive and in sparkling good health, none the worse for wear. The locals will tell you that the chickens kept inside the cathedral are the original fowls, kept alive throughout the centuries by some special dispensation. Well, we saw the chickens, but we couldn't find the resurrected pilgrim or his panting admirer.

Also inside the cathedral, the elaborate sepulcher of Santo Domingo is impressive. He was a champion of the pilgrims and of the Road, being responsible for many hospitals and refuges for pilgrims, especially in the area around the city that now bears his name.

We had breakfast at a very attractive restaurant in the middle of town, where the creamy pastry was marvelous, especially washed down with a good coffee in milk. We then begin the journey towards our next destination, Burgos, crossing through the Sierra de la Demanda and the mythical "Montes de Oca," a mountain chain that welcomes you to Castile with impenetrable forests. The towns you encounter along the way, such as Villafranca Montes de Oca, give you the feeling that the stones of their churches and the roofs of their houses are not anchored to our planet by the force of gravity, but by the force of time itself. Within walls made with stones that were put in place one thousand years ago one feels the presence of lives lived generations ago, of people whose dreams were not so different from ours, who smiled and cried like us, and whose existence on this earth no one remembers.

The people we meet along the way are simple, hard-working folk who when they wish you a safe trip they mean it.

We reach Burgos and head straight for the cathedral, a marvel of Gothic architecture that is now being restored. After a pre-dinner snack of chorizos and blood pudding at a local tapas bar close to the cathedral, we take a short respite at the central riverside park, surrounded by statues of fierce Castilian kings; we then go off and find a small "hostal" with the grandiose name of "Hilton," check in and head back downtown; there we visit Santa Gadea, a church El Cid himself made famous. Back in our

"Hilton," we freshen up and go for a dinner that includes mushroom soup and pork tongue. A television set shows us a "very important" soccer match while we eat. Satisfied, we head to our beds for the night.

It slowly dawns upon us that the owner of the "Hilton" is not a very courteous fellow. We ask him for a place to leave our bikes, and he promptly states that yes, he has a garage, but that will cost us 200 pesetas (about $1.65) per bicycle. We pay. We ask him for towels for the bathroom and he says yes, there are towels, at 200 pesetas each. The soap was also 200 pesetas. What happened next is living proof that, like the medieval *Pilgrim's Guide to Santiago de Compostela* states, you must always be courteous and kind to pilgrims... or else! In the middle of the night, the wash basin in my room woke me with a sound of water traveling at high speeds. Turning on the light I found myself in the presence of a geyser: water was shooting up from the basin in spaced, short spurts. Too tired to try to figure out the unlikely physics behind the inexplicable event, I shut the light and attempted to return to the pleasant dream that was so strangely interrupted.

In the morning we found a very wet innkeeper on the phone frantically attempting to get a plumber to come to his aid, for all the building's plumbing had been knocked out by some mysterious phenomenon. That ought to teach him that the Blessed James works in mysterious ways indeed.

Day 7, Santo Domingo de La Calzada to Burgos. Details.

The last town on the Road to Santiago in La Rioja, 5 kilometers from Santo Domingo, is **Grañón**, a village that grew around a twelfth century castle that guarded the volatile Castile-Navarra border. At one time Grañón had a hospital for pilgrims. It has three religious edifices: the church of San Juan Bautista, the basilica of Nuestra Señora de Carrasquedo, and the Ermita de los Judíos (Hermitage of the Jews), which has a sixteenth century transept.

5 kilometers from Grañón, the first town on the Road in Castile

is Redecilla del Camino. The village consists basically of a row of houses on each side of the Road to Santiago, with the old San Lázaro pilgrims' hospital and a little church with a unique Romanesque baptismal font to make things interesting for the traveler.

1.5 kilometers from Redecilla is **Castildelgado** where, in the place where there once was a monastery and a hospital dedicated to the Apostle Santiago, now stands the hermitage of La Virgen de Campos. In town one can still see the house of the Castildelgados, the family that gave the town its name. The town had been named Villa del Pun (Villaipun), until bishop Jerónimo Gil Delgado gave it his second surname. Outside the town is the fountain of Jaqui (or Jaque), and very close by is Viloria de Rioja, birthplace of Santo Domingo de la Calzada.

9.5 kilometers further on is **Belorado** (called "Belfuratus" in the *Codex Calixtinus*, which means "beautiful and narrow place"). For a long period during the Middle Ages this town was smack on the border of the kingdoms of Navarra and Castile... not an enviable lot. Its church of Santa María dates from the sixteenth century and has an interesting Renaissance reredos. The church of San Pedro is from the seventeenth century, and the hermitage of Nuestra Señora de Belén occupies the spot where once the old "Hospital de los Caballeros" cared for pilgrims. **Belorado**'s patron saint (shared with nearby Cerezo) is Saint Vitores, who is always represented carrying his head under his arm. According to tradition, Vitores was decapitated by the Moslems, but to the surprise of all those present at the beheading, he picked up his head and walked away. He survived in a headless state for three days and nights until he was able to defeat (some say convert) the infidels. There are many caves in this area, many occupied by hermits in the Middle Ages (Saint Vitores is said to have lived in a cave in Cerezo).

4 kilometers from Belorado is the village of **Tosantos**, which has a hermitage called Nuestra Señora de la Peña.

4 kilometers further on the pilgrim reaches **Espinosa del Camino**, a hamlet in whose Asunción parish church is an interesting ancient woodcut of the Crucified Christ.

A hike of 2.5 kilometers takes you to the old Roman settlement of Auca, renamed **Villafranca Montes de Oca** during the Middle Ages, when immigrants from France were settled there. The town is on the strategic springboard from which the pilgrims (or anyone else, for that matter) would begin their crossing of the Oca mountains through the high passes. The "auca" or "oca" is the mythical goose, a mystical symbol of mysterious religious rites since remote Antiquity. Time-worn stones that tell of ancient human habitation in the region show the stylized webbed foot of the goose, a sign left by initiated stone-cutters.

Villafranca Montes de Oca was one of the most important holdings of the medieval kingdom of Castile on the swath of land it occupied along the eastern slopes of the Oca mountains, guarding, as it were, the approaches to the Pedraja pass (Puerto de la Pedraja, whose name may derive from the Celtic "jars," or "goose"), eastern gateway to Castile. Its importance is attested to by the fact that it was an episcopal see up to the year 1076, when the see passed to Burgos. Tradition has it that its first bishop was Saint Indalecio, appointed by the Apostle Santiago himself. Owing to its position on the border of two antagonistic states and its inaccessibility, the region of the Oca mountains was a refuge for outlaws for many centuries.

Villafranca Montes de Oca has many interesting monuments, among which one can point to the church of Santiago Apóstol, dating from the seventeenth century. Santiago Apóstol contains a wood-cut of Santiago and a very large scallop shell (*vieira*). The scallop shell was brought from the Philippines, and is of such dimensions that it serves as a holy water font.

The hermitage of the Virgen de Oca has a thirteenth century image of the Virgin, and next to it is the well where Saint Indalecio's body was thrown after he was martyred (some say they can still see his blood on the stones inside the well); the remains of the Mozarabic monastery of San Félix contains the sepulcher of Diego Porcelos, founder of the city of Burgos. The San Antonio Abad hospital, founded in 1380 by queen Juana Manuel, has an interesting portal with the coat of arms of the Catholic Kings, Fernando and Isabel: it is presently being restored.

5.5 kilometers of steep climb bring you to the Pedraja Pass, at

1130 meters above sea level, and 6.5 kilometers further on (downhill now) you arrive at **San Juan de Ortega**. The town bears the name of a disciple of Santo Domingo who, like his mentor, dedicated his life to helping pilgrims and improving the Road's infrastructure.

Juan de Ortega was born in Quintanaortuño, in the province of Burgos, in 1080. His parents, Vela Velázquez and Eufemia were also of minor nobility (hidalgos). Juan enters the service of the Church and is ordained at Nájera, where he meets Santo Domingo de la Calzada. Getting away from the wars between Alfonso I el Batallador and his wife Urraca, he travels to Rome on pilgrimage and then goes on to Jerusalem. On the way back to Spain he survives a shipwreck thanks to his prayers to Saint Nicholas of Bari, so he promises to erect a church in his name. Back in Spain, he decides to erect the church in one of the most dangerous places along the Road to Santiago, a place in Montes de Oca called Urtica (Ortega), home to a host of thieves and highwaymen. What he builds during the day, the thieves destroy at night, but he perseveres until the thieves give up, too tired to continue tearing down what they know will be right back up the next day. The church is followed by a hospital for pilgrims and construction continues until a whole new community eventually springs up on the site. From San Juan de Ortega the saint goes forth to rebuild bridges at Logroño, Nájera and Santo Domingo, he dries the bogs between Agés and Atapuerca and builds a highway and a bridge there. Close to death, he is taken from Nájera to Ortega, where he dies on 2 June 1163.

San Juan de Ortega is credited with innumerable miracles. His parents are said to have conceived him after 20 years of trying, so he is the saint of fertility. One of the recipients of his miracles is Her Catholic Majesty Isabel, who journeyed to San Juan de Ortega in 1474 after 7 years of unsuccessfully trying to conceive an heir to the throne. Once at the saint's tomb, she had it opened, at which point bees flew out of it accompanied by an exquisite fragrance. One month later she gave birth to prince Juan, and a year later to princess Juana (although her father's name was also Juan, the fact that the queen named the children "Juan" and "Juana" may be an indication of how grateful she was to San Juan de Ortega).

The town's monastery has a hostelry and a twelfth century Romanesque church that is the oldest building in San Juan de Ortega. Inside the church, in the chapel of San Nicolás de Bari, the "miracle of light" takes place twice a year at the equinoxes, 21 March and 22 September. On these days a ray of light enters the temple through a small window at 5 P.M. and first throws light on the capital to the left of the apse, then on the Annunciation, the Nativity and the Adoration of the Magi, taking ten minutes to travel that distance. The church's ciborium was a gift from Her Catholic Majesty Isabel; also worth a visit is the canopy on the church's pinnacle, which recounts in stone, with six reliefs, the life of San Juan de Ortega. The church's apse has rare flared windows that open up in a series of consecutive arches.

A couple of kilometers off the Road is a field that spans the distance between the hamlets of Agés and Atapuerca (from "Alta Porta," the high door to Castile). It was here, in 1054, that Castile ended Navarra's hegemony over the Christian states of the Iberian Peninsula. The battle, fought by the forces of king Fernando I of Castile (reg. 1035-1065) and García el de Nájera, king of Navarra, in the field called "Fin de Rey," is remembered by a carved stone monolith that tells of the event and its consequences. It is said that the Navarran king's entrails, picked up from the battlefield, are buried in the nearby parish church of Santovenia.

Back on the Road and 13.5 kilometers from San Juan de Ortega the pilgrim crosses the hamlet of **Rubena**, and 9 kilometers further enters the city of Burgos.

Founded in the year 854 as a small community (*burgo*) nestled in at the foot of a castle on the Arlanzón river, **Burgos** grew in population and importance, becoming the capital of Castile in the tenth century. Its foundation and growth are directly related to the Road to Santiago; its 35 hospitals for pilgrims, hostels and many other Road-related buildings made it one of the transcendental stops on the Road to Santiago.

The pilgrims enter **Burgos** by Las Calzadas street and proceed along San Juan, Los Avellanos and Fernán González streets, reaching the cathedral. The Catedral de Santa María, whose construction was begun in 1221, was consecrated in 1230 by bishop Mauricio during the reign of Fernando III el Santo (reg. 1217-1252). Mauricio had been to Paris on a trip to prepare Fernando III's wedding, when he saw the work that was being done on the Notre Dame Cathedral. He returned to Burgos filled with the hope of having such a building constructed in his city. Built on the site where an earlier Romanesque church existed, the imposing Gothic cathedral took three centuries to finish.

On the cathedral's exterior is the archbishop's palace; the "Puerta del Sarmental" (French Gothic style doorway with a sculpture of bishop Mauricio in the central column; thirteenth century); the "Puerta de la Pellejería (plateresque style doorway, sixteenth century); the Puerta de la Coronería (thirteenth century); the rose-window with its intricate Star of David design; and the Santa María main doorway (mangled in the eighteenth century). In 1442 master Juan de Colonia began work on the southern spire, toiling continuously until the completion of the northern spire in 1458 (the stylistic influence of southern German church spires is evident). Juan also began the construction of the tower that existed on top of the church's transept, the one that collapsed in 1539 and was eventually replaced by the dome one sees today, the work of Burgundian architect Felipe Vigarny. Also in the exterior and of later construction is the Constable's chapel (Capilla del Condestable). Containing the tombs of the Constables of Castile, it is a Gothic (gótico florido) work by Simón de Colonia, who was named the cathedral's architect (*obrero mayor*) upon the death of his father Juan in 1481.

The cathedral's interior has three naves with a simple apse aisle and only one nave in the transept. The true dimensions of the cathedral are difficult to perceive due to the presence in its interior of a large sixteenth century choir, a characteristic feature of many Spanish cathedrals. There is also a large number of decorative motifs of every style and epoch, owing to the long time it took to complete. The sepulcher of bishop Mauricio is a Renaissance work from the sixteenth century; the chapel of Santísimo Cristo has, in the middle of its reredos, a celebrated thirteenth century image of Christ (*Cristo de los Agustinos,* or *Cristo Vivo*), truly lifelike, sheathed in animal skin with human hair and eyelashes, whose wounds actually seem to be bleeding and whose beard is said to grow. This image is also the object of a legend. It is said a merchant from Burgos, before leaving on a trip to Flanders, promises the Augustinian monks a gift if they pray for his safe return. His business venture goes awry and he is forced to return by sea and without the promised gift. While praying on the ship, he spots a box with a glass cover floating on the waves, and inside the life-sized image of Christ, with His arms folded on His breast. The merchant takes the image back to Burgos as a gift to the Augustinians, and upon entering the city all its bells toll by themselves. Upon opening the box, an inscription is found that certifies the image as the work of Nichodemus, the man who took Christ down from the Cross. As the work of someone so close to Jesus, it is thought that the image is a perfect copy of the Savior's body. The image resisted any attempts at moving it from the Augustinians' church, until 1835, when it was brought to the cathedral. The image is known for its many miracles, and a sixteenth century text describes it as having "resurrected eighteen dead people." People in Burgos will tell you that the image's skin is made from buffalo hide, imported from Beirut, and it inspires such awe that Her Catholic Majesty Isabel, having come to take one of its nails, fainted when she saw how naturally the arm flexed down when the nail came off. Even "El Gran Capitán," Gonzalo Fernández de Córdoba, refused to approach the image, stating that it was not proper to come so close to God.

Still inside the cathedral, the Golden Staircase (*Escalera Dorada*) is a work by Diego de Siloé (1519); the chapel of Corpus Christi is where one finds the famous eleventh century coffer that El Cid gave to the Jewish money lenders Dimas and Raquel as collateral for a loan (full of sand, he told them it was full of silver, and that they should not open it); and the main chapel (Capilla Mayor), which has a fine Renaissance reredos.

Other chapels inside the cathedral are Presentación, San Juan de Sahagún (rococo style, eighteenth century), Visitación, San Enrique (rebuilt in the seventeenth century), Santiago (with an image of Santiago Matamoros, the Moor-slayer, it was rebuilt in the sixteenth century), San Gregorio, Santa Ana (with a Gothic -gótico isabelino- reredos, fifteenth century) and Santa Tecla (eighteenth century).

The cathedral's cloister is Gothic in style (gótico florido) and is from the fifteenth century. The Diocese museum has objects related to El Cid and the Capitular hall with its carved-panel ceiling are also worth a visit.

Other places of interest in **Burgos** are the church of San Nicolás, a Gothic structure with reredos by Francisco de Colonia (fifteenth century); the church of Santa Gadea, where El Cid made king Alfonso VI swear that he had nothing to do with his brother Sancho's murder (present building is Gothic); the arch of Fernán González, built by Philip II in 1592 to honor the first independent count of Castile; the arch of San Martín, a Mudéjar style doorway in the thirteenth century city walls, where, at the left of the entrance, there is a mark on the wall that, according to local lore, records the exact length of El Cid's sword "Tizona"; the church of San Estéban, of Gothic style; the arch of San Estéban, a Mudéjar style doorway with two square towers that was also an entrance to the city through its defensive walls; the church of San Gil, a Gothic structure from the late thirteenth century, containing one of the famous "Burgos Christs," this one has the peculiarity of having a compartment in its back where the monstrance is kept (it can be seen through the Wound on the statue's side); the "Casa del Cordón," a fifteenth century building that owes its name to the stone cordon that decorates its façade, called the "Cordón de San Francisco" and also "Cordón de la Orden Teutónica"; and the church of San Lesmes, a fourteenth century Gothic building that is named after the patron saint of **Burgos**, Lesmes (Adelhelmo), a French monk who helped Alfonso VI conquer Toledo, who on his way back from a pilgrimage to Santiago (1091), stayed in **Burgos** and dedicated his life to aiding pilgrims and improving conditions for all who lived in the area (his sepulcher is inside the church).

In front of the cathedral, where today one finds the "Mesón del

Cid," there used to be housed the first printing press in Burgos and one of the first in Spain. It was founded by Fadrique Alemán, who brought the press from Germany and printed, among many other famous books, the Abad de Oña's *Gramática* in 1485 and Fernando de Roja's *La Celestina* (first edition, 1499).

On the southern half of the city one finds the San Pablo bridge; the "Casa de Angulo," a Renaissance building that houses the **Burgos** Archaeological Museum; the church of San Cosme and San Damián, with a plateresque doorway; the "Hospital de la Concepción," which also has a plateresque doorway; the "Museo del Seminario"; the Carmelite convent, founded by Saint Teresa of Ávila; and the convent of Santa Clara, dating from the thirteenth century.

Some of the most interesting monuments are found on the outskirts of the city. First and foremost is the Miraflores charterhouse (La Cartuja de Miraflores). The Isabelline style building was constructed (1441) on the site where the palace of king Enrique III (reg. 1390-1406) had been. A fire devastated the charterhouse shortly after its foundation, and it was reconstructed, with a church, in the years 1454-1488 in the Gothic style (gótico florido). The church has the mausoleum of king Juan II and his second wife Isabel of Portugal (parents of Isabel the Catholic) done by Gil de Siloé. By the same sculptor is the sepulcher of the Infante Alfonso, brother of Isabel the Catholic, and the reredos of the Life of Christ, in the main chapel (Siloé collaborated with Diego de la Cruz on the reredos in 1490, and they are said to have been gilded with the first gold nuggets brought back home to Spain by Columbus). The charterhouse also contains a statue of Saint Bruno by Manuel Pereyra.

Also in the outskirts of **Burgos** is the monastery of Las Huelgas Reales, built in 1175 by king Alfonso VIII (reg. 1158-1214) on the site of an old royal recreation complex ("huelgas" comes from the old Castilian verb holgar, which means to enjoy). The monastery was intended to receive 100 religious women from the noblest houses of Spain, and it was under Cistercian tutelage. Its church has an unusual pentagonal apse and is built in the Cistercian Gothic style with Romanesque overtones; the cloister is Romanesque, while the reredos is baroque. This church is also the place where Alfonso VIII put the battle standard he captured from the defeated Moors at the battle of Las Navas de Tolosa (1212). The visitor must not leave the church of Las Huelgas without seeing the Mudéjar style Santiago chapel, where an articulate statue of Santiago knighted the kings of Castile by bringing a beautiful battle sword down upon their shoulders (Santiago del Espaldarazo). It is recorded that Alfonso X of Castile was knighted here by the image, and became so devoted to it that he had Abn Abdala, the Moslem king of Granada, knighted also. Other important characters knighted by this Santiago were Edward of England; Philip, son of the emperor of Constantinople; Rudolph, a future king of the Germans; Gaston de Bearn; the marquis of Monferrato among many others. Also interesting is the chapel of Asunción, that of Salvador (done in the thirteenth century in the Mudéjar style) and the royal mausoleum.

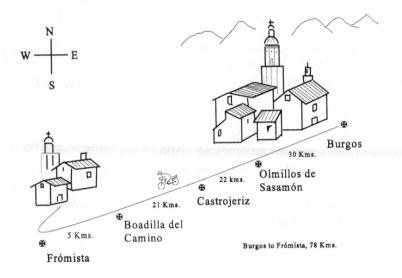

N

W ——— E

S

Burgos

30 Kms.

Olmillos de
Sasamón

22 kms.

Castrojeriz

21 Kms.

Boadilla del
Camino

5 Kms.

Burgos to Frómista, 78 Kms.

Frómista

DAY 8. 7 August 1996. Burgos to Frómista. Incidents.

Out of Burgos after breakfast and a stop at the bank, we head
straight into the Meseta Central, the great Castilian steppes. The most
faithful description I can give is that it is an ocean, only made of wheat
fields and whitish earth. We make our way through flatlands punctuated
by rolling hills and treacherous ravines.

At Hornillos del Camino, a tiny village in the middle of nowhere,
we stop at the local Pilgrims' Refuge, where our credentials are stamped.
There, we are told that the next village has a municipal swimming pool.
We head up the lonely trail, the sun bearing down mercilessly. It's hot.
The heat at times seems to rise from the hot earth, exposed to the sun's
rays for many hours now.

We have seen no one for hours. We take a water stop at the only
tree we've seen on the road for many kilometers now. We move on. The
terrain becomes so flat that the horizon seems exceedingly far; the sky

is endless.

In the distance looms a thunder storm. It approaches slowly. We take our lunch at Hontanas, pool-side at a municipal playground. Some pilgrims next to us seem to be sewing their feet. I later learn that this is the only way to get rid of the troublesome blisters that develop on your feet from so much walking. I feel lucky to travel on a bike. The storm keeps approaching. After buying a delicious ice cream from the playground's cafeteria, we set off again.

At the ruins of the convent of San Antón, the sky opens up. It is 3:30 P.M. We don our rain gear and press on, but we are getting very wet (our 79 cent plastic raincoats do the best they can, which isn't much), and so are our saddlebags. Near Itero del Castillo, at around 5 P.M. we find a 6' x 10' refuge, where we stop to try and dry off a bit. The storm doesn't let up, and the lightning is getting worse. The options are to wait in the little shack until the storm lets up, risking nightfall in the middle of nowhere, or to pedal on, risking the lightning and playing with the strong possibility of catching a bad cold. We keep going in the rain.

When we cross the old bridge on the Pisuerga river into Palencia, it is as if we had plunged into the river: we are soaked.

Arriving in the ancient Roman town of Frómista, we quickly went to Marisa, a family-owned inn where we were told that there were no vacancies, as they were expecting some people from Barcelona who had made reservations months earlier. I quickly convinced the lady innkeeper that it was very late, the weather was horrendous, and the Barcelonans were probably not coming. We got great rooms. After my long, hot shower, I joined my friends for a dinner of fish soup, filet of sole, wine and flan. The food, the wine and the soccer match on television made us forget for a while that we were surrounded by three tables full of Frenchmen smoking. We opened a window and the breathing became a bit easier.

Next morning, as we were having breakfast, the innkeeper advised us that it will most likely rain again today.

Day 8, Burgos to Frómista. Details.

6.7 kilometers out of Burgos the pilgrim crosses the village of **Villalvilla de Burgos**, and 3.5 kilometers further on is **Tardajos**.

Tardajos was a Roman town (Augustóbriga) built on the site of an ancient Celtiberian hamlet that the first Romans in the area identified as "Oter de Alios," or "Garlic Heights"; it had a pilgrims' hospital and its only monument is the parish church of La Asunción, built in the thirteenth century and extensively rebuilt in the fourteenth and eighteenth. Just outside Tardajos the pilgrim crosses the river Urbel (from the Basque "Ur", water, and "Beltza," black).

2 kilometers more take you to **Rabé de las Calzadas**, built on the sides of the Road and, like many of the other little towns along the way, of a marked medieval character. Its name is a derivation of "Riba," meaning "Edge," in other words, it is the town "on the edge of the highway." Its parish church has been reconstructed recently.

7.5 kilometers on is **Hornillos del Camino**, a town built to provide assistance to pilgrims and also formed on each side of the Road to Santiago, which is its "Main Street." Hornillos has a church, Santa María, which is ogival, with three naves and boss vault.

A couple of kilometers north of the Road there is a hamlet called **Olmillos de Sasamón**, a place surrounded by fields of sunflowers and guarded over by the ruins of a fifteenth century castle up on a hill. The village gives the impression of being deserted. Its origin is Roman, and it has a parish church built in the sixteenth century that contains a Renaissance reredos. Olmillos is famous for having been the home of the Cartagena family, to which the famous bishop Pablo de Cartagena belonged. Historians might remember Pablo de Cartagena as Solomon ha-Leví, the rich and powerful Head Rabbi of Castile. After the Pogrom of 1391 (which San Vicente Ferrer helped to start with his preaching) that saw his best and most influential friends die for their faith, Solomon converted to Christianity and, changing his name to Pablo de Cartagena, renewed old contacts within the Christian community and the State administration. His power and influence remained substantial, for he soon became the bishop of Burgos after adopting yet another name, Pedro de Santa María. This rabbi-turned-bishop was an important element in Castilian politics, specially its foreign policy, being instrumental, among other things, in the reconciliation between the Trastámara dynasty and the English House of Lancaster, whose relations had been strained since the wars between Enrique de Trastámara and his brother Pedro el Cruel. Spreading the word that the Cartagena family belonged to the same tribe as the Virgin Mary, Don Pablo cemented his relationship with his newly-adopted religion and gained a wider acceptance from old Christians who might have questioned his motives for converting.

Back on the Road and 11 kilometers from Hornillos del Camino you come to **Hontanas**. It has a medieval pilgrims' hospital (San Juan) and the church of La Concepción.

5 kilometers from Hontanas is the convent of San Antón, a monastery founded in 1146 by Alfonso VII for the "Antonianos," a religious order founded by nine noble knights from France. The monastery is in sorry shape, and it has been unkept since the "Antonianos" were disbanded in 1791. One can still see the remains of a Gothic style church built in the fourteenth century, and still standing is the ogival arch which unites the church and the old pilgrims' refuge and under which the Road to Santiago passes. The monks of San Antón were known by their insignia, the "Tau," a Cross in the form of this Greek letter that was later adopted by the Templars. It was with the "Tau" that they were believed to be able to cure something called "Fuego de San Antón" (Saint Anthony's Fire), an illness similar to leprosy with which some pilgrims and others showed up at their door. One of these knights' main occupations was the search for the relics of Saint Anthony, the Egyptian anchorite. In their comings and goings from Egypt they are said to have come into contact with the esoteric mysteries associated with the cult of Isis and the enigmas deciphered by the devotees of Santa María Egipciaca, a Christian saint who was also an initiate of the mystery religions of Alexandria. The strange powers associated with the Antonianos may be the result of their knowledge of non-traditional medicines and other abilities perhaps frowned upon by the powers that

be and labeled as "Black Arts." Many pilgrims affected by the "Fuego de San Antón" were given specially treated bread and wine to take on their pilgrimage to Santiago, as well as a "Tau" with which to touch the affected parts; most were cured at their arrival in Compostela. A curious note to the story: many pilgrims, upon returning to their original countries, found that the illness returned. Firmly believing it to be the punishment for some new sin committed, they took to the Road again and again knocked at the Antonianos' door. Thus, the Antonianos' fame spread throughout Europe and the monastery of San Antón became well known all over the continent as a place where a "miracle" cure could be obtained. Centuries later medical science found that the illness called "Fuego de San Antón" is a vascular disease which today is called ergotism. The disease is caused by the constant ingestion of the ergot fungus (*Claviceps Purpurea*) that at times infects rye bread. Thus, pilgrims coming from northern Europe, where rye is a staple, brought the infection with them, perhaps exacerbated by the physical exertion of the pilgrimage. After a few weeks in Spain, where bread is made of wheat, the northern Europeans saw their illness disappear; it only reappeared when they returned home and began to consume the infected rye bread again. So the Antonianos were benefitting, perhaps unwittingly, from a cure they had little or nothing to do with: a change in diet was what ultimately cured Saint Anthony's Fire.

A couple of kilometers further you enter **Castrojeriz**, the Roman Castrum Sigerici, a city that has had great influence not only on the Road, but also on the history of Castile. Its name is derived from the Visigothic king Sigerico, who may have built (most probably rebuilt) the castle that can be seen on top of the hill that commands the town (Castrum Sigerici means "Sigerico's Fortress").

Constructed at the foot of a hill with said castle on top, **Castrojeriz** extends along a curve, following the route the pilgrims used to skirt the surrounding elevation. The collegiate church of Santa María del Manzano is a twelfth century Cistercian style building that contains an important collection of art objects, among which is the carving of the Virgin (Nuestra Señora del Manzano), a thirteenth century polychrome stone statue that is said to have been found in a hole in the trunk of an apple tree. This Virgin is said to be very miraculous: king Alfonso X tells of four miracles in his *Cantigas*, all during the construction of the church: one of an overweight mason who was saved as he started to fall from a high scaffold; a quarry worker who fell from the heights and was uninjured; workers who were buried alive in a sand pit and were rescued unharmed, and other workers who were apparently crushed by a rafter but crawled out from under it none the worse for wear. Other valuable objects in this church are the rococo style reredos in the high altar (eighteenth century), a sixteenth century image of Nuestra Señora del Pópulo, an image of Santiago in pilgrim's garb, a seventeenth century painting by Carduccio depicting Saint Jerome, and a Pietá by Brunzino.

Nuestra Señora del Manzano has the tomb of Doña Leonor de Castilla, the wife of king Alfonso IV of Aragón and aunt of king Pedro I "the Cruel" of Castile. In the wars between Pedro I and his brother Enrique de Trastámara, Doña Leonor favored Enrique over her seemingly deranged nephew Pedro. Not being one to forgive and forget, Pedro had his aunt killed (by Moslems, for no Castilians were willing to commit the crime) up in the castle of **Castrojeriz**.

One last bit of information about Nuestra Señora del Manzano: the site on which it was to be built is said to have been indicated by the Apostle Santiago himself, who flung himself from the castle ramparts mounted on his white steed and landed on the selected lot. Four horseshoes that recall the prodigious landing can be seen hanging from the main door.

Castrojeriz also has the church of Santo Domingo, which contains interesting tapestries from the seventeenth century. Next to it is the parish museum. The church of San Juan has a Gothic cloister and tower, both finished in the fourteenth century.

Seven kilometers from Castrojeriz the Road skirts the town of **Itero del Castillo**, the last village in the province of Burgos. Itero del Castillo has a fourteenth century castle and the hermitage of San Nicolás, built in the thirteenth century. A couple of kilometers further on one crosses the bridge called Puente Fitero, or Pontero, on the Pisuerga river, and from there on the traveler is in the province of Palencia, in the region called "Tierra de Campos." Puente Fitero was ordered built by king Alfonso VI on what had been perhaps the oldest border between the old kingdom of León and the upstart breakaway kingdom of Castile.

Once in the province of Palencia, the Road proceeds through Tierra de Campos two kilometers south of the town of **Itero de la Vega**. Should the traveler decide to sidetrack the two kilometers and go to Itero de la Vega, there he will find the hermitage of La Piedad, which dates from the thirteenth century. Inside is an image of Santiago portrayed as a pilgrim. Also in Itero de la Vega is the church of San Pedro, a sixteenth century construction with a thirteenth century doorway. The building that houses the parish archives dates from the eighteenth century, and there is also a Roman bridge and very peculiar dovecots built with stone, adobe and tile.

Back on the Road and 9 kilometers from Itero de la Vega is **Boadilla del Camino**, a little village whose Santa María church (fifteenth century) has a very attractive Renaissance reredos and baptismal font, three naves, boss vaults and a jurisdictional stone column next to the apse, which is fifteenth century plateresque. Boadilla was repopulated by the Christians early in their military drive south against the Moslems, in what is commonly called the "Reconquista," or reconquest of Spain, but it acquired real importance in the twelfth century as a way-station on the Road to Santiago. Boadilla is also the first town on the Road where one sees a different type of construction: stone houses have given way to earth-toned adobe whitened with fine gypsum plaster in the interior. These houses are History come alive: the ancient Roman heating system is still in use, a system where the heat rises from under the floor and is carried by brick ducts; or its variant, the *trebedes* or *glorias*, holes under the rooms that receive the heat from a straw-burning stove. Another bit of History: as in ancient times, wine is stored in caves or subterranean cellars topped by "respiraderos," chimney-like vents that give the place the look of a science-fiction mini-city.

4 kilometers from Boadilla del Camino the pilgrim enters **Frómista**, the ancient Roman "Frumesta." The town owes its name to

the fertile, grain producing region around it (frūmentum is Latin for grain and corn). When the Germanic Visigoths took Spain from the Romans in the fifth century, it became an important administrative center for the new Visigothic kingdom of Spain. Razed to the ground by invading Moslem armies in the eighth century, it was rebuilt and repopulated by advancing Christians in the tenth century, beginning with a castle and later a Benedictine monastery.

The first place to visit in **Frómista** is the church of San Martín, founded in 1066 by doña Mayor, the wife of Navarran king Sancho el Mayor, as part of a Benedictine monastery which no longer exists. It is of the purest Romanesque style (románico palentino), with three naves and three apses, capitals with pilgrims and gargoyles of all types (and figures of men in strange positions that appear to be depicting masonic rites), and an octagonal dome. The horizontal checkerboard bands, first appeared in the Jaca cathedral in Aragón (of which San Martín is a small scale reproduction), that became a trademark for pilgrimage-related constructions, can be observed on the walls of San Martín.

San Martín's restoration is mostly the work of architect Manuel Aníbal Álvarez, who in 1894 tore down all the structures that, with the passage of time, had adhered to the sides of the church. This restoration is not devoid of errors: some of the finest capitals were removed to the "Diputación Provincial de Palencia" and replaced by imitations, and many of the original decorations were also withdrawn, leaving the interior with a swept, barren look. But the structure remains intact: it is the structure of the hall-church, common in the west of France, with three vaulted aisles that are lighted by the windows in the lateral walls. The nave is four bays long and is covered with a barrel vault that is reinforced by transverse arches. There is no clerestory, but the windows in the lateral walls, apses and crossing provide more than sufficient light. Like the nave, the side aisles are covered by barrel vaults with transverse arches; the transepts also have barrel vaults and do not extend beyond the side aisles. The four arches leading into the crossing are of equal height; above them are four windows, and thrown across the angles are squinches with small reliefs of the animals that represent the Evangelists, forming the transition to the high octagonal drum from which the dome rises.

San Martín's central apse is the same height and width as the nave and is covered by a half-dome that is lighted by three simple windows; it opens directly out of the crossing, and there is no choir.

Among the other interesting places in **Frómista** is the church of Santa María del Castillo, constructed in the fourteenth and fifteenth centuries over the ruins of an ancient castle, with a Renaissance doorway, three naves and a monumental reredos in the sixteenth century Hispano-Flemish Gothic style. Santa María has the distinction of housing a bead from Saint Telmo's rosary, kept inside a Renaissance-style iron cage. With his rosary and a torch, Saint Telmo is said to have calmed storms.

The church of San Pedro is from the fifteenth century and has a plateresque doorway; the interior is a mix of Romanesque and Gothic elements, and it contains some interesting paintings from the Ribera school. San Pedro has a monstrance that recalls a legendary event in the history of **Frómista**. The story, as per a document dated in 1453, tells of the manager of the San Martín Hospital, who gets a loan from a Jewish banker named Matutiel Salomón in order to rebuild his recently burned hospital. Unable to repay the loan, he is accused by the banker and is subsequently excommunicated by the Church. He secretly arranges for another loan and is thus able to repay the first. On his deathbed, the manager is about to take Communion when the Host gets stuck to the paten, where it will remain for centuries. Only after confessing to this second loan does the manager get to take Communion, but with another Host.

Frómista's hermitage of Santiago is a sixteenth century Gothic style structure with an interesting thirteenth century sculpture of the Virgin Mary.

The importance of **Frómista** as a Road way-station in the middle of the harsh Castilian plains was reinforced by its strategic position on the spot where the northern pilgrimage route descended from Santander through Reinosa and Cervatos and joined with the Main, or "French" Road.

For centuries, **Frómista** had a very important Jewish population.

Its *aljama* (Jewish quarter) was so large that king Alfonso VII had it incorporated as a "puebla judía," a viable, formal community in its own right. To this day people in the surrounding towns call those from Frómista "rabudos," but few know the origin of the word. It was a commonly held superstition in the Middle Ages that Jews had tails "rabos," such that "rabudos," the tailed ones, referred to the fact that many of the people of Frómista were Jews.

One must not leave **Frómista** without visiting the statue of its most famous son, San Telmo, located in a small plaza very close to the San Pedro church. This statue shows San Telmo, arms open, sailing on a boat and holding a Cross in his right hand. On the plinth is the inscription "San Telmo, 1190-1246, son and patron of this village, patron of sailors." This San Telmo was born Pedro González to a well-to-do family in Frómista. After becoming a priest, he lived a dissolute life, completely unrestrained by convention or morality, until one day, while celebrating his new job as deacon of Palencia, he fell off his horse in a drunken stupor to the great entertainment of all those gathered for the event. Ashamed and disgraced, he decided to leave society and live secluded in a Dominican convent, where he spent his time studying the Classic works of religion and philosophy. This changed his outlook on life, for some years later he went forth to preach the Word as a missionary all over Castile. His fame spread, and he became the confessor to king Fernando III, a job that his newly found modesty and humility did not allow him to keep for long. He quit and went forth again, preaching in Galicia and Portugal while being followed by ever-increasing crowds of people who wanted to hear him and see his miracles. Knowing about his previous affinity for drink and especially for beautiful women, some magnates bought the services of a stunning lady of ill repute, who approached Telmo and began to strip and tease him. Telmo, who began to feel his resolve weaken in the face of such beauty, flung himself on a pyre that was burning close by. From it, he emerged unscathed and with a stronger resolve to withstand the lady's advances. At the age of 56, Telmo, who was preaching in Tuy, France, felt that he was about to die, so he set on the journey back to his beloved

Spain. Just outside Tuy, his condition worsened and he was brought back to that city, where he died. San Telmo is usually (although not in Frómista) represented holding a torch in his right hand (an allusion to the fire that saved him from the temptress) and a ship in his left. The patron saint of sailors, he is said to have calmed the seas during storms using a torch, which is why the curious phenomenon where a light appears above the ships' mast after storms is called "Saint Telmo's Fire." He is also the patron saint of Frómista and Tuy.

Behind San Telmo's statue in Frómista is a restaurant-cafeteria called "Hostería de los Palmeros." Built in the eleventh century, the building previously housed the "Hospital de los Palmeros," a place that tended to Spanish pilgrims traveling to Jerusalem.

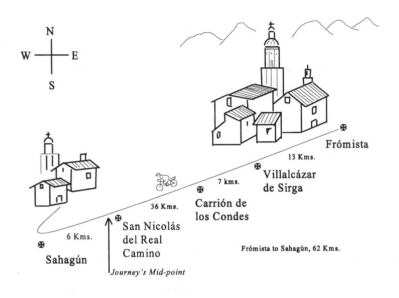

N

W —— E

S

Frómista

13 Kms.

Villalcázar
de Sirga

7 kms.

Carrión de
los Condes

36 Kms.

San Nicolás
del Real
Camino

Frómista to Sahagún, 62 Kms.

6 Kms.

Sahagún

Journey's Mid-point

DAY 9. 8 August 1996. Frómista to Sahagún. Incidents.

We had breakfast, took our bikes out of the garage where they
were stored (no charge) and visited the XI Century church of San Martín.
We left Frómista and took the Road again. This portion is a flat, stone-
filled trail that makes you feel like you're going to loose all the screws in
your bike. Silvio actually loses one, and he fixes the problem using a
twist-tie.

Lunch at Carrión de los Condes was had at a tree-filled, riverside
park. We had our fill of chorizos, mortadella, olives, asparagus, rosé
wine, assorted fruit and white chocolate. All bought some miles back at
a tiny country store run by a little old lady dressed in black who liked to
tell stories. After discharging the content of our bladders in the river (it
was pretty dirty already), we meandered around the park, sat around, and
even managed to drop off in a sweet sleep induced by the wine, the soft

wind in the trees and the sound of the river.

Readying our mounts in order to continue the trip, we were interrupted by a young man who, seeing the shells on our bikes, came to tell us how envious he was of us, how he wished he was in our shoes, traveling on the Road to Santiago. We mount and cross the street to visit the impressive monastery of San Zoilo.

Back on the Road, the trail from here to the next town, Calzadilla de la Cueza, is sixteen kilometers of nothing. We trek through the heat, trying to get some kind of rhythm into our pedaling, to set a steady pace as we forge ahead across the stifling temperatures. We sit a while under the one lonely tree we find on the road. All the flies in Castile seem to live under that tree.

From Calzadilla de la Cueza, where our credentials are stamped, the Road follows National Highway 120 into the province of León and into Sahagún. We are glad that we are no longer on the stone-filled path. In western Palencia and into eastern León the terrain becomes hilly, with tedious climbs and soft drops.

We cross the border into León and there is a soft drop of about two kilometers into Sahagún. After so many medieval villages along the way, Sahagún seems like an important industrial center to us. A gold-orange-light blue sunset welcomes us into town.

Along this part of the Camino de Santiago, the large forms of the "Montes Cantábricos," the great northern range, accompany us to our right, north of us. They don't interfere with us at this point, but two of its arms, the "Montes de León" and the "Sierra de Ancares" will eventually cut us off and make us climb in western León and Galicia.

We came into Sahagún and headed for the local Pilgrims' Refuge. They stamped our credentials and gave us the phone numbers of two "hostales"; the second one I called, "La Asturiana," had room for us, so we headed in that direction.

As we were having dinner, the family that runs the place got a call from Madrid: the elderly father of the lady innkeeper had taken a turn for the worse at the hospital in Madrid where he was being cared for. Everyone there was gloomy.

Day 9, Frómista to Sahagún. Details.

Out of Frómista, the pilgrim enters the region called "Campos Góticos," a large plain that is crossed by small rivers. 4 kilometers from Frómista, at the Ucieza river, the village of **Población de Campos** greets the pilgrim with its parish church of La Magdalena; situated on the highest part of town, it is a baroque structure with three naves. The hermitage of Socorro is a late Romanesque edifice containing an attractive polychrome carving of the seated Virgin Mary (thirteenth century), and the hermitage of San Miguel is also a late Romanesque structure.

3.2 kilometers from Población de Campos is **Revenga de Campos**, a small village with a church, San Lorenzo, built in the baroque style. A couple of kilometers on one comes to **Villarmentero de Campos**: its church of San Martín de Tours contains a plateresque style reredos and a very interesting Mudéjar style carved paneling.

About six kilometers further one comes to the little sanctuary called Nuestra Señora del Río, next to the river Ucieza. Built in the thirteenth century, it contained a sixteenth century alabaster bust of Santiago with a walking stick, a gourd and a hat full of scallop shells. People in the area firmly believe that this statue has the power to cure all types of headaches, a belief that gave origin to a curious custom: pilgrims take a handkerchief and rub it on the statue's forehead; whenever they get a headache, they pull out the handkerchief, rub it on their own foreheads, and make the headache disappear. The bust was recently moved to the Santa María la Blanca church in Villalcázar de Sirga, so nobody is sure whether its curative powers moved along with it.

13.5 kilometers from Frómista is **Villalcázar de Sirga** (called Villasirga in the Middle Ages, its name is very descriptive: "Villa" is a town; "Alcázar" is a fortress, and "Sirga" is an ancient word, probably of Celtic origin, meaning "Road," so this is a "Fortified Village on the Road"). Its one salient monument is Santa María la Blanca, a fortress church of the Knights Templar. Built in the twelfth century in the Romanesque style, Santa María la Blanca has a double-frieze doorway and a Renaissance reredos in the main altar (fifteenth century) made famous by king Alfonso X (reg. 1252-1284) in his *Cantigas*. The White Virgin that gives the church its name is the statue of a sitting Virgin that faces the Santiago chapel. The Santiago chapel is perhaps the most interesting part of this church: it has one of the most enigmatic images of the Virgin Mary, Who is shown holding the Baby Jesus in Her arms while at the same time She is obviously pregnant. The Santiago chapel also holds the sepulcher of the Infante Felipe and his second wife Leonor de Pimentel and is lighted by a large and finely-worked rose window. The Infante Felipe was brother to king Alfonso X el Sabio. In a dispute between the nobles and the king, Felipe took the side of the nobles and was eventually exiled to Moslem Granada, where he offered its ruler his aid against his brother. Of him, the *Chronicles* of Alfonso X state: "You, as the son of a king Fernando [III] and queen Beatriz, and as the brother of king Alfonso, ought better to safeguard the lineage from whence you come and the duty that you owe to it." [29] But Felipe had his reasons for not getting along with his brother. He was educated first in Toledo by Rodrigo Ximénez de Rada, and then in Paris by Albertus Magnus, where he was a classmate of Saint Thomas Aquinas and Saint Bonaventure. Entering the Church, he becomes the Canon of Toledo, Abbot of Covarrubias and Valladolid, and Bishop of Osma and Seville. When Princess Christine of Norway arrived in Spain to marry his brother, king Alfonso X, Felipe's life changed drastically: Alfonso refused to marry Christine and dished her off to his brother Felipe, who was forced to quit the Church (1258) and marry her. Christine died shortly thereafter, some say of a broken heart. Felipe never forgot, and never forgave his brother. His tomb shows his coat of arms and the Crosses of the Knights Templar, while his second wife's tomb shows her holding what is probably a red pepper, an allusion to her last name "Pimentel."

Santa María la Blanca also has the distinction of having been restored by order of, of all people, Manuel Azaña (1880-1940), a chain-smoking, overweight, anti-clerical, anti-Catholic prime minister in the

1930's. This is also the place where legend tells us a young man, having been falsely accused of stealing an ashlar stone, was saved by the quick action of the Virgin, who placed the stone under his feet to prevent his neck from breaking as he was being hanged. A well inside the nave has long been believed to be a secret passageway the Templars used to travel to a concealed underground room where they practiced their enigmatic rites. No evidence has been found to give credence to this belief.

5.5 kilometers from Villalcázar de Sirga is **Carrión de los Condes**, an ancient town steeped in history. Carrión was the capital of a county governed by the Beni Gómez family, counts of Carrión. As we are told by the epic poem *Poema de Mío Cid*, the Infantes (princes) of Carrión married the daughters of Spain's national hero, El Cid (1053-1099), and quickly became his most bitter enemies. Their sarcophagi are in Carrión's monastery of San Zoilo. Readers of the novelist Ramón Pérez de Ayala (1880-1962) should know that San Zoilo is the setting for his novel *A.M.D.G.* (1910), which is essentially an indictment of Jesuit education. It was also in Carrión that king Sancho II of Castile imprisoned his brother Alfonso VI of León, probably in a mansion that used to stand right next to the church of Nuestra Señora de Belén. From Carrión de los Condes was Don Sem Tob, the author, during the times of king Pedro I the Cruel, of *Danza general de la muerte* (*Death Dance*) and of the *Proverbios morales* (*Moral Proverbs.*) Also from Carrión is the celebrated Don Íñigo López de Mendoza, Marquis of Santillana (1398-1458), author of the *Serranillas*, *Canciones* and *Decires*, as well as the *Infierno de los enamorados*, *Doctrinal de privados* and many other popular works. The pen and the sword went together in the times of Santillana: the Marquis fought the in uprisings of the nobility, at times on the side of the king, at times with the nobles; he campaigned against the Moslems and laid waste to the plains of Granada; he also subdued the population of Huelma in the province of Jaén. He was born in a house on # 2 Santa María Street.

Carrión de los Condes' monastery of San Zoilo was an important refuge for pilgrims on the Road to Santiago. Founded in the late tenth century for the Benedictine order, it has been modified through the centuries, to the point where its remaining original Romanesque traits are few. Its cloister is plateresque, from the sixteenth century, and among the many interesting works of art it contains, a painting by Rubens and a Claudio Coello stand out, along with a statue by Gregorio Fernández. The monastery is named for Zoilo, a youth that died for the Faith in Córdoba in the fourth century, during Roman emperor Diocletian's persecutions of Christians. His relics are kept in a silver reliquary; other relics in San Zoilo are those of Saint Felix, Saint Agapius, Saint Moranus, Saint Albert the Hermit and Saint Bona.

Also in **Carrión de los Condes** is the convent of Santa Clara, a thirteenth century building with impressive carved panels. The church of Santa María de la Victoria (also called Santa María del Camino) is a thirteenth century Romanesque structure with subsequent Gothic and baroque additions; it recalls the victory of Bermudo I against a Moslem army, and on the Romanesque doorway one can see a carving recalling a miracle associated with the "Tribute of the Hundred Virgins." The carving has some bulls charging the army of Moslem ruler Miramamolín, as king Mauregato of Asturias is about to hand over the 100 virgins. A gross anachronism, as Miramamolín, the loser in the battle of Las Navas de Tolosa (1212), would not be born for another four centuries. This "tribute" was the payment that the fledgling kingdom of Asturias had to make to the Moslems in southern Spain in order to be guaranteed peace and protection. For centuries, the thought of infidel foreign invaders deflowering the cream of Christian womanhood filled northern Spaniards with hate for the Moslems and with a desire to utterly destroy their civilization. It is interesting that many serious historians now doubt that there was ever such a tribute, and if there was, it only lasted a couple of years in the eighth century when Mauregato was king of Asturias. As negative advertisement against the Moslems, though, it worked wonders. This church of Santa María de la Victoria also has a large reredos done in the Churrigueresque style and several interesting sepulchers.

Carrión de los Condes' church of Santiago was originally built in the eleventh century, and its Romanesque doorway dates from the twelfth. A fire in 1809 destroyed the church but spared the stone doorway, which has a finely sculptured frieze containing one of the best sculptures in all the Road, a God the Father seated in majesty. Its archivolt has 24 figures that represent different trades (cook, blacksmith, shoemaker, etc.), and its capitals are finely sculpted.

The convent of Las Claras and the ruins of the abbey of Benevívere round out a tour of monumental **Carrión de los Condes**.

16.5 kilometers from Carrión is **Calzadilla de la Cueza**, a village that grew at either side of the Road to Santiago, which at this point coincided with the old Roman highway (Calzada), as the town's name implies. Its parish church of San Martín has a Renaissance reredos which used to belong to the old monastery of Tiendas, demolished long ago (its stones were used to build many houses on the area where it stood). The monastery of Santa María de Tiendas was built for the religious-military order of Santiago in the eleventh century, and parts of its original church can still be seen.

Those interested in Roman architecture can take a detour to the village of **Quintanilla de la Cueza**, which is less than 5 kilometers south-southeast from where the Road crosses Calzadilla de la Cueza. There, just outside the village, one can view the Roman hot baths which are next to a house dating back to the second century; the mosaics are impressive.

6.2 kilometers out of Calzadilla de la Cueza one comes to **Ledigos**, (a name derived from the Latin "Letifigus," or "happy") a hamlet which has a church dedicated to the Apostle Santiago. The Road skirts by **Terradillo de los Templarios**, (held by the Knights Templar, to which the townspeople attributed magical powers, like the possession of the "Chicken that Lays the Golden Eggs," supposedly buried here, like in Viana) and then, 5.5 kilometers from Ledigos is **Moratinos**, a small village that probably had a large Moslem population, therefore its name; it has a church named for Saint Thomas Apostle. Less than 3 kilometers on one comes to **San Nicolás del Real Camino**, which used to have a hospital that cared for pilgrims with leprosy and went by the name of San Agustín. Somewhere between Terradillo de los Templarios and San

Nicolás del Real Camino is the mid-pont of the journey that began at the French border near Valcarlos and will end at Santiago de Compostela.

8.3 kilometers from San Nicolás del Real Camino is the first town in the province of León: **Sahagún**. The birth of Sahagún is linked to the efforts of the kings of Asturias to re-populate the devastated no-man's-land that existed between Asturias, in the north, and the Moslem state of Al-Ándalus to the south. Taking advantage of recent Christian successes in the battlefield and subsequent Moslem disarray and civil war, king Alfonso III (reg. 866-910) of Asturias embarked on a major, state-sponsored effort to re-populate the strategic places in this no-man's-land. Of most importance were the sites where the ancient Roman highway (which in many places became overlapped by the Road to Santiago) crossed major rivers. So it was that in 880 A.D. a population center was created where the Roman highway crossed the Cea river, a place where an ancient little hermitage was the only reminder that on that spot the saints Facundo and Primitivo had been martyred. Here, the town of San Facundo (a name that evolved to San Fagún and ultimately to Sahagún) grew and prospered, becoming one of the most important stops on the Road to Santiago. It was re-populated with people from Asturias, Galicia and with Christians coming from the Moslem-occupied south, the so-called Mozárabes, bearers of a rich cultural baggage. (The Mozárabes restored the old monastery of Sahagún in 904 A.D.).

Sahagún, like the rest of Spain, probably doubled its population in the prosperous eleventh century. Texts written by a monk who lived in Sahagún during this period talk of the results of the king's (Alfonso VI) program to re-populate the area around the old monastery: "There came forth from all parts of the universe people with the most diverse occupations, that is to say, blacksmiths, carpenters, leather workers, shoemakers, shield makers and others versed in the most varied arts and occupations; besides there came forth peoples from strange and distant provinces and kingdoms, like Gascons, Bretons, Germans, Englishmen, Burgundians, Normans, Toulousans, Provençals, Lombards and many other traders of diverse nations and strange tongues."

For the newcomers, it must have been quite a step up in their social status to come to **Sahagún**, for the royal document that legalized their situation in their adopted homeland sets some stiff conditions indeed, practically indenturing them to the abbot of the monastery. On the other hand, some important freedoms and exemptions were offered: the market in Grajal (a dependency of the king) was moved to Sahagún, its citizens did not have to pay royal taxes, were exempt from military expeditions (unless the king was surrounded by a hostile force), and they had the right to kill any royal official who attempted to use any of the privileges of his position inside the city limits.

In most places where the Cluny monks became established, a Charlemagne legend was born. In **Sahagún's** case, its legend tells of the epic battles between Charlemagne and the Moslem giant named "Aigolando." Another legendary account tells of the spears of Christian warriors blossoming when planted on the banks of the Cea river, a beautiful tale probably inspired by the rows of poplars that grow there.

Important visits in **Sahagún** include the twelfth century monastery of San Benito. The church of San Tirso is from the twelfth century and is a purely Romanesque structure; built with bricks in typical Mudéjar fashion, it is one of the best-kept examples of Mudéjar art on the Road.

As Christian kingdoms like Asturias expanded, some Moslems were either unable or unwilling to flee south and were left behind in what was now Christian territory. These people are known as the Mudéjares.

San Tirso has an elegant square tower. Also done in the small bricks and wood typical of the Mudéjar style, the church of La Peregrina, founded in 1257, has the lines and general structure of the Gothic style. La Peregrina was part of a Franciscan convent and hospital which is nowadays in sorry shape. The Mudéjar style found in **Sahagún** is typical of the city, and is called "Sahagunina." This particular style can also be seen in the churches of San Lorenzo, La Trinidad and San Juan, with the Mudéjar small brick substituting the large stone of other, earlier constructions. The old monastery of San Facundo achieved great importance after the arrival of the Cluny monks (1080), becoming the most prominent Benedictine monastery (it was called the Spanish Cluny) in all of Spain. All that is left today of the old monastery is the clock tower (Torre del Reloj), a Renaissance arch, some walls and a tomb that tradition holds to be that of the great Alfonso VI, king of León and Castile. Inside there is an interesting image of the Virgin (Virgen del Garrote) holding the Baby in Her left arm and a club in Her right; with the club She appears to be beating the Devil, who is under Her with an expression of pain in his face.

The **Sahagún** fair, instituted in 1153, speaks of the growing commercial importance of the city, which became one of the most prosperous on the Road.

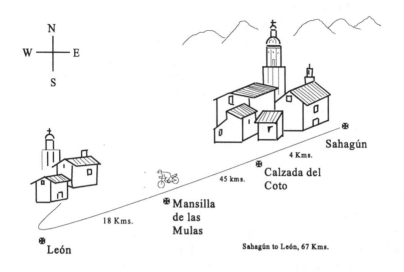

N
W ——|—— E
S

León
18 Kms.
Mansilla de las Mulas
45 kms.
Calzada del Coto
4 Kms.
Sahagún

Sahagún to León, 67 Kms.

DAY 10. 9 August 1996. Sahagún to León. Incidents.

In the morning, as we were getting up, we heard the cries of women and saw the gloomy faces of the men: the old gentleman had died. He reached his Santiago. I hope his Road was fruitful.

After a light breakfast of toast and coffee in milk, we headed for the road, hoping to make it into León (67 kilometers away) by sunset. The terrain here becomes flat again, and the road is a fine gravel which is quite comfortable. We come across small towns like Bercianos del Camino, and see traveling salesmen in vans, which they open up to show the local women their wares. In the small villages where there are no stores, the stores come to them.

A little dog lazily watches me go by. It stares curiously at Rodolfo as he goes by after me, and decides that the third cyclist to ride by is just too much for his patience to bear, so he attacks Silvio, who speeds up and barely avoids being mauled by the tiny (but ferocious) teeth.

At Burgo Ranero we got our credentials stamped, stocked up on food for lunch and had a very nice meal under trees next to a river. The sound of the water and the cool wind in the trees lulled us to sleep for a few minutes. At 3:20 we began pedaling again. The sun is relentless. The terrain is very flat... for now. Trees are as scarce as ice-cream parlors; when we found one, we usually took a water stop. Water is the most important of the elements on the Road to Santiago.

Whatever any cyclist may say about the trials and tribulations of cycling, make no mistake, the one, overriding concern is the pain in your bottom. Legs get firm, resistance increases, but there is no exercise you can do to keep your behind from hurting. Even comfortable seats don't do the trick.

Entering León at 7:30 P.M., we went to the local Pilgrims' Refuge, where they gave us an option of sleeping on the floor there or calling up a few inns. We call the inns and find one, "Covadonga," where Doña Isabel put us up for the night. The plan is to stay all day tomorrow in León, a big modern city, rest a bit, see the sights and wash our clothes. Our bikes spent the night in the dinning room.

Day 10, Sahagún to León. Details.

Out of Sahagún the pilgrim crosses a treeless plain whose monotony is only broken by the rows of poplars that populate the vicinity of rivers like the Cea and the Carrión; this monotonous landscape is constant up to Masilla de las Mulas, 36 kilometers away.

4 kilometers from Sahagún is **Calzada del Coto**, a place where the Road forks into two distinct paths that reunite 32 kilometers further on, at Mansilla de las Mulas. The northern path takes you on the old Roman highway (Trajan's Way) to **Calzadilla de los Hermanillos**, which is 9 kilometers away, and then to Mansilla de las Mulas, 23 kilometers further on. Most people today take the southern path, which offers the comfort of three hamlets, rather than one, in the 32 kilometers

that separate Calzada del Coto from Mansilla de las Mulas. The first of these is **Bercianos del Real Camino**, 5.5 kilometers from Calzadilla del Coto. A little before entering town there is the hermitage of Perales, which at one point was, apparently, a hospital for pilgrims. In Bercianos proper, the church of El Salvador has a carving of Saint John the Baptist and a painting of the Calvary, both from the sixteenth century. 9 kilometers on is **El Burgo Ranero**, a hamlet that is surrounded by small puddles that fill with water (and frogs) in the winter; in these same puddles thousands of storks come together every year in order to begin their migration south. 13 kilometers from El Burgo Ranero is **Reliegos**; and 4.5 kilometers from Reliegos is Mansilla de las Mulas.

Mansilla de las Mulas is the spot where the old Roman highway crossed the Esla river over an also Roman bridge. In the year 1181 Fernando II of León (reg. 1157-1188), the monarch who is best known for having taken the strategic city of Alcántara from the Moslems (1167), gave Mansilla its articles of incorporation and their accompanying "fueros," or laws and rights. Mansilla de las Mulas had, at one time, three hospitals and seven churches. Nowadays the pilgrim can see the remains of the defensive walls (twelfth century) that surrounded the city, the most prominent part of which is the Santa María arch, in the eastern section of the town (through which pilgrims to Santiago entered Mansilla). Also worth a visit are the parish church of Santa María (sixteenth century) and the hermitage of Nuestra Señora de Gracia. The monastery church of San Miguel de la Escalada (a detour of 15 kilometers from the Road) was founded on 20 November of the year 913 by monks from Córdoba and is one of the best conserved Mozárabe constructions along the Road.

San Miguel de la Escalada contains an impressive iconostasis, which is a type of reredos which has religious images painted on it, a large door and two smaller lateral doors; it serves to separate the presbytery and its altar from the rest of the church. Next to the church is a gallery with twelve columns that give support to horseshoe arches and Romanesque capitals.

A couple of kilometers from San Miguel de la Escalada are the remains of mythical Lancia, the last population center of the Astures to fall to the Romans after 200 years of war. Its inhabitants, knowing they were the last free Astures, and theirs the one last bastion of resistance after centuries of fighting for their freedom, died to the last person. The Roman general in charge of the battle (25 B.C.), Titus Carisius, had the hamlet preserved as a tribute to his victory over these fierce peoples of northern Spain, and as the one place that marked the end of a conflict that had endured for two centuries and was the most painful thorn in Rome's side.

Not on the Road to Santiago, the Cistercian monastery of Sandoval, about six kilometers southeast of Mansilla, was built in the twelfth century and has a Romanesque church. Sandoval has an interesting story that explains its founding. A count called Don Ponce, having gained his freedom from a Moslem prison in Morocco, travels the Road to Santiago as a pilgrim. In **Mansilla de las Mulas** he stops at the convent of Carrizo, which his wife has founded in his absence. His wife, a pious woman, was in the habit of washing the pilgrims feet as a sign of humility. When she started to wash the feet of the tired and worn pilgrim that came to her that day, then looked at his hands, she instantly recognized that it was her husband. To give thanks to God for their happy reunion, they took a vow of celibacy and decided to found the monastery of Sandoval.

Back on the Road and 2 kilometers from Mansilla is the hamlet of **Villamoros**; 2 kilometers further the pilgrim crosses the Villarente bridge, one of the longest on the Road, with its 20 arches spanning the Porma river. Having crossed the bridge, the traveler will find a sixteenth century pilgrims' hospital on its western side. 13 kilometers from the bridge the pilgrim enters a city which is one of the major stops on the Road to Santiago: historical León, seat of a Roman legion (Legio), from which its name derives.

Upon arriving at **León**, the pilgrims would cross the Torío river using a bridge called Puente del Castro, proceed to the church of Santa Ana (in the vicinity of which they would find refuge in the hostels available there) and then continue towards the market and down the Rúa towards San Isidoro.

Isidore of Seville (San Isidoro) was arguably the greatest mind in seventh century Europe. Bishop, philosopher, historian, politician, royal advisor, he was a man for all seasons, still highly respected many centuries after his death. The great Fernando I, king of Castile-León (reg. 1035-1065), had al-Mutadid (reg. 1042-1069), the king of Seville who was his tributary, yield the body of Saint Isidore to be re-interred in a newly erected church in León, the church of San Isidoro, slated to be a future pantheon of kings. The *Historia silense* [100] records that a sad al-Mutadid threw a brocaded cover over Isidore's coffin and sighed: "You are now leaving this place, revered Isidore; well you know how much your fame was mine." It was during the dedication of this same church of San Isidoro in 1063 that Fernando I announced to the convened assembly of magnates and bishops that he would partition Castile-León among his three sons, an ill-advised and fateful decision that would largely undo many of his great achievements and conquests. The thirteenth century *Primera crónica general* records his strong-willed son Sancho as saying "In ancient times the Goths agreed among themselves that the empire of Spain should never be divided, but that all of it should always be under one lord." The wars among his sons that followed Fernando's death only served to weaken the Christians and give respite to the retreating Moslems.

Fernando I set out on his last campaign in 1065, when the Moslem king of Zaragoza refused to pay his tribute. Ravaging as far south as Valencia (the same route that El Cid would take a few years later), illness forced him to return to León. There, on Christmas Day 1065, he put his crown and mantle on the altar of this church of San Isidoro, asked for God's mercy and assumed the garb of a penitent. He died two days later and was buried in the church, near his father and his predecessors.

The San Isidoro basilica is the most complete Romanesque complex in Spain. Fernando I had it built (over a ninth century monastery that was dedicated to Saint John) specifically to house the remains of Saint Isidore; its construction took eleven years, from 1056 to

1067, although by the time of Fernando's death in 1065 it was nearly complete. The building has a square tower dating from the seventeenth century, and at the back of the central nave there is a handsome portal with Mozarabic arches. The original Romanesque central chapel was replaced in 1513 by the present chapel, built in the Hispano-Flemish style: in it one finds a silver urn that contains the remains (relics) of Saint Isidore. In the royal pantheon the vaults are decorated with Romanesque wall paintings from the twelfth century, of such beauty that the pantheon has been called the "Sistine chapel of Romanesque art."

San Isidoro also has a library that contains many valuable items, including a Visigothic Bible and a fifteenth century grammar text. It is said that king Philip II, in his quest to bring the remains of all the rulers of Spain to his newly-built pantheon in northern Madrid ("El Escorial," built in the sixteenth century), went to San Isidoro to collect the bodies of the Leonese monarchs, but upon seeing the beauty and elegance of its pantheon changed his mind and left León empty-handed. Doña Jimena, wife of El Cid, is said to have frequented San Isidoro to hear Mass: it was here that she married the hero.

The southern entrance to San Isidoro has a strange zodiac, which must be read from right to left (obviously made by Moslems) that begins with Pisces (Christ's sign) and ends in Aries.

Saint Isidore is said to have accomplished many miracles, among them the conversion to Christianity of Zaida, daughter of the Moslem king of Seville, who became king Alfonso VI's concubine.

Another of the great monuments in the city of **León** is its cathedral, an impressive Gothic-style structure that is also called Santa María de Regla.

The cathedral of **León** was built over a previous Romanesque-style cathedral and it, in turn, had been built over an ancient Roman baths. The present edifice is constructed in the form of a Latin Cross and has three naves; it underwent extensive restorations in the nineteenth century. The western, or main façade has a portal dating from the second half of the thirteenth century: it is divided in two by a mullion that contains an image of the White Virgin, a recurring theme in Gothic cathedrals, and has other fine sculptures. Its other portals are called San Francisco and San Juan. The northern portal has a sculpture called "La Virgen del Dado," or the "Virgin of the Dice." Legend has it that a gambler, furious over losses and debts, threw a set of dice at the Virgin, hitting the Baby in Her arms, Who bled from the impact. The story reminds us of the monopoly that the powerful Jew Çag Aben Benin had in the fourteenth century over the dice gambling racket in the city of León.

The interior of the cathedral is extraordinarily light due to the numerous stained-glass windows (placed from the fourteenth to the sixteenth centuries) that give it its particular look. The main chapel (Hispano-Flemish style, 1513), replaced the previous, Romanesque chapel, and has a plateresque wrought iron gate and a reredos where some fine paintings by the Flemish master Nicolás Francés (fifteenth century)are kept. The Santiago chapel has an image of the Apostle Santiago on whose base the pilgrims used to make a small incision as a remembrance of their passing through. Before leaving the cathedral the pilgrim should visit the Gothic style cloisters (finished in the sixteenth century) and the museum.

Summer months bring an added ornament to the cathedral's exterior: the storks that nest on all its towers.

Another major monument in **León** is the Hostal de San Marcos, a plateresque building built from the sixteenth through the eighteenth centuries. Its main façade is one of the best examples of the Spanish Renaissance style. One of the most interesting images in San marcos is that of queen Isabel the Catholic, flanked by two Classical examples of feminine beauty: Judith, the Jewess, and Lucretia the Roman. The image of Spanish emperor Charles I has an interesting legend: "Better than Trajan and luckier than Augustus." San Marcos was the headquarters of the order of the Caballeros de Santiago de la Espada, and it was here that one of its members, the famous writer Francisco de Quevedo y Villegas, spent four long years in a cold, damp cell.

Through San Marcos' its main portal one enters the cloisters, the "Sala del Capítulo" (Chapter House) with its wonderful carved panels, the main sacristy and the high choir, with its chiseled choir stalls by Guillermo Doncel (who worked on them from 1537 to 1542) and Juan de Juni. Nowadays one of the most luxurious hotels in Spain, it used to be a refuge that cared for the "Christian poor."

There are other interesting monuments in **León**. The church of Santa Ana is from the twelfth century, although it has been restored and reformed; it was constructed over an old basilica where many pilgrims who died here before completing their journey were buried. The old "Ayuntamiento" (City Hall) that is situated in the main square of the city, or "Plaza Mayor," was finished in 1677 and has an outstanding façade in the baroque classical style. The palace of the Guzmán family is a sixteenth century building with a plateresque interior patio. Casa Botines (the present "Ayuntamiento," or City Hall) is a nineteenth century building done by Antonio Gaudí. The palace of the counts of Luna has an interesting fourteenth century stone portal. San Salvador de Palat del Rey is a Mozarabic tenth century monastery that has been completely reformed. The church of San Marcelo has a very interesting reredos in its main chapel; next to this church the hospital of San Antonio Abad cared for pilgrims until its demolition in 1922. The church of Nuestra Señora del Mercado is Romanesque from the twelfth century. The building of the "Obra Hospitalaria de Nuestra Señora de Regla" has a monumental baroque façade dating from the seventeenth century that used to be part of the Marqués del Prado's palace. The marketplace is typically medieval and parts of the Roman walls (third century) and the medieval walls (tenth century) can still be seen.

DAY 11. 10 August 1996. Incidents.

We got up at around nine, having rested well. We headed for breakfast and to a Laundromat, where we had our clothes washed but could not get them dried, as the owner was using the driers for a special job. Back at the inn, Doña Isabel gladly hung them up to dry.

Heading for León's "Barrio Mojado," or "Wet Neighborhood,"

we had a lunch of morcilla (blood pudding), squid, peppers and potatoes, washed down with beer and wine. Then we took in the sights at the cathedral, one of the most striking in Spain, the palace of the Guzmán family and the church of San Isidoro. Back at the inn, we rested a while and then visited San Marcos, a hospital for pilgrims now turned into a luxurious hotel; we then headed for the 10 P.M. blessing of pilgrims at a chapel next to the Pilgrims' Refuge. The nuns' Gregorian chants were eerily beautiful, and the prioress' talk following the service strengthened everyone's spirits. A dinner of paella, squid and veal, washed down with a delicate rosé, flan and coffee, all served by a smiling, 300 lb. lady chef, sends us back to the "Covadonga" inn to sleep and get ready for the tough day ahead. The roughest terrain and the hardest climbs are still to come.

Here in León we witnessed two weddings, one at the cathedral and one at San Marcos. Young people were taking vows to be together and form a family, bringing new life into the world as a consequence. At Frómista we were indirect witnesses to death; at León to the ceremonial union that will result in children and life. That is the nature of the universe, condensed for us in a path leading to Santiago.

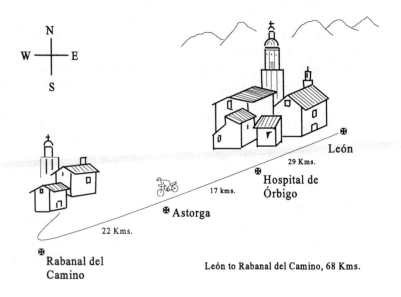

N

W —— E

S

León

29 Kms.

⊞ Hospital de
17 kms. Órbigo

⊞ Astorga

22 Kms.

⊞ Rabanal del
Camino

León to Rabanal del Camino, 68 Kms.

DAY 12. 11 August 1996. León to Rabanal. Incidents.

Last night I was unable to sleep well due to the rich Leonese cuisine of which I have been partaking too eagerly.

I got a wake-up call from Doña Isabel, took a shower, got dressed and readied for the trip. Out of León the terrain seems as flat as it has been for a couple of days now, with once in a while a set of hills to keep us busy. More and more, the mountains ahead of us come into view, their real dimensions coming more into focus. We're due to start the climb tomorrow.

The flat landscape leads us through little villages with medieval churches and stone-paved streets. Old people dressed in black stare at us as we go by, almost always uttering the familiar "hola," or "buen camino" (have a good trip).

In the ancient city of Astorga (Asturica Augusta), episcopal see since the III Century and main population center of the fierce Astures, the people that held-off and defeated the Roman armies for four centuries, we took in the sights at the Gaudí house and the cathedral, had our credentials stamped, and waited for Rodolfo to equip himself with a hefty lunch (I ate only fruit this day up to then).

Out of Astorga, we started to climb the formidable "Montes de León," stopping halfway up the climb to overnight at a one-horse-town called Rabanal del Camino, at 1,200 meters altitude. Although Rodolfo decided to stay at a very comfortable -and expensive- inn, Silvio and I went off to a Pilgrims' Refuge, one equipped with hot showers and somewhat comfortable bunk beds. After securing our places at the shelter, we met Rodolfo for dinner at the inn: pilgrims' soup (red broth with all sorts of beans), salad, stuffed veal with potatoes, and flan. Right before we finished our meal, the electricity failed in the whole town. We finished in relative darkness and headed back to the Refuge, where I didn't get a good night's sleep.

We've been crossing a part of western León that is a cold, windy, desolate place, cycling through little towns that look like history stopped progressing there in the Middle Ages.

Day 12, León to Rabanal del Camino. Details.

Between León and Astorga the Road to Santiago crosses the monotonous Leonese plain. The depressions formed by two rivers which the Road crosses, the Órbigo and the Tuerto, have groves and woods full of alder trees, black poplar, elm and willow. Beyond Astorga the Road starts climbing into the Maragatería region, which is, historically, the place where the most pilgrims became lost; this is one of the least populated regions in Spain, its roads and trails are not very clear as to direction or destination, and it still has healthy populations of wolves, roe deer, otter and wild boar.

6 kilometers out of León the pilgrim comes by the sanctuary of Our Lady of the Road, or La Virgen del Camino, built in 1961 over a sixteenth century oratory. A major attraction in the sactuary are the bronze figures of the Pentecost in the façade, the work of Jos María Subirachs, a member of the "Renacimiento" group of artists that worked in Spain in the mid twentieth century. Elongated and reduced to essential elements, these Pentecost bronze statues recall the mystical exaltation of El Greco's subjects, only that Subirachs's give that impression not with pigment, but with the stark boldness of bronze. This is the place where the Virgin appeared to the shepherd Álvar Simón. Knowing that people wouldn't believe him when he told them of the event, he asked the Virgin for proof to take back to them. She flung a pebble with the boy's sling, and told him that when he returned with the bishop, he would recognize the spot elected for the building of the church because the pebble would have grown to a prodigious size. In times of drought this Virgin is taken in procession to the León Cathedral, from where, it is said, She has never failed to make it rain.

Past the little towns of **Valverde del Camino** and **San Miguel del Camino**, the traveler reaches **Villadangos del Páramo** (Villa de Angos, or "Village of Serpents") an ancient Roman town 19.5 kilometers from León that at one point had a hospital for pilgrims; today it has a church called "Iglesia de Santiago." This church has reliefs in the upper part of the doors that recall -yet again- the Tribute of the 100 Virgins and the Battle of Clavijo, which ended it. A curious mounted Santiago is obviously an eighteenth century work: the sculptor endowed it with a three-cornered hat typical of that century. It was in the desolate plains around Villadangos that the celebrated Battle of Villadangos took place, in the year 1111. Here, in one of the most destructive marital spats in history, Alfonso el Batallador, king of Aragón, defeated the forces of his estranged wife, queen Urraca of León.

4 kilometers from Villadangos is **San Martín del Camino**, with its parish church of Saint Martin. It also used to have a hospital which cared exclusively for poor pilgrims, of which today there remains only an empty lot.

7.5 kilometers from San Martín del Camino is **Hospital de Órbigo**, a town built around a hospital for pilgrims that no longer exists. The town has two churches, San Martín and San Juan, but its most important monument is the thirteenth century bridge, called "Puente del Paso Honroso," or "Puente del Agua," perhaps the oldest of Leonese bridges, with 20 arches spanning the Órbigo river. It was precisely on this spot that from 10 July to 10 August 1434 the knight Suero de Quiñones, after securing the permission of king Juan II of Castile, accomplished his "heroic deed," defeating 68 French, Italian, Portuguese, German and Spanish knights and breaking 166 lances in the process. There were numerous injuries and one knight died: the Aragonese warrior Esberte de Claramonte. This "heroic deed" he undertook for the love

of a woman, doña Leonor de Tovar, who gave him a golden ribbon with blue lettering which he wore on his sleeve during combat. His feat completed and thus purged of this illness called love, he journeyed to Santiago de Compostela as a pilgrim. But he who lives by the sword dies by the sword: 24 years later Suero died in a field between the towns of Barcial de la Loma and Santa Eufemia del Arroyo, in Valladolid, at the hands of a knight called Gutierre de Quijada. Cervantes, in *Don Quijote*, mentions the famous "jousts of Suero de Quiñones," and it may be no coincidence that the Don's real surname is Quijada, like Suero's slayer. Suero is remembered in the Santiago Cathedral, at the Chapel of Relics (Capilla de las Reliquias), where a silver hoop that he donated is kept on the bust of Santiago el Menor.

After crossing the Tuerto river at the hamlet of San Justo de la Vega, the pilgrim comes to **Astorga**, pre-Roman population center of the Astures, a fierce people of northern Spain. It became Astúrica Augusta under the Romans, thrived under the Visigoths, but later became part of the desolated no-man's-land that opened up between Christian Asturias and Moslem al-Ándalus. King Ordoño I (reg. 850-866) eventually repopulated the city, along with León, Túy and Amaya.

Astorga was also the capital of an ancient people called the "Amacos," and tradition has it that its see was founded by no other than Santiago himself. Saint Paul is also said to have come by here in his travels through Spain. The carvings of the cathedral's main portal tell us of both events. Saint Francis Assisi stopped here on his way to Santiago because of illness. During his long recuperation, he was cared for at the "Hospital de San Juan."

During the Middle Ages Astorga had two Jewish neighborhoods, or "aljamas," and one French. There was also a French guild (Rocamador) and an English one (Saint Thomas of Canterbury).

A law from the thirteenth century tells of a special dispensation given to the shoemakers of the city: they were permitted to work on Sundays, because every shoe they made on the Lord's Day would be given as a gift to needy pilgrims to Santiago.

Astorga is the home of Saint Toribio, who almost singlehandedly converted the Germanic Sueves of northwestern Spain to Catholicism. It is also the home of Sampiro, bishop of Astorga, a tenth century chronicler who left us much information about the main events occurring in the kingdom of Asturias during its formative years. One interesting account has to do with king Alfonso III the Great (reg. 866-910), one of the most successful battlefield commanders of Asturias, who devastated Moslem armies and territories for decades. As per Sampiro, Alfonso III may have been deposed by his sons at the end of the year 909. The king then made a pilgrimage to Santiago, led his troops one last time against the Moslems (apparently with his sons' permission) and died in December of 910.

Astorga is also an important crossroads on the Road to Santiago. Christians from the Moslem-controlled south would make their way north up the ancient Roman highway (Vía de la Plata) that began in southern Andalucía and ended in Asturias, where the Romans had silver mines. These pilgrims from Cádiz, Córdoba, Sevilla and other southern cities would reach Astorga and link up with the main pilgrimage road that began at Roncesvalles, turning west here to begin climbing the "Montes de León."

Astorga's importance to the Road is attested to by the fact that at one point it had 22 hospitals for pilgrims. Of these, two are conserved: Hospital de las Cinco Llagas and Hospital de San Juan (twelfth century, reconstructed in the eighteenth). One of its most imposing structures is Saint Mary's Cathedral (Catedral de Santa María). Begun in the fifteenth century, the cathedral has overlapping Gothic (gótico florido), Renaissance and baroque styles, and its main altar has an excellent reredos as well as a Romanesque statue of Mary (Virgen de la Majestad). The carvings in the choir have one image that shows a man smoking a pipe; completed just 25 years after Columbus's first voyage, this is probably the first depiction of tobacco smoking in Europe. On the cathedral's exterior, on a pinnacle on the apse, there is the image of Pedro Mato, local hero of the battle of Clavijo. The battle flag flown by the Christians at Clavijo is kept in the City Hall, a building famous for the two characters sculpted in its façade: called Juan Zancuda and Colasa, they are said to give the hour, but not the quarters, referring not only to the City Hall's custom of ringing bells at the hour on the hour, but to the notion that people from this region are skin flints that hate to spend money.

The Episcopal Palace of **Astorga** is the work of the famous architect Antonio Gaudí (1852-1926). The palace's throne room, the chapel and the Leonese painters' room are worthy of a visit, but for those mostly interested in the Road to Santiago, the palace has a "Museum of the Roads" (Museo de los Caminos) that contains an extraordinary collection of images of the Apostle Santiago.

Other monuments in **Astorga** are the convent/church of San Francisco; the chapel of Vera Cruz (1816); the convent/church of San Bartolomé, originally built by Mozárabes in the tenth century, subsequently restored in the Gothic style; the Fátima sanctuary of the church of San Julián, with a baroque interior and Romanesque capitals in its portal; the church of Santa Marta, decorated in the baroque style;

the convent of Santa Clara; the Diocese Seminary with a cloister by Gaudí, and the remains of an ancient wall that protected the city and was reconstructed in the thirteenth century. The chapel of San Estéban, aGothic style construction, has, between it and the adjacent church of Santa Marta, the underground jail where certain women were walled-in for life, their only link with the outside world being a narrow, barred window through which they received food and drink. I have not found the reason behind this strange practice, and can only conjecture that they were either saintly women hoping to gain the Kingdom of Heaven by their self-torture, of otherwise women of ill repute that were being punished in such a fashion.

For the west-bound traveler, **Astorga** is the gateway to the Maragatería region, a mountainous, windy area that is scarcely populated. Its inhabitants are a historical enigma and theories abound as to where they come from. Some say they are Jews or Arabs or Berbers, some have them as Celts or Mozarabs, others as descendants of king Mauregato of Asturias. A less romantic but more probable explanation might be that they are a group of Astures that became isolated in this remote region and developed their own cultural characteristics. Whatever the case may be, in this region the wayfarer crosses astonishing country, with little towns like **Castrillo de los Polvazares** (just off the Road), **Santa Catalina de Somoza**, (its old pilgrims' hospital is now in ruins), **El Ganso** "The Goose" (which had a monastery and a pilgrims' hospital) with its church dedicated to the Apostle Santiago and the chapel "Cristo de los Peregrinos" (The Pilgrims' Christ), and **Rabanal del Camino**. The Maragatería has ancient Roman gold mine installations tat are still in good shape.

Religious constructions in the Maragatería are of a rustic Romanesque style, and its houses are covered with slate, typical of Maragato construction.

One of the most important villages in the Maragatería is **Rabanal del Camino**, 1,150 meters above sea-level in the approaches to the "Cruz de Ferro" pass. Rabanal has the hermitage of the Cristo de la Vera Cruz; so miraculous that on His day (14 September) a special rite celebrates His many miracles. The church of Santa María, a Romanesque construction with a twelfth century apse that belonged to the Knights Templar; the ruins of the Hospital de San Gregorio; the hermitage of San José, founded by the mule driver José Castro with the bag full of gold that one of his clients never picked up and that, because of his honesty, José didn't even think of keeping for himself. Then there is the "House of the Four Corners" (Casa de las Cuatro Esquinas), the dwelling that sheltered king Philip II (reg. 1550-1598) when he visited the area.

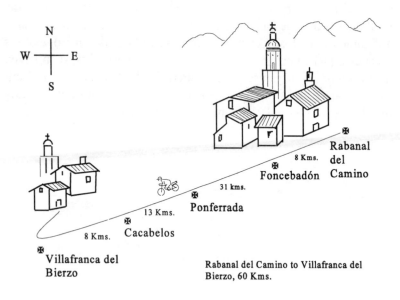

W —— E
N
S

Rabanal
del
Camino

8 Kms.

Foncebadón

31 kms.

Ponferrada

13 Kms.

Cacabelos

8 Kms.

Villafranca del
Bierzo

Rabanal del Camino to Villafranca del
Bierzo, 60 Kms.

DAY 13. 12 August 1996. Rabanal to Villafranca. Incidents.

I got up to find that there wasn't any hot water in the showers at the Refuge, so I washed up as best I could (It's in the low 40's outside, not counting the wind-chill factor) and woke Silvio up. After retrieving our bicycles, who had spent the night in a barn full of animals, we had breakfast at Rodolfo's inn and headed out a little after nine in the morning.

We were in León's Maragatería region, with temperatures barely reaching 40 degrees Fahrenheit, (in the middle of summer) a stiff wind right in your face and a very steep climb. This place is the image of desolation: set in an epic landscape of high mountains and deep valleys, the little towns you cross were abandoned long ago, the only remnants of their past life being parts of walls to houses that have been uninhabited for decades, perhaps centuries. How someone could have survived at such altitude in such desolation with the cold and the constant wind is a mystery.

As I pedaled through Foncebadón some signs of life appear: some cows chew lazily in a fenced-in space behind a house that seems structurally sound, the only one in the whole town. I can only wonder what the life of that family is like.

Continuing the climb, I reach the "Cruz de Ferro," the famous iron cross at the top, at 1,500 meters, that announces that you've made it. A simple sign scribbled on the ground says: "Take heart, pilgrim, Santiago is closer, and so is Heaven." After that climb, that is the most eloquent statement that could possibly be found there.

The iron cross divides the Maragatería region from El Bierzo, a place that can be described as a gigantic, deep bowl, the rim of which is formed by the "Montes de León" on the east and south, the Ancares range to the west, and the colossal "Montes Cantábricos" to the north.

The descent into El Bierzo is a 15 kilometer drop through a curvy road which can be very dangerous, for great speed and curves don't mix very well.

As I zoomed down into Molinaseca and Ponferrada I couldn't help but wonder at the amazing landscape that surrounded me. I was looking down at both towns as from an airplane, the buildings and the cars looked like ants down below. In ancient Ponferrada, the Roman "Pons Ferrata" (Iron Bridge), I had lunch by myself, went into a medieval church and saw the castle of the Knights Templar. Knowing that my companions were as much as two hours behind, I then went to the local Pilgrims' Refuge and hung a note on the door for them, telling them that I would go on to the next town and wait for them there. I thought it over, though, and decided to stay put right there. One and a half hours later they rolled into town.

After they had lunch, we started for Villafranca del Bierzo, one of the most striking towns of the whole trail. Set among mountains, it has kept its Middle Ages look very well, its houses being very modern inside, while outside the narrow streets, stone walls and wooden balconies filled with flowers talk of a bygone era of noble knights and famous ladies.

I called a couple of places and found rooms at the "Hostal Comercio," set in a XV Century building. Everything was slanted in the place, my bed threatened to throw me off all night and several pieces of furniture, tied to the wall with rope, kept a menacing guard over me. After the trying climb of the "Cruz de Ferro," I slept like a baby.

This, of course, after having a hefty dinner of "empanada de carne" (meat pie), caldo gallego (Galician soup), a steak with potatoes and flan for dessert. The ever-present rosé washed it down very well.

A good dinner was essential, for the next day would be the most trying, physically and mentally, of the whole trip: the climb up to the imposing "Cebreiro" and "Alto del Poio" passes, the doors leading out of the El Bierzo bowl and into green Galicia.

Day 13, Rabanal del Camino to Villafranca del Bierzo. Details.

In the ascent to Rabanal del Camino and the "Cruz de Ferro," the pilgrim is crossing the "Montes de León," the imposing mountain range in western León province. The area -especially past Rabanal- has many abandoned villages, testimony to the harsh living conditions that it offers. From Astorga to the "Cruz de Ferro" (Iron Cross) the traveler is involved in a steady and trying climb of over 600 meters in 25 kilometers, an average climb of over 24 meters per kilometer.

5.5 kilometers out of Rabanal in a steady climb is **Foncebadón**, a nearly-deserted hamlet that was very important in the Middle Ages due to its strategic position on the Road. In the eleventh century a hospital for pilgrims was founded there, as well as a church and a pilgrims' refuge, of which only ruins remain.

A couple of kilometers from Foncebadón, at the top of Mount Irago (1,500 meters above sea level), the pilgrim at last reaches one of the oldest monuments on the Road to Santiago, the "Cruz de Ferro," a simple iron Cross on a rustic pole standing on a pile of rocks that at a certain point served as the boundary marker between the region of the Maragatería and the region of El Bierzo. Most probably because of the dizzying elevation of the place, there used to be an altar dedicated to the god Mercury, protector of travelers, in pre-Christian days. The pagan ritual had the travelers deposit a pebble to the god to ensure a safe arrival, a custom later followed by Galician agricultural workers journeying to Castile and, lastly, by Christian pilgrims on their way to Santiago. The constantly growing pile talks of the continuing popularity of the ritual. Once the travelers reach this iron Cross, they should be glad to know that the next 35 kilometers are basically downhill. If one looks south from the "Cruz de Ferro," the imposing and mythical Mount Teleno (2,288 meters above sea level) can be seen. It was associated in ancient times with the cult of Mars, the god of war.

2.5 kilometers from the Cruz de Ferro is an abandoned hamlet called **Manjarín**, and 8 kilometers further down is **El Acebo**, one of the few remaining hamlets in the area graced by human habitation. **El Acebo** is very typical of this region: its houses have slate roofs, exterior staircases leading to the second floor and large portals opening to the street. Its main attraction is the Romanesque church of San Miguel, with a beautiful wood carving of Santiago.

An interesting detour can be taken from El Acebo: a small trail leading southeast down the valley will take you to **Compludo**, a few kilometers south of the Road to Santiago. There, the traveler can see the oldest working forge in Spain, built by the Visigoths in the early eighth century. For well over a millennium, the forge has been set in motion by the rush of water flowing from a nearby stream, which powers the levers and cams that move the hammer; the same water-powered contraption created the pressure that makes air blow through the forge to cool it.

Back on the Road and 2.5 kilometers from El Acebo the pilgrim crosses the hamlet of **Riego de Ambros**, and 2.5 kilometers down is **Molinaseca**, with its Romanesque bridge over the river Meruclo Molinaseca has some interesting places, like the "Santuario de la Virgen de las Angustias," an eighteenth century sanctuary that unfortunately is in very bad shape; the town's parish church has a portal and a tower which are Neoclassic in style; there is a pilgrims' hospital, the house of queen doña Urraca, and the mansion of the famous Balboa family, with its impressive towers. Molinaseca, Like Puente la Reina in Navarra, has a system of street cleaning that uses the waters of the nearby river Miruelos, which run through the streets, leaving them clean.

7 kilometers from Molinaseca is **Ponferrada**, which owes its name to its bridge, made of granite held together with iron staples, (Pons is "bridge," ferrata is "made of iron") built in the twelfth century by the bishop Osmundo of Astorga on the site of a previous Roman bridge.

One of the most surprising monuments in **Ponferrada** is the twelfth century castle of the Knights Templar, one of the most prominent military orders in Spain, charged with defending the region and caring for the pilgrims (often serving -it is said- as bankers for travelers strapped for cash). Built in 1178, its massive construction surprises the historian, who knows that in this period there were no military threats in the area to justify such a building. It is said that the castle is full of Templar symbolism, from the triple wall, alluding to the three oaths of the Knights, to the Rose, at the entrance, symbol of those initiated into the Order, the Tau and many others, like the twelve towers that represent the twelve constellations, the zodiacal symbols, or -more likely- the twelve Knights that are said to guard the Grail. All these symbols, united with the belief that the Templars were able to rescue the Holy Grail and the Arc of the Covenant from the Temple in Jerusalem, (which they guarded, yes, with *twelve* Knights in a secret place) give credence to the theory that the Grail and the Arc were secretly brought here, a peaceful and secluded place at the end of the known world, and at the disbanding of the Order were hidden in a secret place (Galicia?), only known to the highest members of their hierarchy, now gone underground in the guise of other organizations (Masons? Hospitaliers?). The fact remains that such a mighty fortress in this remote and peaceful region has little or no justification unless one thinks of the mythical projection and elusive practices of the Templars, which would lead one to theorize that they were, in fact, hiding something. The recurring symbol of the Holy Grail along the Road, especially in northwestern León and Galicia, puts more wood on the fires of theory.

Also prominent in Ponferrada is the basilica of Nuestra Señora de la Encina, a sixteenth century structure dedicated to the patron saint of El Bierzo, Our Lady of the Ilex, found by the Templars in an ilex around the year 1200. The church of San Andrés is baroque, seventeenth century, with baroque reredos and the "Cristo de las Maravillas," an image from the late twelfth century. The convent of the Concepcionistas is from 1542; the Clock Tower is the only thing left of the ancient defensive wall that surrounded the city; the Hospital de la Reina was founded in 1486 and is still functioning, and the church of Santo Tomás de Ollas, 1 kilometer outside the city, is a tenth century Mozarabic construction.

2.5 kilometers out of Ponferrada the Road skirts by **Columbrianos**, a hamlet that was already ancient when the Romans arrived in the first century B.C.; it has a church with three naves and a dome. 4 kilometers further on the Road crosses **Camponaraya**, a town that used to have two hospitals for pilgrims, La Soledad and San Juan de Jaberos; it has a church, San Ildefonso. 4.5 kilometers on the traveler reaches **Cacabelos**, a town that has a sixteenth century parish church, Nuestra Señora de la Plaza, that contains a Romanesque apse from the twelfth century. Next to the church there is a plaza with an interesting portico. The town has a "National Archeological Museum" that should be visited because of its many interesting pieces of diverse origin, ranging from the area's prehistoric inhabitants to the Celts, Romans, Sueves and Visigoths. The Cistercian monastery of Carracedo is from the tenth century and has some Romanesque elements.

The area around **Cacabelos** has some interesting sites. South of Cacabelos, down the Cúa river is Las Médulas, the largest gold mining center the Roman Empire had on the Iberian Peninsula. Pliny the Elder (who lived in nearby Castrum Bergidum for a long time), writes that 20,000 lbs. of gold a year were extracted by the miners of Las Médulas. The scarring of the landscape has left unusual formations that are now covered by chestnut groves. West of Cacabelos is Castrum Bergidum, an ancient Celtic hamlet that has been declared a national monument.

Back on the Road, 3 kilometers past Cacabelos the pilgrim goes by the hamlet of **Pieros**, and 7 kilometers on he reaches Villafranca del Bierzo.

Villafranca del Bierzo owes its existence to the Road to Santiago. A hospital (San Roque) had been built there to aid pilgrims and give them a place to rest before attempting the climb to El Cebreiro and Alto del Poio; the town grew around it, being populated mostly by Franks.

In what used to be the San Roque hospital there is now the Convento de la Anunciada, where the tomb of San Lorenzo de Brindisi and the pantheon of the Marquis are found, as well as a beautiful tabernacle.

Villafranca del Bierzo has a special privilege that sets it apart from other towns on the Road: at the "Puerta del Perdón" in the church of Santiago, any pilgrim who felt unable to continue on to Santiago de Compostela, due to illness or total exhaustion, would get his or her plenary indulgence (jubileo) without having reached Compostela. The church where this happens, "Iglesia de Santiago," was built in 1186 in the Romanesque style. Its portico shows the *twelve* Apostles, strangely in pairs, with two twin Adorations of the Magi. The Templars, of course, were involved in its construction.

The palace of the Marquis of Villafranca is a castle-like structure built by the first Marquis of the town in the fifteenth century. The convent of San Francisco is located in front of the church of Santiago and was built in the thirteenth century with a Mudéjar style church. The collegiate church of Santa María is from the sixteenth century and has a plateresque reredos. The Hospital de Santiago was one of the five hospitals Villafranca had, today it is the college of Divina Pastora. Other sites are the Water Street (Calle del Agua, where two famous characters, Father Sarmiento and Enrique Gil y Carrasco lived), the Main Square (Plaza Mayor) and the "Convento de la Concepción."

One must not leave **Villafranca del Bierzo** without visiting its park, where a fountain has the statue of a Roman goddess that was brought from Bergidum Flavium: Cauca, infernal daughter of Vulcan. Those interested in the Spanish Inquisition (which wasn't even remotely as harsh as its sister Inquisitions in England, Italy and France), might want to take a look at the Torquemada family house, where the famous Head Inquisitor Tomás de Torquemada, Jew turned Catholic zealot, spent much time.

One more note: Villafranca del Bierzo was the capital of the short-lived province of El Bierzo (17 April 1822 - 30 November 1833), which seceded from León and styled itself as the "fifth province of Galicia." Some political graffiti on walls along the Road still recall with nostalgia an "independent" or "Galician" El Bierzo and express the hope that in the future they will again be "free."

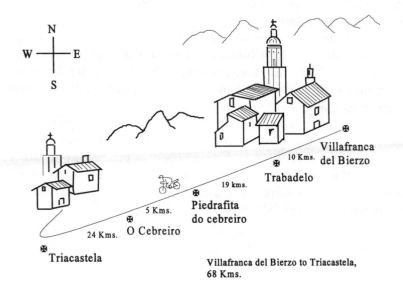

N
W — E
S

Villafranca
10 Kms. del Bierzo

Trabadelo

19 kms.

Piedrafita
do cebreiro

5 Kms.

24 Kms. O Cebreiro

Triacastela

Villafranca del Bierzo to Triacastela,
68 Kms.

DAY 14. 13 August 1996. Villafranca to Triacastela. Incidents.

After breakfast and a cold shower we rolled out of Villafranca del Bierzo through a tunnel and started the climb out of León and into Galicia. Here, the trail climbs up the sides of mountains with green valleys and rivers below. Green. Everything is green and the air is cool. The silence is only broken by the wind in the trees, the rumble of a river making its way through the valley, and the cry of an eagle flying high overhead. The scenery is breathtaking, with little or no sign of human habitation until one crosses a tiny village like Herrerías or La Faba, where one of its 12 inhabitants is sure to wish you a safe trip.

I've left my two companions far behind long ago, right after leaving Villafranca. At a certain point after passing La Faba, I meet up with a group of 6 pilgrims that are surprised to see someone with a bike on this particular branch of the Road. Apparently, I missed the sign directing cyclists in another direction. So I had begun climbing up to Cebreiro on a very narrow trail meant for nimble people on foot, not for someone with a bicycle. Too late to turn back, I decide to press on.

In spite of the unlikely hike pushing my bicycle (which I've affectionately started to call Babieca, after El Cid's famous horse), I'm not sorry I took the wrong turn: the scenery is like nothing I've seen before, green woods, tiny villages on the other side of the valley, and a view of many miles below. So the wrong turn turned out to be the right turn.

A couple of hours after beginning this hike, I run out of water. A few kilometers up I see a tree which seems to have pink and yellow flowers. Just when I think I'm hallucinating, I see that the apparent flowers are towels, hung there by a young lady that has taken some time off her own pilgrimage and is having a siesta. As I walk by pushing the bike she opens her eyes and asks what in the world is someone doing up there with a bicycle. I'm tempted to respond that I want "to go where no cyclist has gone before," but instead I explain my oversight of the directional sign. She must have detected that I was in bad shape at that point, for she offered me the little water she had. I took only a sip and started to walk on, but a bit further up she caught up with me and offered some company, asking if I needed help with the cumbersome bicycle. I refused the help, for she was weighed down herself, but I was very grateful for the kind offer and for the company. It may just be that, at so many meters of altitude, you find exceptional beings that don't exist anywhere else; after all, up here you *are* closer to Heaven. Her name was Paz, Spanish for peace.

As we got to Cebreiro and the highway, we said good-bye. Here, the trail follows the highway all the way to Triacastela. I still had to climb to the "Alto del Poio," at 1,337 meters, but the highway was a welcome change.

After Alto del Poio, the descent into Triacastela (which is only 665 meters in altitude) is exhilarating, for you get straightaways followed by curves that really challenge the cyclist, who at that point can develop speeds of 65 kilometers per hour. This part of the trip is not devoid of danger: I learned that in 1993 two cyclists lost their lives in this stretch, and only this year a number of cyclists have ended up in the hospital with broken bones and other ailments. The trick is not to get overly excited and apply the brakes consistently.

Arriving at Triacastela at 5:45 P.M., I went to the Pilgrims' Refuge there, a modern, comfortable facility like none I had seen on the trail. It even had separate rooms with four beds each. I signed up for three beds, took a hot shower, shaved, and sat in a sort of Florida room in the back to catch up on my diary entries.

At around 8:30 P.M. a pilgrim came looking for me, with a message that my companions had just arrived, having taken the bicycle-friendly branch of the trail, which runs on a national highway and is quite a bit longer than my short-cut. He said they were in town, at a local restaurant (I would have guessed that part of it), so I picked them up and left them at the Refuge, from where, after a shower and a rest, they set off to meet me at an inn where we would have some outstanding Galician cuisine accompanied by Paz, who arrived in Triacastela at approximately the same time my companions did.

DAY 14, Villafranca del Bierzo to Triacastela. Details.

The region the pilgrim is now in the middle of, El Bierzo, has for many centuries been a center of eremitic monasticism, a place where hermits could come to get away from it all and to lead lives of retreat and prayer.

This particular interpretation of Christian duties called eremitic monasticism has its origins in the ancient Christian lands of North Africa and the eastern Mediterranean. Very early in the history of the Church, enthusiastic Christians began to separate themselves from society and move to lonely places where they could lead the lives of hermits. Surviving with an absolute minimum of food and clothing, their time was spent in prayer, fasting, and contemplation. Celibate and frugal, they endured rigorous fasts and self-inflicted scourgings, and some even developed ingenuous forms of asceticism, like St. Simon the Stylite, a hermit who lived on a pillar for many years.

Monasticism was brought to the Western Church by St Athanasius around the year 340 A.D. Becoming a type of hero for Spaniards, eremitic monks did not lack for admirers, and occasional crowds would make excursions from population centers to watch some favorite saintly hermit perform picturesque penances and self-punishments (outside Spain, St Simon is said to have attracted large crowds to view him on his pillar). But this popularity, for most hermits, defeated the purpose of their retreat from society, so they searched for the most desolate, secluded places imaginable. In Spain this was El Bierzo, a place literally cut off from the world by the surrounding mountain ranges. South of Ponferrada is the Mozarabic church of Peñalba de Santiago, in a place that used to be called "La Tebaida Leonesa," now the Valley of Silence; this lonely place owes its name to the popularity it enjoyed among the silent hermits who made it their home.

Leaving Villafranca del Bierzo, the Road skirts by the villages of **Pereje** (medieval hamlet that used to have a pilgrims' hospital dependent on El Cebreiro's hospital); **Trabadelo** (a hamlet that was donated by Alfonso III to the church at Compostela); **Vega del Valcarce** (with its fourteenth century ruins of the castle of Sarracín, built over a ninth century fortress, and the clastle of Castro de Veiga); **Rutilán**, a village whose original name is English (Rutilán is a corruption of "Land Route"), and where one can find, inside a small chapel, the cave in which Saint Froilán lived in the ninth century (Froilán is said to have cursed a pair of rabbits that were gnawing at his documents, and since then no one has seen a rabbit in the area); and finally **Herrerías**, 19 kilometers from Villafranca del Bierzo.

In a Papal Bull, Pope Alexander III mentions **Herrerías** with the name of "Hospital de los Ingleses," or "Englishmen's Hospital." In its church many pilgrims who died in the area were buried. 3.5 kilometers further and the Road crosses **La Faba**, the last hamlet in León province. From La Faba to El Cebreiro, the next hamlet, the Road climbs 350 meters in 3.5 kilometers, a dizzying average of 100 meters per kilometer, or one meter up for every ten ahead.

Crossing into Lugo province one is at last in Galicia, region which geology tells us is the oldest part of the Iberian Peninsula, and whose first hamlet is **El Cebreiro** (O Cebreiro to the locals). El Cebreiro is the door to Galicia on the Road to Santiago; it is a small hamlet of "pallozas," the typical construction of Galicia's Ancares region. (The palloza is a round house with a roof of elm and rye straw. It gives its inhabitants good protection from the cold and wind of the winter). House foundations uncovered in ancient nearby Celtic "castros" (fortified hamlets) show the same round forms as present day pallozas, certifying the latter's origin as Celtic.

O Cebreiro's old hospital and monastery, said to have been founded by Saint Giraldo de Aurillac, used to give refuge to weary pilgrims who had just made the climb from El Bierzo. The church of Santa María is a pre-Romanesque ninth century structure that is steeped in tradition. In its chapel of the Santo Milagro one can view the reliquary (with its beautiful Chalice) that recalls the famous Eucharistic miracle according to which the bread for the Mass became transformed into flesh and blood. The legend tells us that late in the twelfth century a man from Barxamaior came to the chapel to hear Mass on a cold, snowy and windy day. The priest, upon seeing him arrive, exclaimed "Look at what bad shape this poor man is in; give him bread and wine!" As if to remind the priest of their symbolic and sacred nature in the Mass, the bread and wine promptly turned to flesh and blood to the astonishment of everyone present. Two centuries later the pious queen Isabel la Católica, traveling through El Cebreiro on her way to Santiago, donated two silver phials to the church in which to keep the flesh and the blood; these are kept next to a Romanesque Chalice wherein the miracle is said to have taken place. An image of the Virgin is next to the Chalice, and it holds a Baby Jesus which -tradition has it- opened His eyes wide in astonishment upon seeing the prodigious event, remaining thus even to this day. The two sepulchers in the church are said to be those of the two protagonists of the story.

Although a very small hamlet (9 houses at last count), **O**

Cebreiro was a very important stop on the Road; its hospital was closed and became ruined until 1965, when a "mesón" (rustic restaurant) was opened on the restored premises.

Leaving O Cebreiro the Road skirts by the hamlet of **Hospital de la Condesa** which, as its name suggests, has a refuge for pilgrims founded in the eleventh century. 7.5 kilometers from O Cebreiro the Road crosses **San Juan de Padornelo**, a hamlet that used to belong to the order of the Hospitalarios de San Juan; the hamlet's chapel has been converted into a covered cemetery.

After San Juan de Padornelo the Road goes up to Alto de Poio, at 1337 meters above sea level and 9.5 kilometers from O Cebreiro; it then comes down through **Fonfría**, which used to have the "Hospital de Santa Catalina," built in 1535 and demolished in the nineteenth century, **Biduedo**, and then comes into **Triacastela**, 11.5 kilometers from Alto de Poio.

Triacastela derives its name from the Latin "Three Castles," and its origin was the castle-monastery of San Pedro y San Pablo. Its main street coincides with the Road to Santiago, and along it there used to be several pilgrims' hospitals and even a jail for pilgrims. The jail still stands, with very curious and interesting carvings on its walls and doors, done by jailed pilgrims, among which one can still see the rooster, symbol of liberty among the French. Its Church of Santiago is from 1790 and the ruins of one of its hospitals, Hospital de la Princesa, can still be seen, along with a parish Cross dating from the twelfth century.

According to tradition, upon leaving Triacastela the pilgrims would take a limestone that they would carry to the lime ovens at Castañeda, the providers for the construction of the Santiago Cathedral.

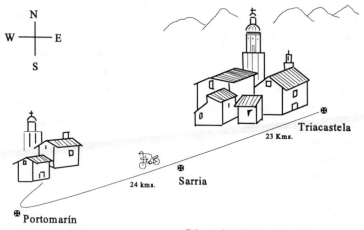

N
W —+— E
S

Triacastela
23 Kms.

Sarria
24 kms.

Portomarín

Triacastela to Portomarín, 47 Kms.

DAY 15. 14 August 1996. Triacastela to Portomarín. Incidents.

Slept late. After breakfast we left Triacastela and biked through the green countryside, through trails bounded by thick bushes or stone walls covered in a lush, green muck. In a thrilling downhill ride through a patch of trail bounded by walls and covered by trees, we felt as though we were in a tunnel. It is here that Rodolfo falls a fifth time, trying unsuccessfully to dodge yet another rose bush. He's not hurt, even though the tumble was considerable. I marvel at his ability to bounce and roll.

The trail here becomes part rock and part mud, as the overflowing creek next to it decides to try a pilgrimage to Santiago and takes over the path. We walk the bikes for about two kilometers until we come to a paved road that coincides with the trail.

Winding up and down the rolling hills, the trail takes us to Sarria, where we stop for lunch at a restaurant called "Londres", whose advertisements we've been seeing for a few kilometers. Lunch was incredible. First course, a pot of beef stew, a pot of Galician soup and a plate of pork ears. Second, baby squid, rack of lamb and pork ribs. Yogurt, fruit and ice cream come next, topped off by a good strong coffee. All was nicely washed down by red wine, "tinto" in these parts.

After that, we pedal (a little more slowly) to Portomarín, on the Miño river, Galicia's most important waterway. Here we stayed at Perez's Inn, where we also had a hefty dinner; being up on a hill overlooking the river, the climb up to Portomarín had made us hungry. We watched a soccer game and to bed.

DAY 15, Triacastela to Portomarín. Details.

Not on the Road, but seven kilometers from where it crosses Triacastela, is the great monastery of San Xulián de Samos, one of the most powerful in Galicia. Originally Visigothic and dating from the sixth century, some claim that it was founded by Saints Julián and Basilisa and the Abbot Abedico and the Abbess Sarra in the year 759, mostly to house monks fleeing from the Moslems in the south. The monastery has undergone successive additions and reconstructions (mostly in the seventeenth and eighteenth centuries) to the extent that not much of the original structure is left. Samos is located in a valley of the Ouribio River, a valley so narrow that one of its monks, the famous eighteenth century writer fray Benito Jerónimo Feijoo, once wrote that the only visible horizon at Samos was Heaven.

In front of the monastery is the tenth century Mozarabic church of El Salvador.

Back on the Road and 8.5 kilometers from Triacastela is **Sarria**, an important population center in the Middle Ages. A tower and parts of the walls of its ancient castle are still standing. Its parish church of San Salvador is a Romanesque construction with a Gothic main portal. The convent and church of La Magdalena was founded by Augustinian monks in the thirteenth century and is done in the Isabelline Gothic style; it had a hospital founded by Italian pilgrims that shut in 1896. Sarria's Hospital de San Antonio is in front of the edifice that houses the court. The medieval bridge, Ponte Aspera, has only one arch, and the hermitage of San Lázaro had a hospital for lepers. Sarria is the birthplace of writer Fray Luis de Granada and of artist Gregorio Fernández.

King Alfonso IX died in **Sarria** in the course of a pilgrimage to Santiago de Compostela. Death did not deter him: he still finished the pilgrimage and was interred in the cathedral at Compostela next to his father, king Fernando III.

4 kilometers from Sarria is the town of **Barbadelo**, whose parochial church, Santiago de Barbadelo, is a good example of Galician rural Romanesque architecture, although it has undergone extensive renovations through the centuries. The symbols on its tympanum, the Rose and the Cross, speak of the mysterious hands of the Templars, who left behind, here and all along the Road, enigmatic markers leading to a secret only known to them.

The Road then crosses the town of **Ferreiros**, founded as an iron foundry by the monks at Samos ("ferro" means iron in Galician, "ferreiros" are foundry workers,) continues north of **Paradela** (which has an eleventh century church, San Miguel), and reaches the Miño River at **Portomarín**, 19.4 kilometers from Saria.

The original medieval village of **Portomarín** became submerged under water when the nearby dam of Belesar was built. The new Portomarín was built on higher ground and many of its monumental treasures were transferred, stone by stone, to the new location. Among these are San Nicolás, a thirteenth century Romanesque fortress-church that belonged to the military order of San Juan de Jerusalén. Another surviving monument is the Romanesque church of San Pedro (1182), with a portal that opens out through three beautiful archivolts. Other interesting places in **Portomarín** are the hermitage of Santa María de las Nieves, the palace of Berbetoros and the sixteenth century house of the count of El Pozo.

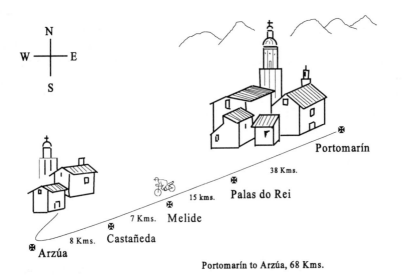

N
W ─┼─ E
S

Portomarín

38 Kms.

15 kms. Palas do Rei

7 Kms. Melide

8 Kms. Castañeda

Arzúa

Portomarín to Arzúa, 68 Kms.

DAY 16. 15 August 1996. Portomarín to Arzúa. Incidents.

Early breakfast. Climbing the 215 meters up to Palas del Rey, Silvio stopped and got off his bike to take a closer look at a little piece of paper that was hanging on a traffic sign. He disappeared all of a sudden, falling into a ditch by the side of the road. As he crawled out, he shouted that he was alright, although later on he had to put a bandage on his leg because of some bleeding.

The rest of the day went without incident, up and down the green Galician hills until we reached Palas del Rey, where we had an outstanding lunch of octopus.

Forging ahead, the terrain becomes a constant, tedious up and down, to the point where I begin to remember the Castilian plains with fondness.

When we reached Arzúa, a mere 35 kilometers from Santiago, we decided to stay there for the night. We got comfortable rooms at the Caballeira inn, had a dinner of Spanish omelette and a special treat, white rice, a staple for those of us brought up on Caribbean cuisine. We hung around the dinner table watching yet another soccer match and listened to the melodious sounds of the Galician language, being spoken all around us by a few old gentlemen who, apparently, arrived to visit the innkeeper and his family. Hours after beginning our dinner, we got up from the table and turned in for the night.

Wanting to arrive in Santiago in top shape and looking it, I had the innkeeper's daughter wash and dry my clothes, for a nice fee, of course.

DAY 16, Portomarín to Arzúa. Details.

Out of Portomarín the Road proceeds through **Ventas de Narón**, a place where Galician and Asturian troops fought a major battle against the army of Moslem leader al-Hakem I. It was a great victory for the Christians, who killed the two field commanders of the Moslem army, abd-Ala and al-Delkrim. The Road then goes by the hamlet of **Hospital de la Cruz**, which as its name states, used to have a pilgrims' hospital, then on to **Ligonde**, whose stone Cross reminds the traveler of its own pilgrims' hospital, and then on to **Palas do Rei**, 23 kilometers from Portomarín.

Palas do Rei (from the Latin "Palacium Regis," or "palace of the King", Visigothic king Witiza, that is) has the church of San Tirso, a Romanesque structure with a simple portal. It also has the impressive castle of Pambre.

9 kilometers from Palas do Rei the Road crosses **Leboreiro** (from the Latin "Campus Levurarius," due to the abundance of rabbits, or "lepusoris") now in the province of La Coruña; here the pilgrim treads on the ancient Roman highway. Leboreiro is a typically medieval town, where one can still see the big old house that served as a pilgrims'

hospital and, in front of it, the Romanesque church of Santa María. Santa María has in its tympanus an image of the seated Virgin. The Virgin's image on the Main altar was found next to a puddle, from which water began to flow, emanating mysterious lights at night and attractive smells in the day. Once taken to the church, the Virgin mysteriously returned to the puddle at night, a situation that continued until the Virgin saw a sculpted image of herself in the church's portal. Townspeople say that the coquettish Virgin went to the puddle at night to comb Her hair.

4.5 kilometers onward the pilgrim crosses the "Ponte Furelos," a bridge that is probably of Roman origin, and enters **Melide**, a strategic point on the Road. It is in Melide that the "Northern" or "Coastal" Road, coming from the Basque region, Cantabria and Asturias and proceeding inland from Ribadeo, joined up with the main or "French" Road to Santiago de Compostela. Its importance was compounded by the fact that it was the headquarters in Galicia for the "Cofradía Hospitalaria del Sancti Spíritus," a very important brotherhood that provided sundry services all along the Road (the present-day parish church had been the church of the Sancti Spíritus Monastery).

The church of Santa María, in the middle of town, is from the twelfth century, and its western portal contains cryptic inscriptions and signs arranged in a semi-circlethat have been associated by some scholars with the Runic writings of the Druid Celts, and by others with the Templars and their enigmatic, cabalistic rites. The church of San Pedro is Romanesque, with a fine portico from the twelfth century. **Melide**'s convent of Sancti Spíritus had a pilgrims' hostel dating from 1375. The chapel of El Carmen and the regional museum of "A terra de Melide" are worth a visit, as is Melide's surrounding area, which is rich in megalithic remains and ancient Celtic "castros."

A few kilometers past Melide is **Castañeda**, where one can still see the two lime ovens that supplied the construction of the Santiago Cathedral; this is where the pilgrims deposited the calcite stones they had picked up at Triacastela.

14.5 kilometers from Melide is **Arzúa**, center of a region known for its outstanding cheeses, an industry so important to the locals that they've erected a monument to cheese vendors and even celebrate an annual cheese-fest on the first Sunday in March. The Gothic style chapel of La Magdalena is the only thing left of the old Augustinian convent where pilgrims put up for the night. The "Casa Consistorial" (Town Hall) is from the twelfth century, and the old jailhouse and the "Casa de Azulejos" (Tile House) are also interesting.

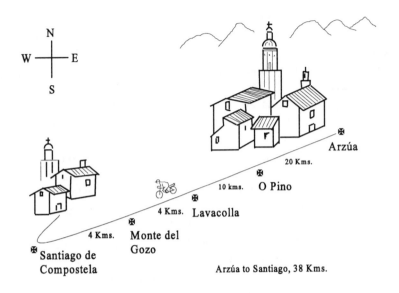

N

W ——+—— E

S

Arzúa

20 Kms.

O Pino

10 kms.

4 Kms. Lavacolla

4 Kms. Monte del
Gozo

Santiago de
Compostela

Arzúa to Santiago, 38 Kms.

DAY 17. 16 August 1996. Arzúa to Santiago. Incidents.

The big day. Today we arrive at Santiago. As I pack my clean clothes, this is all I can think about. We paid the innkeeper, said our goodbyes and had some breakfast at a local cafeteria. And off we went.

I hardly noticed the terrain in the excitement of arriving. I pedaled easier and with more energy than ever. Definitely, Santiago was pulling me in.

After a stop at the airport to inquire about my flight home, we keep rolling up to Monte del Gozo, the Mount of Joy, where at last one can see the city of Santiago sprawling below. The monument at the top tells us we are almost there.

After drinking some water, I mount my bike and literally sprint into the city, asking passers by as I go the shortest route to the cathedral, the goal and end of our journey. They eagerly give directions and always have something nice to say.

I can see the towers of the cathedral above the roofs. Cutting through some Medieval streets, through arches and down stairs, I make a left turn and there I am, at the Obradoiro, in front of the Santiago Cathedral. I can only marvel in silence. It's 4 P.M. on the 16th of August, 1996.

My companions arrive. Congratulations are in order. We pedaled around to the Pilgrims' Bureau to get our last stamp and receive our "Compostela," a Latin document that confirms that we've completed the pilgrimage and are now part of that select army of people who have done so. They're closed until 5 P.M., so we wait around in a café, have a beer and return. We get the last seal and the Compostela.

After securing rooms at the XII Century "Seminario Mayor," right next to the cathedral (parts of the Seminario are from the XVIII Century), Rodolfo treats us to dinner at the most expensive restaurant in Santiago. It's his late father's birthday, and he always celebrates it in this way. After dinner, the owner treats us to seven bottles of Orujo, a local firewater. We have too much of everything and limp back to the Seminario. The physical part of the Camino de Santiago has ended.

We spend a week in Santiago and around Galicia (in a rented car) seeing the sights and even reaching the end of the world (Finisterre). I fill up my emotional and spiritual luggage with Spain before heading back home.

DAY 17, Arzúa to Santiago. Details.

From Arzúa the Road crosses the hamlets of **Ferreiro**, **O Pino**, **Burgo** and comes to **Lavacolla** (also Labacolla), 26 kilometers from Arzúa and next to the modern Santiago International Airport; this is where the pilgrims would wash their private parts before heading into Santiago, a symbolic ablution that also had useful and practical effects.

3 kilometers from Lavacolla is the **Monte del Gozo**, also called Montjoy, Montxoi and Colina de San Marcos, a hill from where the

pilgrim gets a first glimpse of the city of Santiago de Compostela. Monte del Gozo used to have a twelfth century church dedicated to Santa Clara, but today there is only the San Marcos hermitage and a modern monument celebrating Pope John Paul II's visit to Compostela.

Pilgrims coming in groups would run up the hill at **Monte del Gozo**, each individual trying to be the first to see Santiago from the summit. The first one to do so would be proclaimed "The King" by his fellows, a title that would often be perpetuated in names and surnames throughout Europe, such as the French Le roi (Anglicized to Leroy).

Once on Monte del Gozo, those pilgrims that rode horses would dismount and walk the rest of the way (6 kilometers) into Santiago de Compostela.

The Main (French) Road to **Santiago** enters the city through "Concheiros," where the scallop-shell vendors had their shops, descending then down the Rúa de San Pedro, by the convent of Bonaval and the stone Cross called "Cruceiro do Home Santo" to the "Porta do Camiño," or "Puerta Francígena," the gate in the old medieval wall that allowed entrance to the inner city. Through the gate the pilgrim then walked down Casas Reales street to the Plaza Cervantes, then to Azabacherías, a small square in front of the cathedral's North Portal, where he would enter the church (except for Holy Years, when the Puerta Santa de la Quintana is used).

Once inside the cathedral, the pilgrim performs a series of age-old rites, beginning in the "Pórtico de la Gloria," where he puts his hands in the indentations formed by the many thousands of other hands that preceded his, then, on the other side of the mullion, he will bump his head three times on the stone head of Master Mateo, popularly known as "Santo los Croques," master sculptor of the "Pórtico de la Gloria" who placed an image of himself on his marvelous work. Bumping his head might transfer, it is hoped, some of his genius to the pilgrim.

From there, the pilgrim proceeds to the crypt, where he visits the tombs of Atanasio and Teodoro and the reliquary ark (*Arca Marmórea*), depositary of the Apostle's remains (some say that the body of Prisciliano, a famous heretic, is actually contained therein), ascending afterwards to hug the image of Santiago el Mayor in the middle of the high altar. He will then exit the cathedral and walk around to the Pilgrims' Bureau, where he will get the final seal on his credential and receive the "Compostelana," the document that credits its bearer with having completed the pilgrimage properly.

Santiago de Compostela is a city founded by pilgrims for pilgrims, a city that guards Spain's most important symbol and one of Christianity's holiest shrines. It is precisely its status as a city of pilgrims that gives Santiago its very cosmopolitan feel, sustained by the continuous influx of people from the most diverse cultural backgrounds. It is also this status that makes it a monumental city.

The outstanding monument in the city of **Santiago de Compostela** is the cathedral, marvel of eleventh century architecture in Spain and jewel of the Romanesque style. Begun in 1078, it is an eloquent tribute to its visionary founder, bishop Diego Peláez, who envisaged a monument the likes of which had never before been seen in Spain, where the greatest previous Romanesque structure (outside of Catalonia) was the small San Isidoro pantheon in León.

It is necessary to think that from the beginning of his tenure as bishop in 1071 (perhaps even before then), Peláez had been planning the construction of a cathedral worthy of crowning the pilgrims' long journey to Compostela, but all his plans could not preclude problems. Even before starting work, there was a dispute over the lot to be occupied by the structure, as the monastery of San Pelayo de Antealtares had a church that joined with Saint James's tomb on its eastern side. The great cathedral could not be built without including the Apostle's tomb, but the monks of San Pelayo, led by the abbot San Fagildo, were not about to surrender it without a fight. Without resolving the issue, Peláez had his crew begin digging the foundations, so that when the matter reached king Alfonso VI, he was compelled to propose a compromise: bishop Peláez received the lot, which penetrated the precincts of San Pelayo de Antealtares, and the abbot San Fagildo received the rights and revenues deriving from three altars in the east end of the new cathedral. The agreement was signed on 17 August 1077.

Much has been said about the foreign influences on the style and architecture of the cathedral, yet the architect who planned and built it is almost certainly a Spaniard. The *Codex Calixtinus* names "Bernardus senex," or Bernard the Elder, as the "mirabilis magister," or marvelous craftsman, who, along with an unidentified "Rotbertus" began to build the structure, "cum ceteris lapicidibus circiter quinquaginta...," or with about fifty other stone cutters. This Bernard the Elder is almost certainly Bernardo Gutiérrez, treasurer of Santiago and later chancellor of king Alfonso VII, who was forbidden by bishop Diego Gelmírez to go on a pilgrimage to Jerusalem because his services in the building of the cathedral could not be spared (*Historia Compostelana*, iii, 8). Bernardo Gutiérrez also built an impressive fountain in front of the North Portal of the cathedral and died in 1134. A man who planned and then began the construction of the cathedral in 1078 definitely would have been a "senex" if he lived to 1134, a sobriquet he acquired late in life and which passed on to the *Codex Calixtinus* as his distinguishing surname.

Replacing a modest church built there in 899 in the Asturian style of Naranco, the great church which Bernardo the Elder and Don Diego Peláez began in 1078 is, to this day, substantially the same as it was built, although through the centuries it has been overlaid with rich decorations and has suffered some modifications, such as the impressive Churrigueresque baroque façade by Casas y Novoa.

As one walks around the exterior structure at ground level almost nothing of the original church can be seen, but in the interior, in spite of the modifications, the Romanesque core of the building is evident in the general layout of the nave and the transepts, which are just as they were when they were completed in the early twelfth century.

The earliest and most original part of the cathedral of **Santiago de Compostela** is its easternmost section; this part has a sanctuary in the form of a semicircle that is surrounded by an ambulatory from which five chapels radiate. Above the sanctuary is a quadrant-vaulted triforium and a clerestory with windows that reach the vault of the apse. The bottom part of the sanctuary has been completely covered by the exuberant baroque decoration that was placed there between 1660 and 1669, and there is reason to believe that the underlying, original structures were damaged in the process. Such was the fate of the capitals of the eight monolithic columns, which were found to have been destroyed when in July of 1932 a government architect by the name of Ferrant opened up part of the baroque decoration and took a look, discovering extensive damage.

The ambulatory and four of its five original chapels have gone relatively unchanged over the centuries: San Salvador, directly behind the high altar, is square when seen from the exterior, but inside the niches placed in the angles make it semicircular. A baroque wall screens all of the eastern part of the cathedral, so the eastern façades of the chapels are covered over, but San Salvador's original blind arches in the lateral walls are still intact. As are the original capitals of the entrance arch, where angels holding scrolls present king Alfonso VI and bishop Diego Peláez to an audience that admires them, presumably for having been responsible for building the cathedral.

There is a window between each of the five chapels that serve to light the ambulatory: below the window that opens between the chapels of San Salvador and San Pedro there is the portal through which the monks of San Pelayo de Antealtares (who, because of the compromise of 1077, were given the rights to three altars in the eastern sector: those in San Salvador, San Pedro and San Juan Apóstol chapels) entered the cathedral. Nowadays tat portal is only open on Holy Years (Jubileo).

The chapel of San Pedro (which is now dedicated to the "Virgen de la Azucena) has undergone extensive alterations, but its original semicircular form and three shafted windows can still be seen. The original San Andrés absidiole no longer exists, having been replaced by the eighteenth century chapel of Nuestra Señora del Pilar; the chapel of San Juan Apóstol is still there, but has been enlarged by a domed altar: its roof has a badly weathered sculpture of what appears to be a winged lion with the head of a bearded, long haired man. The original chapel of Santa Fe (now called San Bartolomé) keeps much of its original structures intact: it has a quintuple arcade and the middle three arches contain windows, while on the roof the stone figure of a four-legged, winged creature is ridden by a man-like creature with the feet of a frog.

The ambulatory has a triforium gallery over it which contains windows that introduce light through the quadrant vault; on the outside these windows originally had columns on either side, but after later modifications which included fortifications, battlements were added above the original ambulatory cornice and the whole ambulatory roof was raised.

Coming through the vault of the apse are five clerestory windows; the exterior of the clerestory has twisted columns and cusped arches between the windows.

Many historians of architecture and specialists see a definite break in the pattern of construction between the eastern part of the church and its western counterpart, a possible interruption in construction that is marked by a long vertical joint shaped like an inverted "J." If, in fact, there was such an interruption, the most likely explanation can be found in the political upheavals that followed the death in 1065 of king Fernando I of Castile-León. We might remember that at his death Fernando had split his kingdom among his three sons, giving Castile to Sancho (Sancho II, reg. 1065-1072), León to Alfonso (Alfonso VI, reg. 1065-1109), and Galicia to García (reg. 1065-1071). Don Diego Peláez had been made bishop by Sancho, king of powerful Castile, with whom Peláez had cast his lot (Sancho had deposed his brother García of Galicia in 1071 and sent him into exile in Seville). But Sancho's improbable death at Zamora after having defeated his brother and the Leonese army in 1072 left Peláez out in the cold: his protector, the man whom he had supported was dead, his enemy, Alfonso, was now in command.

Although it is true that they got along well for some years (the cathedral was begun in 1078), eventually Alfonso put Peláez in prison, and many years would elapse before another bishop, Diego Gelmírez (consecrated in 1101) would take over and complete the cathedral, becoming so powerful that he practically ruled Galicia. It is entirely possible that, with Peláez in disgrace and imprisoned, funds dried out and construction came to a halt until the brash new bishop got things going again.

The cathedral is built in the shape of a Latin Cross, with a large central nave in the Romanesque style. Other interesting chapels within the church are "Cristo de Burgos," with Churrigueresque reredos; Communion; Santa Catalina; San Antonio Corticela, with a Romanesque portal from the thirteenth century; Espíritu Santo, originally from the thirteenth century, widened in the fourteenth and containing seven tombs; Reliquias, where a reliquary/bust is said to contain the head of Santiago Alfeo, cousin (some say brother) of Jesus Christ (the bust has metal fetters around its neck, the gift of Suero de Quiñones), and Mondragón, with a sixteenth century grille and terracota reredos.

The cathedral's cloister is done in the Gothic style called "gótico florido." Next to it are the cathedral archives, the museum and the library, where many important manuscripts are kept. The capitular has impressive Flemish tapestries, and the royal pantheon, the main chapel and the crypt (also called the old cathedral and attributed by some scholars to Master Mateo) are important visits within the cathedral.

On the exterior, on the western side, the main façade (Obradoiro) is a late addition (1738) and is in the baroque Churrigueresque style. Its designer, Casas y Novoa conceived it as a gigantic reredos, as if it were a screen behind an altar. On this side a large staircase allows access into the building. On either side of the western façade there is a tower: to the left is the "Torre de la Carraca," or "Tower of the Rattle," where to this day a rattle is kept that is used (as it has for centuries) to call the faithful to Mass during Holy Week; the tower on the right is the "Torre de las Campanas," or "Tower of the Bells," older than its twin.

In 1168, king Fernando III (reg. 1158-1188) gave the archbishop of Santiago, Pedro Gudesteiz, the privilege of constructing the narthex known as the "Pórtico de la Gloria." This famous portico, masterpiece of the late Romanesque and masterwork of Mateo, who finished it on April 1, 1188, is now hidden from outside view by the Obradoiro façade. The "Pórtico de la Gloria" is clearly divided into three sections that summarize Christian theology, conveying a message through the figures that grace the three arches that give access to the nave. If the pilgrim stands across from the portico in the narrow area covered by cross vaults, he or she will see Saint James twice: once in his usual place next to the other Apostles, and once seated in majesty, just under the image of Christ in Majesty, in the mullion that parts the entrance. In this second image Saint James is holding a walking stick in the form of the symbolic Tau, while on the other hand he holds a scroll that reads "Misit me Dominus" (The Lord has sent me). He rests his feet on two young lions. Under him in the mullion is the Tree of Jesse (Christ's Family Tree), with the indentation caused by the thousands of pilgrims who throughout the ages have put their hands on it.

On the other side of this mullion or central column, facing the nave, the figure of a kneeling man strikes his chest. The accompanying stone sign used to say "Architectus," which is why it is taken to be the image of Master Mateo himself. It is said that as penance for his sins, he was put in that position so that he might never enjoy his prodigious work. Bumping one's head to his is supposed to covey some of his wisdom over to the person doing the bumping. Many local university students have been known to frequent the figure in times of desperation.

One of the most popular figures in the "Pórtico" is that of Daniel, whose smile conveys a sense of worldly joy, even sensuality. If one follows his gaze, one sees that he is looking at queen Esther, who is in front of him. Esther has lowered her head. It seems that tradition has it that Esther was endowed with ample breasts, and thus she was originally sculpted by Mateo. But the figure (along with the undauntedly admiring Daniel) became the focus of popular attention, forcing an overly pious bishop to order the breasts reduced to the dimensions we see today.

On the tympanum, above the central arch, a seated Christ shows His wounds accompanied by the four Evangelists, Mark, Matthew, Luke and John, the 24 Elders of the Apocalypse playing various instruments and a row of angels carrying the symbols of the Passion of Christ. The left arch represents the Old Testament, with an allegory of the Synagogue, the Prophets and Adam and Eve. The right hand arch is an allegory of the vices stalking the pagan world. Some of the figures are on the columns of the embrasures, and the Elders/musicians are in the curve of the arch, which forms an attractive archivolt over the central door.

The other two major portals leading into the cathedral are Azabachería, whose eighteenth century façade is the work of Ferro Caaveiro based on a 1758 design by Ventura Rodríguez, and Platerías, which is the oldest façade in the cathedral.

Platerías has a double row of semicircular arches splayed with triple archivolts and is decorated with numerous sculptures, some of which are mentioned in the medieval *Pilgrims' Guide*, while others that are now in Platerías are mentioned by that same *Guide* as being in the northern façade, "Azabachería." Apparently, when the original Azabachería façade was demolished in the eighteenth century, some of its sculptures were transferred to Platerías and set there in an almost chaotic fashion. Platerías' original bas-reliefs are to the right and left of the entrance, level with the columns. Among the best bas-reliefs are "Abraham's Sacrifice," "David playing the Viol," and the "Creation of Man."

Because of its dimensions, the cathedral is a typical Pilgrimage church. The ample central nave allows the faithful to hear Mass while large lateral naves and the ambulatory allow the throngs of pilgrims to circulate freely throughout the church, visiting the chapels, the crypt, etc. without interfering with the Service.

Before leaving the cathedral to visit other sites in **Santiago**, the pilgrim should look at the Romanesque tympanum on the western end of the southern nave, where a bas-relief tells the story of the battle of Clavijo. On the eastern end one can see the ninth century baptismal font from where Moslem general Almanzor's horse drank after the great Moorish leader took and pillaged the city late in the tenth century.

Another interesting place in the cathedral is the tomb of Galician bishop Muñiz, a mysterious character who they say was very well versed in the Black Arts. Perhaps because of this reputation, his tomb is not very visible, being behind the "Pórtico de la Gloria." One Christmas Eve, tradition has it that Muñiz ate a meal in Rome, where he was visiting. Dissatisfied with the taste of the food, he flew back to the Santiago cathedral, where he was in time for morning prayers the next day. Once a year the cathedral chapter says prayers for Muñiz in the chapel of Soledad, and on special holidays the canons' religious procession stops by his tomb and prays in silence.

Should you be in **Santiago** on the 6th of August, don't miss the Mass that has been offered for centuries every year in the cathedral for the soul of Charlemagne; another tradition is played out on the 25th of July, Day of Santiago, when a lantern in the Berenguela tower is lit to orient the pilgrims towards the church.

Among a number of different styles, the Romanesque and baroque churches in Santiago are the most numerous. The most ancient church in the city, about 300 years older than the discovery of the Apostle's tomb, is the church of San Fiz de Solovio, which dates back to the sixth century. It has gone through some rebuilding, especially in the twelfth century, when its Romanesque façade was built.

The monastery of San Pelayo de Antealtares, has a Classical style church with Churrigueresque reredos, but perhaps its most impressive feature is the large wall that closes off one of the sides of Plaza de la Quintana.

Reconstructed in the seventeenth century, the monastery of San Martín Pinario was founded in 899, and it became one of the most famous and influential in all of Galicia. Behind it it has a church, San Martín, built in 1590. Its façade looks like a reredos split into three parts, with reliefs that represent St. Martin along with other characters from his life. The main reredos is an imitation of the Cathedral's, the choir-stalls have a representation of the life of the Virgin on their backrests, and the Main Altar is Churrigueresque.

Among the other churches and constructions in the city, the most outstanding are as follows: The church of Santa María del Camino is an eighteenth century construction with a high-relief of the Magi; the Casa de Bazán is a magnificent edifice from the sixteenth century; The church of San Benito del Campo is one of the oldest in the city, dating from the tenth century; the Palacio de Don Pedro is in the Gothic style and contains the Pilgrimage Museum; the church of San Miguel dos Agros dates from the beginning of the nineteenth century and is neoclassical in style; the Casa de la Parra is an interesting baroque style construction; the House of the Canons (Casa de los Canónigos, Puerta Real) was built in the seventeenth century and is next to the "Tower of the Clock" (Torre del Reloj), which dates originally from 1316 and houses one of the most powerful bells in the world; the palace of bishop Gelmírez was built in the eleventh century by the first archbishop of Santiago, Diego Gelmírez, and it is one of the most important civil constructions done in the Romanesque style; the Hospital Real was founded by the Catholic Kings, Isabel and Fernando, and it has an impressive plateresque front (today it is an expensive hotel called "Hostal de los Reyes Católicos"); the Rajoy Palace is from the mid eighteenth century; the Colegio de San Jerónimo was built in 1501, but its front is from the fifteenth century.

It would be an encyclopedic effort indeed to detail all the important constructions in Santiago. A summary list of other places that should be visited includes The Colegio Mayor Fonseca, a Renaissance building with a lovely plateresque patio; the palace of the Marqués de Bendana, done in the baroque style much like the Casa Deán; the palace of Santa Cruz de Ribadulla, neoclassical; the Casa de las Pomas; the Romanesque church of Santa María, twelfth century, the baroque convent of Nuestra Señora de los Remedios; the University of Compostela, founded in 1501; the baroque church of La Compañía; the convent of Belvis; the convent of Las Madres Mercedarias; the baroque convent of San Agustín; the also baroque church of Nuestra Señora del Pilar; the church of Santa Susana; the monument to the great Galician writer Rosalía de Castro; the twelfth century collegiate church of Santa María la Real del Sar, which still has its original Romanesque portal and a cloister with charmingly slender columns and capitals that are attributed to Master Mateo himself (the church is visibly leaning, and efforts have been made to stop it from bowling over); the monastery of Santa María del Conxo, founded in the eleventh century and reconstructed in the seventeenth, containing Churrigueresque reredos, an image of Santiago as pilgrim by Ferreiro and a Christ by Gregorio Fernández; the convent of Santo Domingo, in whose Gothic chapel are housed the remains of famous Galicians, among which is Rosalía de Castro (its annex houses the Museum of the Galician People and the Municipal Museum with its wonderful triple spiral staircase by Domingo de Andrade); the convent of Santa Clara, with a façade that is considered one of the most significant constructions in Galician baroque, ornamented with lavish volutes and heavy stone cylinders; the monastery of San Francisco, said to have been founded by St. Francis Assisi when he came to Santiago as pilgrim in the year 1214, with a church that was reconstructed in 1613 that contains a sculpture of the Saint in its atrium by Francisco Asorey, a Santiago native; and the twelfth century church of Santa María Salomé, with its beautiful Romanesque portico.

The city's squares and plazas are not to be overlooked, specially Azabacherías, on the north arm of the Cathedral, or Quintana (Literatos), where the Puerta Santa (Holy Door), decorated with twelfth century Romanesque statues, opens during Jubilee Years, or Platerías, next to the famous cathedral portal, where we find the "Fountain of the Horses" (Fuente de los Caballos), from the nineteenth century, and the baroque "Casa del Cabildo," or Obradoiro, where one observes the impressive façade of the Cathedral, contiguous to the Cathedral's plateresque cloisters over which rises the "Tower of the Treasury" (Torrecilla del Tesoro).

Conclusions

The Road to Santiago, contrary to popular belief, does not make you a different person. It does give you a very focused perspective on the person you are. Each day, as you confront different situations, you tend to watch yourself react. You're in a strange land of tiny villages, huge mountains and endless plains where the intonation given the language by the locals at times throws you off. You monitor your body and your psyche much of the time: when you ache, when the sun burns your skin, when you're lonely, when you become irritated with your companions for the most trivial reasons.

I noticed that all three of us made the trip alone, although we were together much of the time. We traveled on the Road the same way we travel through life: for Rodolfo the Road itself was the important element, the act of traveling, slowly enough to take in everything as you go. Silvio was intent on making friends and on being known and remembered by the people we met on the Road, telling anyone who cared to listen about his life back in New York. For me, arriving was the all-consuming passion: I drove my body and my mind more than I should have, seeing as much as I could at the fastest pace possible. All for naught, as I usually ended up waiting for my companions under a tree somewhere on the Road. Little by little, though, I came to comprehend that this Road, like life, must be traveled primarily from the *inside*, rather than from the *outside*. What goes on inside of you is by far more important than the incidental phenomena of the physical road.

I can only explain my passion for arriving as the result of my being a modern man. I've become convinced that there is a jackpot waiting for me just beyond the bend; I just have to be fast enough and work hard enough to achieve it. So I travel fast through life, working the extra hours, speeding from place to place, but the jackpot always remains beyond the next corner, around the next bend in the road. And no one has told me what this jackpot actually *looks like*, so I keep struggling to reach it without knowing if I've already caught up with it, or even passed it without recognizing it. Yet somehow it always seems further up the road.

My experiences here, moving to the daily rhythms of this ancient trail, seeing tranquil and joyous life of the people in its villages, enjoying, like them, the little wonders that life offers constantly, all have given me new insight into what bliss is, have shown me that the rat race does not have a finish line, that it is unnatural, that it works against the individual's ability to be happy, that it keeps you from finding your true destiny and fulfilling it. Many individuals chasing this jackpot might just give up, seeing themselves as failures. At the point where they find themselves at odds with their society, they will have fallen off the edge of the world, speeding into the endless void of meaningless existence. On the Road to Santiago it's easy to see that the meaningful things in life are never beyond the rainbow, but always right in front of you.

Looking at the history of this great nation I have just spent over two weeks traversing, I can establish a parallel between it and this rat race that absorbs modern urbanites. Beginning in the XVI Century, Spaniards set out to conquer the world, and they basically accomplished their goal. As a reward for their superhuman effort they didn't get much of anything in return: the gold gained from far-off lands first went to pay for extravagant items; after that it began to pay for basic necessities, for the nation stopped producing things it could just obtain elsewhere with gold. Needing gold to survive now, the Spanish pushed themselves more and more, seeking the jackpot beyond the next mountain, and then the next, until no more riches were to be found and the nation fell into the great void of meaningless existence. After that shock, it is now evident that contemporary Spaniards have begun to take stock of the real paradise that belongs to them, right here and right now, on the Iberian Peninsula.

As far as my attitude upon arriving in Roncesvalles to begin the Road, it's not surprising that I though of the journey in terms of *overcoming* the obstacles speedily, of making my way swiftly to that finish line called Santiago de Compostela. But the Road brought home to me that the real journey is not in the trail that supports the wheels of your bicycle, but in the way you progress and develop *inside*. This urge to *overcome* is natural to all human beings, but we've distorted it into an endless struggle to achieve what is, in its essence, not achievable, for it will always remain just ahead of you, just beyond your reach. Because there *is* no finish line.

Eating a superb meal at any little inn along the Road, the hours would go by without being noticed; enjoying the food became a most memorable event, and nobody hurried us so that our seats could be occupied by other customers (as a matter of fact, the owners were many times sorry to see us leave, for they were truly interested in us). The innkeepers' families and friends were sure to show up at any moment and sit and sip coffee, basking in the knowledge that their lives are important. In my circle of friends, we would probably have considered such activity as an inconceivable waste of time. As if we actually *saved* time. Time will pass, whether you are *saving* it by rushing around like a chicken without a head, or just sitting around a table, like the folks that live in the towns on the Road to Santiago, enjoying friendships and cementing lifelong relationships.

Looking at them it's easy to see how I am a product of a society that employs people like so many unimportant screws in a huge machine whose main goal is its own well being. I go to fast-food restaurants and become agitated when I take too long to finish a meal, thinking that I'm keeping the next person from eating. The question is, why do I run so much? Am I actually saving time? If I'm saving time this way, why don't I have time to do anything? Perhaps because I'm always too busy trying to save time.

For a professor who spends his life in front of a class or behind a desk, driving in an air-conditioned car and avoiding stairs, the first feeling I got as I tackled the first kilometers on the Road to Santiago was that of breaking molds that had constrained my life up to now, of taking chances, out in the middle of nowhere with nothing but a bike and my wits to guide me. In this sense, the Road to Santiago was the fulfillment of an old dream, one I imagine we are all endowed with, of living life to its fullest, of taking risks, of experiencing a marvelous adventure, of being free, traveling on the road that comes from all points and leads to your own self, to a place where, upon arrival, you will see yourself in a wonderful new light.

An adventure like this allows the individual to envisage the world as a myriad of wonderful possibilities: the ability to do it is what separates us from other living things and makes us human.

But this is not an easy thing to do. We often tend to stifle and inhibit our imagination, prevent it from exploding within us in all its vigor. We set rigid parameters within which to lead our lives, doing the same thing day in and day out, the time we wake, the place we have lunch, what we eat, the people we see. We repeat our routines because we are certain that these routines provide us with the best lives available. This keeps us in a shell outside of which we dare not stray; we forget that life is an adventure.

So we come to judge the value of our existence by how many times we go to a good restaurant, watch good movies, or go on vacation to a strip of sand with a palm tree on it. We are unaware of the life outside our shells, with its trials, pain, sweat, joys and ultimate fulfillment. Real happiness is in the struggle of adventure and in the uncertainty of combat against the elements and against your own weaknesses. A person who finds this happiness is endowed with wings.

Perhaps this is the reason why the actual arrival at Santiago was not quite as sweet as the imagined arrivals; the goal, though precious, did not mean so much once I had reached it, the prize was not so great once it had been attained. We must remember that if we add up all the goals attained in the span of our lives, they don't add up to much: real life is lived in the spaces that precede the moment of arrival, in the steps taken towards the goal, in the effort put forth and in the dreams that powered the effort. It is not the goal that makes us wise and contented, but the dreams forged and the road taken to arrive there.

On the airplane, now far from Santiago, I can still hear its cathedral bells tolling. I can still feel the heat of the Castilian steppes and the intense cold of the Navarran summits. Perhaps for me the Road has not yet ended. It might never end. All things considered, I'm now more than ever aware that it's not a transgression to search for the joy in life;

that it's not a sin to break the shell and grow wings. God has made you, but only you can make your destiny. Go to Santiago. Meet your ghosts. Unfurl your wings. Make your own Road.

ULTREIA.

Top left: Alfonso (author) in Pamplona.
Top right: Alfonso (*right*) and Silvio (*left*) relax in León in front of lion and "Covadonga" inn.
Bottom, from left to right: Silvio, Alfonso, and Rodolfo in Burgos.

Top left: León Cathedral.
Top right: Street in León.
Bottom: Frómista.

Top, and bottom left: Castille.
Bottom right: Santo Domingo de la Calzada.

Top: Irache Monastery.
Center: Sunflower field in Castile.   *Bottom*: Torres del Río.

Views in Galicia.

Opposite, Top: Castle of the Knights Templar.
Center: Break in a small town in León.
Bottom: Villafranca del Bierzo
This page, Top: Road views in Galicia.
Bottom: Alfonso crossing from León to Galicia

Santiago de Compostela.

APPENDIX I.

The "Codex Calixtinus" and the "Pilgrim's Guide to Santiago de Compostela" (XII Century).

The *Codex Calixtinus,* also known as the *Liber Sancti Jacobi,* is a series of Latin documents written at different times by several individuals. In the XII Century they were brought together as a single text and revised, as they all dealt with the same subject: Saint James. The name *Codex Calixtinus* stems from the belief, held by many, that Pope Calixtus II (1119-1124), a devout fan of Santiago and the Road, had a major role in the creation of the text. A number of manuscript copies of the *Codex* are conserved: the most important one, consisting of 225 folios, is kept in the archives of the Santiago Cathedral; another important one is incomplete and is known as the Ripoll manuscript. This second one is kept in Barcelona.

The *Codex Calixtinus,* as it has come down to us, consists of five different compilations which are commonly referred to as books. The first one is a collection of liturgical pieces meant to be used for the cult of Santiago on two specific days: 25 July, the day he was martyred, and 30 December, the day his remains undertook the uncanny voyage in the stone vessel. This first book is very important as a reference for medieval liturgical music.

The second book is known as the "Book of Miracles," or *Liber miraculorum*, a collection of 22 miracles attributed to Saint James, 18 of which are said to have been recorded by Pope Calixtus. It is interesting to note that 21 of the miracles occur between 1080 and 1110, the most important period in the consolidation of the Road, with the last miracle taking place in 1135.

The third book is basically a glorification of the cult of Santiago; a sort of commercial spot calling for the upgrading of the See of Santiago, where the remains of the Saint are kept. Of greater interest in this book are the two versions of the account of the transfer of the Saint's body from Palestine to Spain. The account is not only prefaced by Pope Calixtus II, but it is also "certified" by a certain "Pope Leo," widely believed to be Pope Leo III (785-816).

The fourth book, called the *Historia Turpini*, is an "historical" account which is prefaced by Turpin, "archbishop of Reims and companion of Charlemagne in Spain." The account purports to relate, from an eyewitness perspective, the adventures of the French king on Spanish soil, the encouraging words offered him by Saint James himself, and the epic and improbable battles that allowed Charlemagne to free Galicia from Moslem control.

But it is the fifth book of the *Codex* which concerns us here the most. This book, called the *Pilgrims' Guide to Santiago de Compostela*, has been called the first tourist guide in history. It's not certain who is actually responsible for this book, or how many hands contributed to its making, but the apparent author of one of its sections, Aimery Picaud, has often been proposed as the most likely editor/compiler. Having been put together from several disparate accounts, the *Guide* is very uneven, with very short chapters that seem to be the result of hasty editing by the compiler; these next to long chapters that most likely owe their length to the nature of their content, which probably interested the compiler more than what is contained in the smaller chapters.

The one unifying element in the *Guide* is its orientation: at every turn it seems to sing the praises of the French: the peoples of Spain are more worthy if they resemble the French, less so if they are not French-like. In his value-judgements, Galicians are the best of the Spanish because they are the closest in character to "our French people," while the Basques and Navarrans are quite animalistic owing to their lack of resemblance with the French. As you may have guessed, Aimery Picaud was a Frenchman.

The following translation of the Santiago Cathedral's archival copy of the *Pilgrim's Guide* is meant to give the reader a first-hand historical sense of the Road to Santiago, for this is a document that every person who is interested in the Road should be familiar with. After eight centuries, this document can still prove somewhat useful to pilgrims undertaking the trip, for the physical characteristics of the Road and the terrain have not changed very much in that period.

In the interests of being brief, I have excerpted much of chapter eight, by far the longest chapter, with its long lists of mostly French saints, the miracles attributed to them and other sundry details which might not be the main interest of the modern pilgrim to Santiago.

The other chapters I've translated whole. Where appropriate, I have included notes at the end of selected chapters.

Here Begins Book V of Saint James the Apostle

Summary of the Blessed Pope Calixtus

If the knowledgeable reader seeks for the truth in this, our work, he is sure to find it in this codex, as have many people who bear witness to the truths contained within it.

Chapter I   The Routes of Saint James.

Chapter II The Day's Journey on the Apostle's Road.

Chapter III   The Names of the Towns on this Road.

Chapter IV   Three Hospices of the World.

Chapter V The Names of the Travelers Who Restored the Road of the Blessed James.

Chapter VI   The Bitter and the Sweet Waters.

Chapter VII The Types of Lands and Peoples along the Road

Chapter VIII   The Saintly Remains that May Be Visited on This Road and the Passion of Saint Eutropius.

Chapter IX   Details of the City and the Church of Saint James.

Chapter I
Of the Routes of Saint James.

There are four roads that lead to Santiago. These all converge and form a single road at Puente la Reina, on Spanish soil. The first crosses Saint-Gilles, Montpellier, Toulouse, and the pass of Somport; the second crosses Notre-Dame of Le Puy, Sainte-Foy of Conques and Saint-Pierre of Moissac; the third goes through Sainte-Marie-Madeleine of Vézelay, Saint Léonard in the Limousin and the city of Périgueux; the fourth traverses Saint-Martin of Tours, Saint-Hilaire of Poitiers, Saint-Jean-d'Angély, Saint-Eutrope of Saintes and the city of Bordeaux.

The road that goes through Sainte-Foy, the one that traverses Saint-Léonard, and the one that cuts through Saint-Martin meet at Ostabat and, gaining the Cize Pass, join at Puente la Reina with the road that comes down from Somport. From there, a single road leads as far as Santiago.

Chapter II
The Day's Travel on the Apostle's Road.
Pope Calixtus

There are three short day's journeys from Somport to Puente la Reina: the first from Borce, a village at the entrance of the Somport on the Gascon side, up to Jaca; the second day from Jaca to Monreal, and the third from Monreal to Puente la Reina.

From the Cize Pass as far as Santiago there are thirteen days' stages on the journey. The first day you travel from the village of Saint-Michel, at the entrance to the Cize Pass on the Gascon side, to Viscarret: this stage is short. The second stage leads from Viscarret to Pamplona, and it is also quite short. The third stage goes from Pamplona to Estella; the fourth one, from Estella to the city of Nájera, must be made on horseback, as is the fifth day's travel from Nájera to a city named Burgos. The sixth day you proceed from Burgos to Frómista; the seventh from Frómista to Sahagún; the eighth from Sahagún to the city of León; the ninth from León to Rabanal del Camino; the tenth from Rabanal to Villafranca del Bierzo, after surmounting the high passes of Mount Irago and reaching the mouth of the river Valcarce; the eleventh stage is from Villafranca to Triacastela; the twelfth from Triacastela to Palas del Rey; and finally the thirteenth day -a short stage- you proceed from Palas del Rey as far as Santiago.

[NOTES. To journey mostly on foot from the Pyrenees to Galicia in 13 days seems to be a superhuman feat indeed. The same journey took us 16 days on mountain bikes. Realistically, and under the most favorable conditions, a strong pilgrim would take more than twice that period of time to make the journey. I can offer no explanation as to why the compiler(s) of the *Guide* would give such a seemingly careless account of the journey's stages, other than to say that they may not have made the journey themselves, or that in the interests attracting more pilgrims they made it seem shorter than it really was.]

Chapter III
Of the Names of the Towns on this Road.

These are the towns on the Road to Santiago from the Somport to Puente la Reina: first, at the foot of the mountain on the Gascon [north] side is Borce; once on the summit you find the hospice of Santa Cristina, then Canfranc, followed by Jaca, then Osturit, and then Tiermas, where there are continuously running hot royal baths; then there is Monreal and finally Puente la Reina.
From the Cize Pass until one reaches the basilica in Galicia, the most important towns to be found are: first, at the foot of the Cize Mountain and on the Gascon [north] side there is the village of Saint-Michel; once having overcome the summit, one reaches the hospice of

Roland and then the town of Roncesvalles; next is Viscarret, then Larrasoaña, then the city of Pamplona, then Puente la Reina, and next Estella, where the bread is good and the wine is excellent, the meat and the fish abundant; indeed a place exuberant with all sorts of pleasures. Then comes Los Arcos, then Logroño, then Villaroya and next the city of Nájera. Next come Santo Domingo de la Calzada, Redecilla del Camino, Belorado, Villafranca, the Oca forest, Atapuerca, the city of Burgos, Tardajos, Hornillos del Camino, Castrogeriz, the Itero del Castillo Bridge, Frómista and then Carrión de los Condes, a well-managed and industrious town that has bread, wine, meat and all types of produce in abundance. Next is Sahagún, affluent in all kinds of merchandise, where there is a meadow in which, as is reported, the shining spears of victorious warriors, planted there for the glory of God, once bloomed. Next comes Mansilla de las Mulas, and next León, a royal and courtly city that is brimming with wealth.

Then come Orbigo, the city of Astorga, Rabanal del Camino called the captive, the Mount Irago Pass, Molinaseca, Ponferrada, Cacabelos, Villafranca del Bierzo at the mouth of the river Valcarce, Castro Sarracín, Villaus, the Cebreiro Mountain Pass and then the hospice at its summit. Next is Linares del Rey and right after it Triacastela, already within Galicia and at the foot of the aforementioned mountain. There, the Pilgrims are given a stone which they carry with them to Castañeda in order to make lime for the construction of the Apostle's basilica. Following these are the towns of San Miguel, Barbadelo, the bridge over the river Miño, Sala de la Reina, Palas del Rey, Libureiro, Santiago de Boente, Castañeda, Villanova, Ferreiros, and at last Compostela, the Apostle's most excellent city, replete with bounteous delights. The city guards the precious body of the Blessed James, for which it is recognized as the happiest and most magnificent of all the cities in Spain.

I have sparingly enumerated the towns above and day's journey so that the pilgrims who set off for Santiago, after listening to this, may anticipate the expenses needed for their trip.

Chapter IV
Three Hospices of the World.

God has, in a most particular way, instituted in this world three columns that are greatly necessary for the upkeep of his poor, they are the hospice of Jerusalem, the hospice of Mount-Joux, and the hospice of Santa Cristina on the Somport Pass. These hospices, set up in places where they are greatly needed, are holy places, the house of God for restoring the saintly pilgrims, providing rest for the weary, consoling the sick, providing for the salvation of the dead, and giving aid to the living. Thus, those who built these holy places, whomever they may be, will doubtless partake of the kingdom of God.

Chapter V
The Names of the Travelers Who Restored the Road of the Blessed James.

Here are the names of some of the travelers who in the times of Diego, archbishop of Santiago, of Alfonso, emperor of Spain and Galicia, and of pope Calixtus, prior to the year 1120 and under the reign of Alfonso, king of Aragón and of Louis the Fat, king of France, for the love of God and the Apostle rebuilt the Road to Santiago from Rabanal as far as the bridge over the river Miño: Andrew, Roger, Alvito, Fortus, Arnold, Stephen and Peter who reconstructed the bridge that had been demolished by Queen Urraca.

May their souls and those of their assistants rest in eternal peace.

[NOTES. This Diego is Diego Gelmírez, Bishop in 1100 and Archbishop of Santiago from 1120 to 1140. "Alfonso, emperor of Spain and Galicia" is Alfonso VII, the Galician son of Raymond of Burgundy and Urraca. Born in 1105, he became king of Galicia in 1111 and king of León and Castilla in 1126; he was also proclaimed "Emperor of Spain," a largely symbolic title, in 1135. "Alfonso, king of Aragón," is Alfonso I the

Warlike, king of Aragón and Navarra (1073-1134), second husband to Urraca, daughter of Alfonso VI of León and Castilla. "Louis the Fat" is Louis IV, born in 1081 and king of France from 1108 to his death in 1137. "Queen Urraca" is the wife of Alfonso I, daughter of Alfonso VI and mother of Alfonso VII. An impetuous woman, she led a military campaign against her own son and defended Castilian independence by force of arms when her husband Alfonso I attempted to absorb León and Castilla into Aragón-Navarra. During military operations against her husband, her troops destroyed the very important bridge on the Miño River.]

Chapter VI
Of the Bitter and Sweet Waters Found Along This Road.

These are the rivers found from the mountain passes of Cize and Somport as far as Santiago: descending from Somport there is a salubrious river called the Aragón which waters Spain; from the Cize Pass there issues a healthy river which is called by many the Runa; it crosses Pamplona. Two rivers, the Arga and the Runa, flow by Puente la Reina.

Towards the east, at a place called Lorca, there flows a river called Salado. Beware of drinking from its waters or watering your horse in its stream, for it shall be fatal.

While we proceeded towards Santiago, we met two Navarrans seated on its banks who were sharpening their knives. These people make a living from skinning pilgrims' mounts after they drink the water and die. When we questioned them, they lied to us, telling us that the water was healthful and safe to drink. Believing them, we proceeded to water our horses, but no sooner had we done so, than both of them died. The men skinned them on the spot.

The river Ega flows by Estella: its water is sweet, healthful and excellent. On the other hand, by a town called Los Arcos flows a deadly stream, and beyond Los Arcos, next to the first hospice, in other words, between Los Arcos and that hospice, there flows a stream that is deadly to horses and men. By the town called Torres, still in Navarra, there is a stream that is equally deadly to horses and men that drink its waters. From there to a town called Las Cuevas there flows an equally deadly stream. Yet by Logroño there flows a large river named Ebro which is healthful and has plenty of fish.

The waters of all the rivers one finds between Estella and Logroño are truly fatal to the men and horses that drink them, their fish being no less dangerous to eat. If anywhere in Spain or in Galicia you eat either the fish people call barbel, or the one the people from Poitou call alose and the Italians clipia, or even the eel or the tench, you will surely die soon after or at the very least fall ill. If, after eating them, someone did not fall ill, this is because he was healthier than most people or because he had dwelled in that country for a long period. All the fish and the flesh of beef and pork from all of Spain and Galicia will cause foreigners to get sick.

These are the names of the rivers whose waters are sweet and healthful: the Pisuerga, which flows under the bridge at Itero del Castillo; the Carrión, which flows by Carrión; the Cea, by Sahagún; the Esla, by Mansilla de las Mulas; the Porma, under some large bridge between Mansilla de las Mulas and León; the Torio, flowing by León under the encampment of the Jews; the Bernesga, which flows by the same city, on the other side, towards Astorga; the Sil which waters Ponferrada in Valverde; the Cua which waters Cacabelos; the Burbia which flows under the bridge at Villafranca del Bierzo; the Valcarce which flows in its own valley; and Miño that flows by Puertomarín. Besides these, there is a certain river that is located about two miles from the city of Santiago, in a wooded place, which is called the Lavamentula because French pilgrims that go to Santiago, for the love of the Apostle, in that place wash not only their virile member, but, having shed all their clothes, wash the dirt off their whole body. The river Sar, flowing between Monte del Gozo and the city of Santiago, is considered healthful, as is the river Sarela, which flows westward on the other side of the city.

If I have thus given a description of these rivers, it is so that pilgrims on their way to Santiago do their best to avoid unhealthy waters and choose those rivers which are good for them and their mounts.

[NOTE. The general aversion felt by the author(s) towards Basques and Navarrans is manifested clearly in this chapter. This ill feeling is again shown, with even more passion, in subsequent chapters. The encampment of the Jews mentioned here can be no other than Castro de los Judíos, a small community very close to the city of León. The place called Lavamentula, where travelers wash their "virile member," is present-day Lavacolla; mentula is the Latin for penis, Lavamentula, therefore, is the "washing of the penis." Lavacolla is a mere modern version of Lavamentula, as "colla," in old Romance, means scrotum.]

Chapter VII
The Quality of the Land and of the People Along this Road.

On the Road of the Blessed James by way of Toulouse, after crossing the river Garonne, one first enters the land of Gascon; afterwards, having attained the Somport Pass, one enters the country of Aragón and then, as far as the bridge on the Arga [Puente la Reina] and beyond, the land of Navarra. If one comes by way of the Cize Pass, however, one finds, after Tours, the country of Poitou, a well-managed land that is blessed and excellent. The people of Poitou are strong and warlike, extraordinarily skilful in the use of bows, arrows and lances in times of war, bold in battle, fast in running, seemly in dress, noble in features, clever in language, generous in rewarding others and prodigal in the hospitality they offer. Afterwards comes the land of Saintonge. After somehow crossing an estuary and the river Garonne, one arrives in Bordelais, a region excellent in wine, abundant in fish, but of rustic language. Those of Saintonge already speak a rustic language, but those of Bordelais speak an even more rustic one. From here, one needs to travel three days, for people who are already tired, to get across the land of Bordelais.

This place is desolate and devoid of all good: there is no bread, wine, meat, fish, water or springs; it is hard to find a village here. The sandy and flat land abounds in wild boar, honey, millet and panic-grass. If you chance to cross it in the summer, be careful to guard your face against the huge flies that greatly abound there and which are called by the people wasps or horseflies. On top of all this, if you are not careful to watch your feet, you will soon sink up to your knees in the quick-sand that is found everywhere.

Having crossed this region, one reaches the land of Gascon, rich in white bread and excellent red wine, covered by forests and meadows, streams and healthful springs. The Gascons are fast talkers and verbose, given to mockery, lecherous, drunkards, prodigal in food, dress poorly and are careless in the ornaments they wear. But they are efficient in battle and are generous in the hospitality that they provide for the poor. When they sit around the fire, they are accustomed to eating without a table and drinking all of them out of only one cup. As a matter of fact, they eat and drink a lot, wear wretched garments and lie down brazenly on a rotten, thin straw litter, the servants together with their master and mistress.

Upon leaving that country, always on the Road to Santiago, one finds two rivers that flow near the village of Saint-Jean-de-Sorde, one on the right and one on the left, one called a stream and the other a river. You cannot cross them without a raft. May their ferrymen be damned! Although both streams are quite narrow, they usually demand one coin from each man, be he rich or poor, whom they ferry over; for a horse, disgracefully, they extort four. Their boat is quite small, made from a single tree, not made for ferrying horses. When you board this boat, be careful not to fall into the water outside the boat. It is best to embark with only a few passengers, for if the boat is overloaded, you will soon be in peril.

It is also common for a ferryman, after receiving his fee, to have such a large number of pilgrims board his boat that it capsizes, drowning the pilgrims in the waves. At this point the boatmen, having plundered the dead, fiendishly celebrate.

After that, and near the Cize Pass, one reaches the Basque Country, on whose sea-shore, in the north, is the city of Bayonne. This land, whose language is savage, is wooded and mountainous, devoid of bread, wine and every food for the sustenance of the body, except that there are plenty of apples, cider and milk.

In this country, near the Cize Pass in the town called Ostabat and in Saint-Jean and Saint-Michel-Pied-de-Port, there are evil toll-gatherers who for certain will be perfectly damned. In fact, they actually approach the pilgrims with two sticks, forcefully extorting a toll from them. If any traveler should refuse to give them his money when they demand it, they beat him with the sticks and take away the toll money while cursing him and even searching through his pants. These people are fierce, and their country is uncivilized, wooded and barbarous. Their savage countenance and their brutal speech scares the wits out of those who see them, and although according to the rules and regulations they must not demand tribute from anyone but merchants, they unjustly profit from pilgrims and other travelers. At those times when they are supposed to receive, as is customary, four or six coins for a certain service, they charge eight or twelve, in other words, double.

For this reason we hereby censure and beseech these toll-gatherers as well as the King of Aragón and other magnates that profit from their tribute, as well as those who are in complicity with them, like Raymond de Soule, Vivien d'Aigremont, the Viscount of Saint-Michel and all their descendants, together with the ferrymen and Arnaud de la Guigne and all his descendants, as well as the other lords of the lands traversed by said streams who unjustly profit from the tolls collected for the crossing; also the priests who confer upon them the penitence and the Eucharist and celebrate Mass for them or otherwise admit them into church. All these people, until they expiate their sins through a long and public penance and show restraint in the collection of these tributes, be they instantly excommunicated not only in the episcopal sees of their own lands but also in Saint James's Basilica in the presence of pilgrims. Should any prelate, no matter who he may be, pardon them for the sake of charity or interest, may he be struck down with the sword of anathema.

It must be known to all that these toll-gatherers should, under no circumstances, collect a toll from the pilgrims, and that the ferrymen that I've mentioned should not demand for the crossing of two men -and this, provided they are rich- more than two coins; for a horse, as stipulated by the rules, one coin only. No tribute at all should be asked from a poor man. Besides, these ferrymen should have boats that are large enough to fit men and their mounts safely.

On the Road to Santiago, in the country of the Basques, there is a very high mountain that is called Port-de-Cize, either because it is the door that opens the way into Spain, or because it is through that mountain that goods are transported from one country to the other. The ascent to the mountain is eight miles long, and the descent is also eight miles; it is in fact so high that it seems to touch the sky. When you ascend to its summit, you feel that you can touch the sky with your hand. The Sea of Bretagne and the Western Sea can be seen from its summit, and also three kingdoms: Castilla, Aragón and France. On this summit there is a place called Charles's Cross; it was here that Charles, on his way to Spain with his armies, opened a passage with axes, hatchets, pickaxes and other tools, and it was here that for the first time he erected a Cross and, on his knees, said a prayer to God and Santiago facing Galicia. It is here that pilgrims, falling on their knees and facing the land of Santiago, offer a prayer and plant their own crosses like standards. Truly, up to a thousand crosses can be found there, and for that reason that place is the first prayer-station of the Road to Santiago. It was on this same mountain, before the advent of Christianity in Spain, that the Navarran and Basque fiends would not only rob the pilgrims going to Santiago, but would also ride them as if they were asses shortly before slaying them. Near this mountain and further to the north there is a valley called Valcarlos, where Charles himself made camp with his army after his warriors had been slain at Roncesvalles. Many pilgrims wishing to avoid climbing the mountain take that route.

After descending from the summit, one finds the hospice and the church with the rock that the great Roland, with a triple stroke of his sword, split from top to bottom. Next one finds Roncesvalles, the place where a large battle took place and in which King Marsile, Roland, Olivier and forty thousand Christian and Moslem soldiers were killed.

After this valley there is the land of Navarra, rich in bread, wine, milk and livestock. The Navarrans and the Basques are very much alike: they eat the same food, wear the same clothing and speak the same language, although the Basques can be recognized readily by their complexion, for they are whiter than the Navarrans. The Navarrans wear short black garments that come down to their knees, just like the Scots, and their footwear, called <u>lavarcas</u>, is made of uncured, hairy leather that is fastened around the foot with leather straps; they cover the bottom of the foot only, leaving the rest bare. They also wear dark wool cloaks that reach their elbows, fringed like a cape and called <u>sayas</u>. They dress most poorly and eat and drink in a most revolting manner. In their household, the servant, the master, the maid and the mistress eat from only one dish that contains all the food mixed together, and they don't use spoons but their hands. They also all drink from a single cup. If you see them eating, you will surely mistake them for dogs or swine gorging themselves, and if you hear them speak you will mistake them for barking dogs. Their language is, to be sure, a most barbarous thing: they call God <u>Urcia</u>; the Mother of God <u>Andrea María</u>; bread is <u>orgui</u>; wine is <u>ardum</u>; meat is <u>argui</u>; fish is <u>araign</u>; house is <u>echea</u>; the master of the house is <u>iaona</u>; the mistress is <u>andrea</u>; the church is <u>elicera</u>; the priest is <u>belaterra</u>, which means beautiful land; grain is <u>gari</u>; water is <u>uric</u>; king is <u>ereguia</u>; and Saint James is <u>Iacona domne Jacua</u>.

This is a most barbarous nation, different from all others in habits and character, its people being malicious and black in color. They have ugly faces and are depraved, perverse, treacherous, disloyal, vitiated, lecherous, drunkard, violent, ferocious and savage, insolent, false, blasphemous, uncouth, cruel, irritable, incapable of virtue but well-versed in all manner of vices and inequities.

In malice they are like the Getae and the Moslems, and in every aspect inimical to our French people. Given the chance, a Navarran or Basque would slay a Frenchman for a coin. In some of their lands, namely Vizcaya and Álava, when the Navarrans get saucy, men and women show each other their intimate parts. These Navarrans also use animals for incestuous fornication. It is said that the Navarran places a latch-lock on his mule or horse's behind such that he alone has access to it. He also kisses lasciviously the vulva of women and mules.

For this reason, the Navarrans are berated by anyone who is sensible. Despite all this, they are courageous in battle, clumsy in the assault of fortresses, reliable in the payment of the tithe, and constant in their offerings at the altar. Each day, when they go to church, the Navarrans make an offering of bread, wine, wheat or something else to God.

The Navarrans and Basques always wear a horn around their neck wherever they go, in the manner of hunters, and it is their custom to carry two or three javelins, which they call <u>auconas</u>. Upon entering their houses, they whistle like a kite, and when hiding out in secret places, they contact their companions by singing like an owl or howling like a wolf. In this manner they remain undetected.

They say that these people are the descendants of a race of Scots because they are similar to them in their habits and appearance. It is said that Julius Cæsar sent three nations to Spain, and that these were the Nubians, the Scots and the tailed ones from Cornwall. Being that the Spaniards refused to pay him tribute, he ordered them to run-through all the males with a sword, sparing only the women. The invaders entered the land from the sea, and after destroying their ships, they proceeded to devastate everything by sword and fire, from the city of Barcelona to Zaragoza, and from the city of Bayonne to the mountains of Oca. Yet they were unable to proceed beyond these areas because the Castilians, arrayed for combat, defeated them and expelled them from their territories. Fleeing as well they could, they reached the maritime mountains that lie between Nájera, Pamplona and Bayonne, towards the sea, in the land of Vizcaya and Álava. Once settled there, they built many fortresses and, having slain all the males, took their wives by force. With these women they produced children who were called Navarrans by succeeding generations.

For this reason the Navarrans can be described as not a true nation, that is to say, they do not proceed from a true lineage or authentic stock. Besides, the Navarrans first took their name from a certain city called Naddaver, which lies in the lands from which they originally came. The Blessed Matthew, apostle and evangelist, preached in this city in early times and converted it to the Lord.

After this land, one crosses the Oca wilderness in the direction of Burgos. After that is found the land of the Spaniards: Castilla and its territories. This land is abundant with treasures such as gold and silver; it has plenty of textiles and robust horses, bread, wine, meat, fish, milk and honey. But it has very little wood and is full of wicked and vile people.

Afterwards, having crossed the land of León and cleared the passes of Mount Irago and Mount Cebrero, one arrives in the land of the Galicians. This land has plenty of wood and great rivers, meadows and orchards, excellent fruits and transparent streams. But it is poor in cities, towns and plough-fields. Bread, wheat and wine are hard to find, but rye bread and beer are plentiful, as are livestock and beasts of burden, milk and honey. Ocean fish, although very large, are poor in number, but the land is full of gold, silver, textiles, fur and many other goods as well as valuable Moslem merchandise.

Galicians are the best among the boorish peoples of Spain, for they are the ones whose habits most closely resemble those of our French nation, although they are irascible and quarrelsome.

[NOTES. This chapter illustrates a number of problems faced by the traveler of the period. For one, it gives a good account of the difficulties attending the crossing of rivers and of the knavery of those ferrymen who preyed on the pilgrims who had no choice but to get across. Also, the toll-gatherers seem to have been an obstacle to the traveler as great as surmounting a high pass, as some, thinking of themselves as an extension of "the long arm of the law", felt inclined to beat travelers who did not want to pay the requested sums. It is also evident that the writer has a deep-seeded anti-Basque, anti-Navarran bias, as he again singles out these people for virulent attacks in which, in effect, he not only derides their habits and language, but questions the legitimacy of their lineage by making them out to be the descendants of the three British peoples sent to Spain by Cæsar (he mistakes the Numians of Devonshire for Nubians of Ethiopia). In fact, if there is an autochthonous people in Spain, it is the Basques, who at one point occupied the whole country and have been there, before any other known group, since time immemorial.]

Chapter VIII
Saintly Remains on the Road and the Passion of Saint Eutropius.

SAINT Place of Association		Feast Day
Trophimus	Arles	29 December
Cæsarius	Arles	1 November
Honoratus	Arles	16 January
Genesius	Arles	25 August
Giles	Arles	1 September
William	Toulouse	28 May
Tiberius	Banks of the River Hérault	10 Nov.
Modestus	Banks of the River Hérault	10 Nov.
Florence	Banks of the River Hérault	10 Nov.
Saturninus	Toulouse	29 November
Foy	Le Puy	6 October
Mary Magdalene	Vézelay	22 July
Leonard	Noblat	6 November
Fronto	Périgueux	25 October
Euverte	Orléans	-
Martin	Tours	11 November
Hilary	Poitiers	13 January
John the Baptist (head)	Angély	24 February
Eutropius	Saintes	-
Roland	Blaye	-

Seurin	Bordeaux	23 October
Paladins of Charlemagne:		
Olivier	Belin	-
Gondebaud, King of Frisia	Belin	-
Ogier, King of Dacia	Belin	-
Arastain, King of Bretagne	Belin	-
Garin, Duke of Lorraine	Belin	-
Domingo	Santo Domingo	-
Facundo	Sahagún	27 November
Primitivo	Sahagún	27 November
Isidoro	León	-
James	Santiago de Compostela	-

Chapter IX
Characteristics of the City and the Church of Santiago.

One finds the city of Santiago de Compostela between the rivers Sar and Sarela. The Sar flows in the east, between Monte del Gozo and the city, whereas the Sarela flows to the west. There are seven gates through which to enter the city: the first is Puerta Francesca; the second is Puerta de la Peña; the third is Puerta de Subfratribus; the fourth is Puerta del Santo Peregrino; the fifth is Puerta Fajera, which leads towards Padrón; the sixth is Puerta de Susannis; the seventh is Puerta de Mazarelos, through which the Precious Bacchus enters the city.

Churches of the City.

In this city the churches are ten in number, of which the most notable is that of the most glorious Apostle James, son of Zebedee. Situated in the center of the city, the Church shines splendidly. The second church is that of the Blessed Apostle San Pedro [San Pedro d'Afora], a monastery church near the French Road. The third, San Miguel, is called the Church of the Cistern [San Miguel dos Agros]. The fourth is that of San Martín the Bishop, which is a monastic church as well and is called Pinario. The fifth, Santa Trinidad, is used as a place of burial for pilgrims. The sixth, Santa Susana the Virgin, is next to the stone road. The seventh is San Félix [San Fiz] Martyr. The eighth is San Benito [San Benito del Campo]. The ninth, San Pelayo [San Payo], is behind the basilica of Saint James and has a door that leads into the basilica situated between the altar to Saint Nicholas and the altar of Santa Cruz.

Measurements of the Church

Saint James's Basilica is as long as the height of fifty three men, measuring from the western portal to the altar of San Salvador. It is as wide as the height of thirty nine men, measuring from the French [north] Portal to the south portal. Inside, its elevation is equal to the height of fourteen men, but from the outside no-one can tell its length and height.

The church has nine aisles on the lower level and six on the upper level; it also has a very important head in which one finds the San Salvador altar, a crown of laurel, a body, two members and eight small heads with an altar in each.

There are nine naves, six of moderate size and three large ones. The principal nave runs from the west portal to the four middle piers which command the church. This nave has an aisle on its right side and another on its left. There are two other large naves in the two transepts, of which the first runs from the French [north] Portal to the four piers of the crossing, and the second from the piers to the south portal. Each of these naves has two lateral aisles.

The three main naves reach the church's heaven [vault], and the six aisles reach the middle of the supporting arches. The large naves are as wide as the height of eleven and a half men, the height of each man being eight palms.

The largest of the naves has twenty nine piers, fourteen on each side and one on the inside between the two portals facing the north and separating the vaulted passageways. In the naves of the cross [transepts] of this church, from the French to the south portal, there are twenty six piers, twelve on the right and the same number on the left, with two more in front of the doors on the inside, separating the arches of the entrance and the portals.

The crown of the church has eight single columns surrounding the altar of the Blessed James. The six small naves that are above, in the palace of the church [galleries] are the same length and width as the corresponding aisles under them. They are supported on one side by walls, and on the other by piers which ascend to the top from the large naves below, as well as by the double pillars that stone cutters call mid-arch reinforcements.

There are as many piers in the lower part of the church as in the naves on top, and there are as many waist-band reinforcements in the section below as in the triforia above. In the aisles of the triforia there are also, between the single pillars, two identical shafts which are called reinforced columns.

One cannot find one crack or flaw, as it is built admirably, being large, spacious, luminous, with graceful dimensions, well proportioned in width, length and height, of incredibly marvelous workmanship and, like a royal palace, built on two levels.

When you walk through the aisles of the triforium above, if you came up sadly, when you see the outstanding beauty of this church you will no doubt leave happy and delighted.

The Windows.

There are sixty three windows in this basilica, and above every altar surrounding the ambulatory there are three. In the church's heaven [upper level], around the altar of the Blessed James, there are five windows that give this altar good light. Above, in the triforium, there are forty three windows.

The Portals.

The church has three main portals and seven small ones. The main one opens to the west, another to the south, and the other to the north. Each of the main portals has two entrances, and each entrance has two doors. The first of the seven small portals is the Portal de Santa María; the second is the Vía Sacra; the third is San Pelayo; the fourth is Cañonica; the fifth is Pedrera; the sixth is similarly called Pedrera; and the seventh is that of the Grammar School, which also gives access to the palace of the archbishop.

The Fountain of Saint James.

When we Frenchmen enter the basilica of the Apostle, we do so from its northern side; in front of this entrance and next to the Road is the hospice of the poor pilgrims of Saint James, and further on, past the Road, there is a parvis that has nine descending steps. There is a wonderful fountain at the bottom of the parvis like there is no other in the world. The fountain sits on a base of three stone steps that support the most beautiful stone basin which is round and hollow like a dish, so large that fifteen men could easily bathe in it. There is in its middle a column of bronze of good height, wide in its base and made of seven square panels. There are four lions very close to its top which shed water through their mouths, quenching thus the thirst of pilgrims and of the general population. The water coming from the lions pours directly into a catch-basin below, where, through a hole, it escapes into the ground. One cannot see where the water comes into the fountain, as one cannot see where it goes. This water is sweet, healthy, clear, excellent, warm in the winter and cool in the summer. All around the column just mentioned, below the lions' feet, there is the following inscription engraved:

I, Bernard, being the treasurer of the cathedral, erected this monument for the salvation of my soul and that of my parents, on the third ides of April of the year 1160 of the era. [11 April, 1122]

The Parvis of the City.

As we've stated, behind the fountain one finds the parvis, all paved with stones. Scallop shells, the symbol of Santiago, are sold there to the pilgrims, as well as wineskins, shoes, deer-skin travelers' bags, side-bags, leather straps, belts, every type of medicinal herb, all sorts of drugs and much more. On the French Road you find money changers, innkeepers and all sorts of merchants. In length and in width, the dimensions of the parvis are a single stone throw.

The North Portal [Azabachería].

The north portal of the Santiago basilica, also called the French Portal, is beyond the parvis. It has two entrances with beautiful carved ornaments on both of them. There are six columns on the outside of each entrance, some made of marble, some of stone, three on the right and three on the left, or six to one entrance and six to the other, making for a total of twelve. There is a column between the two portals, on the outside walls, in which the Lord, seated in majesty, gives a blessing with His right hand while holding a book with His left. Around His throne, the four Evangelists gather as if holding it up. On the right is a representation of Paradise inside of which the Lord appears yet again to reproach Adam and Eve for their sin; on the left another image of the Lord appears expelling them from Paradise.

In the same place there appear sculpted images of saints, beasts, men, angels, women, flowers and other beings the details of which we cannot give here because they are very numerous. It should be mentioned that in the entrance to the basilica, above the left door, on its tympanum, the Annunciation to the Blessed Virgin Mary is represented with the angel Gabriel speaking to her. Again on the left, on the side entrance above the doors, the months of the year are sculpted along with many other beautiful works. Two large and ferocious lions are placed on the outside walls, one on the right and the other on the left, looking as if they were guarding the doors. Four apostles are represented above the jambs, each of them holding a book on the left hand while raising the right to give blessing to those entering the basilica. In the left entrance Peter is standing on the right and Paul on the left; in the right entrance the Apostle John stands to the right while the Blessed James stands to the left. Above each apostle's head there appear ox-heads in high relief, carved in the uprights.

The South Portal [Platerías].

As we've stated before, there are two entrances and four door-leaves on the south portal of the Apostle's basilica. Above the doors, on the first register of the entrance on the right, the Lord's Betrayal is represented in an excellent manner. The Lord appears here tied to a column by the hand of the Jews; there He is whipped with leather straps; further on Pilate appears on his throne as if he were judging Him. Above, on another register, there appears the Blessed Mary, Mother of the Lord, with her Son in Bethlehem, and the Three Kings, come to visit and offer Him presents; further on the star and the angel warn Them not to return home through Herod's lands.

On the jambs of that same entrance there are two apostles that seem to be guarding the door-leaves, one on the right and one on the left. In the same fashion, in the other entrance, to the left, on the door jambs there are two more apostles, and on the first register of that entrance, above the doors, the Temptation of the Lord is sculpted. In front of the Lord stand some repellent angels who look like monsters; they set Him up on the pinnacle of the Temple; still others offer Him stones and entreat Him to transform them into bread; still others show him the worldly kingdoms, offering them to Him if He, on His knees, adores them -may that never come to pass! Yet there are other angels, white, as they are good, behind and above Him, ministering to Him with incense burners.

On that same portal there are four lions, one on each side of both entrances. There are two more ferocious lions above the pier that rises between the two entrances, the rump of each pressing up against the other.

There are eleven columns on the sides of this portal, five on the right entrance and five on the left, with the eleventh placed between the two entrances dividing the portal arches. Some of these columns are of marble, others of stone, and all sculpted marvelously with figures of flowers, men, birds and beasts. These columns are made of white marble. We must not forget to mention that there is a woman next to the Temptation of the Lord who holds in her hands the filthy head of her lover, beheaded by her own husband, who forces her to kiss it two times a day. Ah, what a fitting and admirable punishment was given to this adulterous woman, one that should be recounted to everyone!

On the top register above the four door-leaves, in the direction of the triforium, there is a shining stone ornamentation which is splendid. The Lord stands there, Saint Peter on His left holding the keys, and the Blessed James on His right between two cypresses in the company of Saint John, his brother. Finally, on the right and left sides, the rest of the apostles appear. So, above, below, to the right and to the left, the whole wall is abundant with adornments: flowers, men, saints, beasts, birds, fishes and many other things whose details cannot be described here. We must point out that there are four angels above the archivolts of the passageways, each with a trumpet announcing the Day of Judgement.

The West Portal [Obradoiro].

The west portal has two entrances, and it excels the other two in its magnificence, size and workmanship, for it is larger, more beautiful and made more splendidly than the others. On the outside it has a very large stairway with many different marble columns that are decorated with men, women, animals, birds, saints, angels and flowers, all ornamented in different styles, a decoration which is so abundant as to make it impossible to describe in detail. On the top it shows the Transfiguration of the Lord on Tabor Mountain, sculpted splendidly.

The Lord is there in an impressive cloud with His face shining like the sun, His garments glittering like snow while His Father speaks to Him from above; Moses and Elias, who are together with Him, appear speaking to Him about His destiny, to be fulfilled in Jerusalem. Saint James is also there, along with Peter and John: to them, before anyone else, the Lord revealed His Transfiguration.

The Towers of the Basilica.

Of the nine towers of this church, two will be above the portal of the fountain, two above the south portal, two above the west portal, one above each of the two corkscrew staircases, and another, the largest, above the crossing, in the middle of the basilica. Because of them and of the many other truly precious works, the basilica of the Blessed James shines in magnificent glory. It is all constructed out of bright, brown, living stone, hard as marble. The interior is decorated with several paintings, and the exterior is covered perfectly with tiles and lead. Of all of the things we have herein described, some parts are completely finished, while yet others await completion.

The Altars of the Basilica.

The altars of the basilica follow this order: first, next to the French [north] Portal, which is on the left, there is the altar of San Nicolás; after it is the altar of Santa Cruz; then, in the ambulatory, the altar of Santa Fe, Virgin; then, the altar of San Juan, Apostle and Evangelist, brother of Saint James; then, the altar of San Salvador, located in the large chapel in the apse; There follows the altar of San Pedro Apóstol; then San Andrés; then San Martín, Bishop; and finally the altar of San Juan Bautista. Between the altar of Santiago and the altar of San Salvador one finds the altar of Santa María Magdalena, where masses are sung for pilgrims in the morning. Above, in the triforium, there are three more altars, of which the most important is that of San

Miguel Arcángel; to the right of this one is the altar of San Benito; and the other, to the left, is the altar of San Pablo Apóstol and San Nicolás, Bishop. The archbishop's chapel is located here.

The Body and the Altar of Saint James.

Up to now we've given the distinctive features of the church. Now we'll deal with the venerable altar of the Apostle. The venerated body of the Blessed James rests under the high altar, which has been erected with great reverence in his honor. It rests within a casket of marble in a most remarkable vaulted tomb of outstanding workmanship and harmonious dimensions.

It is impossible to move the body, as is well known and was witnessed by San Teodomiro, bishop of the city, who discovered it long ago and found he could not move it from its place. Shame on those who, from beyond the mountains, claim to have a part of him or even the entire relic. Actually, the whole body of the Apostle rests here, favored by excellent lighting of paradisiacal carbuncles, constantly honored with delicate, soft fragrances, decorated with impressive heavenly candles and worshiped by diligent, attendant angels.

Above the tomb can be found a small altar which, it is told, was built by his disciples and which, for the love and respect of the Apostle and his disciples, no-one has destroyed. Also, above this one there is a marvelous, large altar that is five palms high, twelve long and seven wide. This measurement I obtained with my own hand. So the small altar is contained by the large one in such a way that it covers it on three sides: the right, the left and the back, being open in the front so that, at the removal of the silver antependium, the old altar may be seen without hindrance.

Should someone be pleased to donate, in devotion to the Blessed James, an adornment for the altar or linen cloth for covering the altar, it must be nine palms wide and twenty one palms long. But, if for the love of God and the Apostle you should wish to send a linen cloth to cover the antependium, you must be sure that it measures seven palms wide and thirteen palms long.

The Silver Antependium.

The altar front [antependium] that covers the face of the altar is a magnificent work of gold and silver. In the middle is a sculpture of the Lord's throne around which are twenty four elders in the order in which the Blessed John, James's brother, saw them in his Apocalypse: twelve on the right and twelve on the left, forming a circle and holding in their hands zithers and gold phials full with perfume. The Lord in majesty is seated in the middle: in His left hand the Book of Life; with His right He is giving His blessing. Around the throne, as if they were holding it up, are the Four Evangelists. The Twelve Apostles are on the right and left: three in the first row on the right and three on top; the same occurs on the left, three on the row below and three on the row on top. Finally, splendid flowers are shown everywhere, and magnificent columns serve to separate the Apostles. Of marvelous and superior workmanship, this antependium has these verses inscribed on its top:

Diego II [Diego Gelmírez], Bishop of Santiago, made this antependium in the fifth year of his tenure [1105]. He paid from the treasury of Saint James eighty silver marks less five.

Below it, there appears this inscription:

Alfonso [Alfonso VI] was king, and Raymond, his son-in-law, duke, when said bishop completed this work.

The Ciborium of the Apostle's Altar.

The ciborium covering this revered altar is magnificently decorated, inside and out, with paintings, drawings and sundry other ornamentation. It is square, rests on four columns and, in height and width, it is most harmoniously executed.

The first interior register has the eight principal virtues, as celebrated by Paul, in the form of women: two in each of the corners. There are angels, standing straight, over the heads of each woman; they hold up with raised hands the throne that is at the summit of the ciborium. In the middle of this throne is the Lamb of God, holding a cross with its foot. Here, there are as many angels as virtues.

On the first outer register there are four angels announcing, with trumpets, the Resurrection on Judgement Day: two are on the front and two on the back. There are also four prophets on this register: Moses and Abraham on the left and Isaac and Jacob on the right, each holding in his hand a scroll containing his prophecies.

The Twelve Apostles are seated in a circle on the top register. On the front, the Blessed James is right in the middle, holding a book in his left hand and giving a blessing with his right. There is an apostle on his right and another on his left, all in the same register. There are also three other apostles on the ciborium's right side, while on the left there are also three as well as on the back. Appearing to guard the altar, four angels sit on the upper cover. In the four corners of this ciborium, at the base of the upper cover, there appear the Four Evangelists, each in his own likeness.

While the interior of the ciborium is painted, the exterior is both sculpted and painted. On the top of the exterior an end-structure has been set up that has a triple arcade: within it the Divine Trinity has been represented, the person of the Father under the first arch facing west; the person of the Son is under the second one, facing southeast; and facing north, under the third arch, the person of the Holy Spirit. On top of this structure there is a shining silver ball on which stands a precious silver cross.

The Three Lamps.

Three large silver lamps hang in front of the Blessed James's altar, there to honor Christ and the Apostle. The middle one is very large and is constructed excellently and in the shape of a large mortar. This lamp contains seven alveoli that represent the Seven Gifts of the Holy Spirit, each one with a wick set in it. These alveoli are fed with only balsamic oil, myrtle, benjamin or olive. The largest one is in the middle of the others; on each of the two surrounding it there are two images of the apostles, sculpted on the outside.

May the soul of Alfonso, King of Aragón [Alfonso I the Warlike], who is said to have donated them to Santiago, rest in everlasting peace.

Dignity of the Church of Saint James and its Canons.

By rule, no-one celebrates mass at the altar of the Blessed James unless he is bishop, archbishop, pope, or cardinal of this church. According to a long-established practice, in the church there are seven cardinals that celebrate the Holy Mass on this altar. Their endowments and privileges were authorized by many popes and were particularly confirmed by Pope Calixtus. This dignity, stemming from a long and venerated tradition, should, for the love of the Apostle, never be stripped from this basilica by anyone.

Stonecutters of the Church and Their Work from Start to Finish.

The master stonecutters that first worked on the construction of the basilica of the Blessed James were named Master Bernard the Elder, a master craftsman, and Robert, as well as about fifty other stonecutters who persevered in their work under the most faithful administration of Wicart, Prior Segredo, and Abbot Gudesindo, when Alfonso was king of Spain [Alfonso VI] and Diego I

[Diego Peláez], a great soldier and generous man, was bishop.

The construction of this church commenced in the year 1116 of the era [1078 A.D.]. Counting from the year it was started to the year in which Alfonso, valiant and famous king of Aragón [Alfonso I the Warlike, also known as Alfonso VII, king of Aragón and Navarra] died, there are fifty nine years; from its start to the year in which Henry, king of England, was murdered, there are sixty two years, and to the death of Louis the Fat, king of France, sixty three. Such that, from the year in which the first foundation stone was laid until the last stone was placed, forty four years elapsed. [1078-1122. *The author's computations with regards to the deaths of these kings is erroneous.]

From the first moment, this church has shined by the light of the Blessed James's miracles: herein the sick have been healed, the blind have seen, the dumb have spoken and the deaf have heard, the lame have walked and the possessed have been exorcized and, furthermore, faithful prayers have been answered, wishes granted to those who've knocked at its door, the afflicted have known consolation, and foreigners of all nations have come in great numbers to bring their gifts in praise of the Lord.

Dignity of the Church of Saint James.

It should not be forgotten that the Blessed Pope Calixtus [Calixtus II], fondly remembered, because of the love he had for the Apostle and to honor him, transferred the archiepiscopal dignity to Santiago from Mérida, where it was formerly held in the land of the Moslems. Upon doing this, he ordained and confirmed Diego [Diego Gelmírez], a great noble, as the first archbishop of the apostolic see of Compostela.

[NOTE. "The era" refers to the Spanish Era, a system of counting years which was used throughout Spain. The Spanish Era begins counting in 38 B.C., the year in which Spain was formally incorporated into the

Roman Empire. For this reason it is always 38 years ahead of the Christian Era, such that 1116 of the Spanish Era, the year given for the start of construction on the Santiago Cathedral, is 1078 A.D.

Concerning the chapter's introduction, of the seven gates that lead into the city, the Puerta Francesca is present-day Puerta del Camino, in the northeast of the city, the place where pilgrims on the French Road entered Santiago. There are no traces of the original gate in place today. Nowadays the place is the intersection of Casas Reales, Ruedas and Aller Ulloa streets. Puerta de la Peña was in the north side of Santiago; of it nothing remains except a street named for it, between present-day Calle de la Fuente de San Miguel and Calle de los Laureles. The Puerta de Subfratribus, today's Puerta de San Martín, is in the east of the city at the end of San Francisco street, close to the San Martín Pinario monastery. The Puerta del Santo Peregrino is now the Puerta de la Trinidad, in western Santiago, where pilgrims that continued on to Finisterre left the city. The Puerta Fajera, in the southwest, has the same name today; it leads out to the Alameda de la Herradura gardens. The Puerta de Susannis was located at the modern intersection of Seura, Huérfanas, and Fuente de San Antonio streets. Nothing remains of this gate. The seventh gate, the Puerta de Mazarelos, also known as Puerta del Mercado, is still in place as the modern "Arco de Mazarelos", at Mazarelos street close to the Plaza de la Universidad.

Regarding the churches of the city, San Pedro d'Afora, as its name suggests, was outside the city walls, close to the Puerta Francesca; San Miguel dos Agros is one of the most ancient churches in the city, probably set next to an ancient cistern; San Martín Pinario is a large complex of structures (second in size only to the Cathedral) the first of which were erected in the IX Century by the Benedictines; the Capilla de la Trinidad, which used to be next to the Puerta del Santo Peregrino, was constructed in 1128 and demolished in 1930; the church of Santa Susana was the old church of Santo Sepulcro, consecrated by Diego Gelmírez in 1105, changing its name to Santa Susana soon after the relics of Saint Susana (stolen from Braga in 1102) were enshrined there. The original façade can still be seen in spite of the many renovations of the

XVII and XVIII Centuries; San Félix, or San Fiz, is the oldest church in the city, being in place long before the "discovery" of the tomb of Saint James in the early IX Century, probably dating to the VI. Destroyed by Almanzor in 997, it was rebuilt by Diego Gelmírez early in the XII Century and was renovated in the XVIII, but the Romanesque portal is still in place; San Benito del Campo is also an ancient structure, but it has undergone extensive renovations throughout the centuries, most important of which is that of the ubiquitous Diego Gelmírez in the early XII Century and that of the XIX Century; San Pelayo (San Payo) was established in the year 813 by king Alfonso II under the name of Saint Peter (San Pedro de Ante,altares). It is very close to the Cathedral and was extensively reconstructed by Diego Gelmírez in the early XII Century; although its monastic complex underwent extensive renovations in the XVIII Century, it still retains some important Romanesque sculptures; the church of Santa María Virgen, like San Félix, pre-dates the Cathedral and existed as an independent structure on the site where the Cathedral stands today. It was incorporated as one of the chapels inside the Cathedral, that of Santa María de la Corticela.

Concerning the Cathedral, we must note that it has undergone extensive renovations since the writer gave us its description in the *Guide*. Also, the author uses the future tense in some of his descriptions of its structures, indicating that many were not completed at the time of writing; the subsequent incorporation of the church of Santa María into the Cathedral building is a clear example. Many of the sixty three windows are today blind. The many chapels in the Cathedral have, throughout the centuries, fluctuated in number, undergone transformations and changed names, such that any attempt at identifying all of those given in the *Guide* will be tentative at best. To a large extent, the same may be said of the seven small portals. Of the three main portals, the first one described is the North Portal, as this is the end of the all-important French Road that consolidates at Puente la Reina. It is also called Portal de la Azabachería, from the word "azabache", Spanish for obsidian. Right outside this gate, where today vendors have set up tents where they sell T-shirts, figurines and other little objects that tourists find endearing, there used to be vendors, probably using the same type of tents, that sold images of Santiago, seashells and other objects, all made of obsidian. The façade described in the *Guide* was demolished in the XVIII Century and replaced by the neoclassical one we see today, although some of the original reliefs, of Romanesque style, were incorporated into the top part of the South Portal. The South Portal is also called Portal de las Platerías because of the many silversmiths (plateros) who worked and peddled their wares right outside (as they do to this day). Of the original portal, work of Esteban, master sculptor and master builder of the Pamplona Cathedral, little is left. Many of the figures on it now, especially on the upper part, are not original but re-used from the other portals, mostly Azabachería. Of interest is the inscription MCXVI, probably dating the beginning of construction at 1116 of the Spanish Era, which corresponds to 1078 of the Christian Era. The West Portal is the most important of all, today facing the Plaza de Obradoiro. What is described in the *Guide* about this portal was completely demolished in the XII Century to make way for the famous Pórtico de la Gloria (completed in 1188), which stands today in eloquent praise of its maker, Master Mateo. So not much is left of the original sculpted figures, as most were lost after the demolishing of the original portal and the earlier popular uprising against the ecclesiastical authorities in 1117, which targeted the Cathedral for destruction as the most visible symbol of the Church's power. Some of the pieces survived and were transferred to the South Portal.

Concerning the nine altars the author describes in the Cathedral, they line up as follows: with the first being San Nicolás, they are the five chapels on the ambulatory and the four on either side of the transept's eastern wall. Their fate is varied: the San Nicolás altar, dedicated in 1102, no longer exists, it used to be in what today is the passageway to the chapel of Santa María de la Corticela (Saint Nicholas, patron saint of travelers, was, of course, very important in Santiago. He is the patron of the university of Santiago Compostela.); the altar of Santa Cruz, or Holy Cross (reputed to hold a piece of the Cross of the Crucifixion), was replaced by the Concepción chapel (also called Prima) in the sixteenth century; the altar of Santa Fe was also replaced by the chapel of San Bartolomé, but most of the original altar is still in place; the altar of San Juan Evangelista (brother of James) underwent major reconstruction in the XVI Century and was re-dedicated to Santa Susana; the altar of San Salvador is now the chapel of the King of France, "Rey de Francia," the chapel closest to France (easternmost) and originally the largest; Saint Peter's altar (San Pedro) was also dedicated in 1102, re-dedicated in the XVI Century as the chapel of Doña Mencía de Andrade, it is today the chapel of Nuestra Señora de la Azucena, having kept the original Romanesque construction; the San Andrés altar, last one on the apse, was demolished in order to make room for the large chapel dedicated to the Virgen del Pilar (also called Monroya), in the early XVIII Century; San Martín suffered the same fate, being demolished at about the same time as the two previous ones, giving way to the Puerta Real (Quintana), which was opened there.]

Chapter X
Distribution of the Offerings in Saint James's Altar

Seventy two canons, which correspond to the seventy two Disciples of Christ, serve this church according to the rule of the Blessed Doctor Isidore of Spain. Among them are divided the oblations of the altar of Saint James, each week a different canon. The first canon is in charge of the oblations for the first week; the second canon for the second week, the third for the third, and so on to the last one.

On Sundays, according to tradition, the oblations are divided into three, the first part being assigned to the hebdomadary, and the other two parts are consolidated and then divided into three; one is given to the canons for the communal meal, another is for the maintenance of the basilica, while the third goes to the archbishop. The oblations of the week between Palm Sunday and Easter Sunday are given, as is customary, to the poor pilgrims of Santiago that are lodged in the hospice. In effect, if divine justice were to be properly applied, the tenth part of the oblations of the altar of Saint James would be given to the poor who show up at the hospice.

All poor pilgrims, in fact, must be received with complete hospitality at the hospice the first night after the day of their arrival, this for the love of God and the Apostle. Sick pilgrims must be cared for there, until such a time as they die or they recover from their illness. This, indeed, is the practice at Saint-Léonard, where, regardless of the number of pilgrims that arrive there, they are all provided with sustenance. In addition, it is also customary to give to the leprous of the city the oblations obtained at the altar each Sunday, from early morning to the hour of terce. If any prelate of this basilica should, by fraudulent means alter the destination of these oblations as it has been described, may his sin ever stand between him and his Maker.

Chapter XI
The Appropriate Welcome for the Pilgrims of Saint James.

All pilgrims, be they rich or poor, whether they return from or proceed to Santiago, must be received charitably and respectfully by everyone. All who welcome such pilgrims, giving them lodging, will have as their guest not only the Blessed James, but the Lord Himself, who thus spoke in the Gospels: "Whomever welcomes you, welcomes Me." Many have brought upon themselves the Wrath of God by refusing to receive the pilgrims of Saint James or the indigent.

Such as what happened in Nantua, a city between Genève and Lyon, where a weaver refused to give bread to a pilgrim who requested it and immediately some of his linen fell to the ground and ripped down the middle. Or in Villeneuve, where a woman stored bread under hot ashes. When, in need, a pilgrim of Saint James asked for bread and she answered that she had none, the pilgrim stated: "May the bread you have turn into stone!" When the pilgrim was at a considerable distance from the house, this greedy woman went to the ashes intending to retrieve her bread, but found only a round stone there instead. Repentant, she set out to look for the pilgrim, but did not find him.

Two French knights were returning one day from Santiago and, destitute, asked for lodging in the city of Poitiers, for the love of God and Saint James, from the house of Jean Gautier to the church of Saint-Porchaire. But no lodging was offered to them. At last they were received by a poor man in the last house of the street that is next to the basilica of Saint-Porchaire. That same night, and by divine vengeance, every house on that street burned to the ground, from the first where they requested lodging to the last, sparing only the house of the man who welcomed them, by divine grace. In all, about one thousand houses were destroyed by fire.

For this reason, all should know that pilgrims of Saint James, be they poor or rich, have the right to hospitality and to diligent respect.

This is the end of the fourth [fifth] book of Saint James. Glory to him who wrote it and glory to him who reads it.

This book has been properly received by the Church of Rome. It was written in several places: Rome, Jerusalem, France, Italy, Germany, Frisia and mainly in Cluny.

[NOTES. Although the text states "fourth book" (codex quartus), the manuscript shows obvious signs of tampering, of changing the in in quintus to ar in quartus (fifth to fourth). But this is the fifth book of the original Codex Calixtinus; only in the XVII Century was the Pseudo-Turpin book (book IV) deleted from the manuscript, at which late stage the Guide (book V) became book IV.]

APPENDIX II

GLOSSARY OF ARCHITECTURAL TERMS.

☙　Apse. A semi-circular (or polygonal) vaulted space that terminates a church. In Christian churches, which run from west to east, the apse is located at the extreme eastern end. Romanesque churches usually have semicircular apses, while later churches generally have polygonal apses. Apses may be flanked by chapels at the base.

☙　Arcade. A structure that is composed of a series of arches that are supported by columns.

☙　Architrave. The lower part of the entablature. A horizontal beam placed directly on the capital that spans the columns or piers like a lintel. Generally, the architrave is not ornamented, so as to form a contrast to the richly-decorated frieze.

☙　Archivolt. Set of moldings that decorate an arch on its exterior vertical facing, covering the full extension of the arch's curve and ending on the impost. Also used to describe the inner curve of an arch or the structural parts of the inner curve.

      ❧   Baroque. The baroque style has its origin in fifteenth century Italy, where masters and artists began taking liberties with the traditional notions of Classical Antiquity, re-ordering elements and themes in order to achieve a more personal expression. Although maintaining the canons of Classical Antiquity as their artistic ideal, baroque architects were deeply concerned about expressing "space," which is why they abandon the straight, geometric lines of the Renaissance and give preference to the curve, a more dynamic line. The baroque structure does not exist independently, but is an integral part of the place where it is built. As such, the façade of the building is very important, while in the interior the lines and angles of the structure virtually disappear under the overwhelming ornamentation of flowers and animals on the abundant cornices and Solomonic columns (twisted and contorted in form). Baroque sculpture is conceived as a function of the building in which it will be placed, as a part of the dynamic whole, an element tat will give mobility and life to the static architectural lines.

      ❧   Bay. An opening in a wall that may be rectangular or curvilinear. A bay may serve as a door, in which case its lower part is called the groundsill, and it may serve as a window, in which case the lower part is the sill. The upper part of a bay is called the lintel when it is horizontal, and it is called an arch when it is curvilinear. The divisions that are formed by the arcades of nave, cloister or gallery are at times also called bays, especially in Gothic architecture, as is the space between columns in Classical architecture.

      ❧   Boss. The block, or keystone at the place where the ribs of a ribbed vault intersect. Usually richly sculptured, the boss conceals the collision of the different ribs and their moldings, and give extra dead-weight for countering the outward thrusts of the vaults.

     ɸ   Capital. An ornament that is the upper part and crowning feature of a column, set on top of the shaft. Capitals act as the transition between the column and the structure it is there to support, be it a lintel, an arcade or an architrave. As a norm, capitals have distinctive sculptural decoration.

     ɸ   Churrigueresque. Named for José de Churriguera (1665-1725), "Churrigueresco" is a variant of the baroque style of architecture that stresses that style's penchant for exuberant ornamentation. The distinguishing features of the Churrigueresque are the extraordinary decoration of the reredos, and the concept of the church façade itself as a reredos, such that the exuberant decoration begins on the outside of the structure. Churrigueresque altars take the form of temples surrounded by Solomonic columns, twisting and covered with flowers, vine shoots and leaves. On the cornice are abundant figures that seem to want to escape from their surroundings. These elements are best seen in Churriguera's Main Altar in the church of San Estéban in Salamanca and the Main Altar at Capilla del Sagrario in Segovia.

         Most representative of this style is Pedro de Ribera (? - 1742), who completed the façade at Madrid's Hospicio de San Fernando and the church of Monserrat, with its characteristic tower.

         Other Churrigueresque structures in Spain are the sacristy at the Cartuja de Granada, the church of San Luis in Seville and, of course, the Obradoiro façade at the Santiago de Compostela cathedral.

     ɸ   Ciborium. A canopy of wood or stone that rests on four columns, especially one covering an altar and shaped like an overturned cup.

     ɸ   Cloister. A construction that is part of a monastery or adjoins a church. It is a covered gallery, surrounded by a pierced arcade, that completely surrounds a garden or courtyard. Cloisters, which are built in the shape of a quadrangle, were areas set apart for meditation, study, reflection and relaxation, and in some cases they have recesses or carols where the monk could sit. A lavatory is frequently found at cloisters also, as cloisters usually lead to the refectory, which is the dining room of a monastery or convent.

❧ Clerestory. Part of an interior wall which rises above the adjacent roof. It has windows which admit light.

❧ Corbel. A bracket of stone (or other material) that projects from the side of a wall and serves to support a cornice, the spring of an arch, a balustrade or another structure.

❧ Cornice. The decorative molded upper part of the entablature that projects beyond the frieze.

❧ Crossing. In a cruciform church, the place where the transept crosses the nave.

❧ Entablature. Supported by columns, the entablature is a superstructure that is divided horizontally, top to bottom, into cornice, frieze and architrave. Its height varies from four to five times the diameter of the shaft of the column that supports it, depending on its order.

❧ Frieze. A horizontal part of the entablature situated between the architrave and the cornice (today the term is also applied to the broad border which sometimes runs around a room between the top of the wallpaper and the cornice, and also to a painting or sculptured bas-relief whose length is considerably greater than its height). In religious architecture, friezes became important fields for figured sculpture, giving the artist a wide area in which to develop a narrative from which people who could not read could derive instruction. Sculptured-narrative friezes invite the viewer to follow the story line by walking along the length of a particular area of the building.

❧ Gable. The vertical triangular wall between the sloping ends of a gable roof.

❧ Gothic. A style of architecture produced in Spain from the early thirteenth century to the early sixteenth. Gothic architecture evolved from the Romanesque and for decades both styles overlapped. The term "Gothic" was overtly pejorative in its inception, used to describe a style that was crude and rustic if compared with the superior decorum of Classical architecture. It was naturally associated with northern Europeans (Goths), the barbarians who succeeded in destroying (in the fifth century) the superior civilization of Mediterranean peoples.

But the term "Gothic" began to lose its negative connotations when it was demonstrated that one of its most characteristic features, the pointed (ogival) arch, was in fact more efficient than the Romanesque semicircular arch as a load-bearing structure. Other Gothic characteristics such as the ribbed vaults and flying buttresses demonstrated to the critics that Gothic architects were superb structural engineers.

The rib vaulting, for example, has visible diagonal cross-arches of stone or brick. These "ribs" act as a permanent scaffolding that provide a stiff, cut-stone center for the vault. As such, a rib vault is a stone canopy that rests almost entirely upon the diagonal ribs, which transfer the weight and dynamics directly down to the springing point of the vault. In prior vaulting the entire vault took part in that transmission, the whole shell acting in unison.

A characteristic element in Gothic structures is the flying buttress, a type of buttress that stands apart from the main structure and is connected to it by an arch. Flying buttresses have two parts: 1- a "flyer arch" that transmits the thrusts from the vault across the aisle to the 2- "upright support" (buttress), that extends outward from the building's outer walls.

      𝓮𝓵 Impost. The lowest stone in an arch, from which it springs.

      𝓮𝓵 Isabelline. Also called the Hispano-Flemish style, it is a style of architecture and decoration that is associated with the reign of Isabel I of Castile (1474-1504), the Catholic Queen. During this period, architectural forms and designs were introduced into Spain from the Low Countries that mingled with the native Mudéjar style. The two main creative centers of the Isabelline were Toledo, where don Álvaro de Luna, Master of the Order of Santiago, was its great patron, and Burgos, where archbishop Alonso de Cartagena was its great supporter. Valladolid and Palencia would later become important centers of Isabelline constructions, particularly the latter with its great patron Fray Alonso de Burgos, the Dominican bishop of Palencia.

      The Isabelline style made its appearance in Toledo around 1450, when John II was king of Castile. At this point, the Mudéjar style had reached its pinnacle, and the influence of the Low Countries was making itself felt very strongly. It was c. 1440 when Hanequin de Bruselas arrived at Toledo, bringing the richness of Netherlandish decoration to his architectural work in the city. But it was his disciple Juan Guas who blended what he learned from Hanequin with Mudéjar forms to invent the new style, crystallized in his most famous works, the monastery of San Juan de los Reyes in Toledo (1476), the Palacio del Infantado in Guadalajara (1480) and the Colegio de San Gregorio in Valladolid, begun by Guas in 1487.

      𝓮𝓵 Lintel. A horizontal beam that is used as a finishing piece over a door or window.

𐤀 Mozarabic. A term used to describe the art of Christians living in areas of Spain under Moslem domination. It is also used for Christians who emigrated from Moslem areas beginning in the tenth century, hoping to resettle areas in the north that had been recently conquered by the Christians. Mozarabic art and architecture represent a reassertion of traditional Visigothic culture, a revival of the old forms by people who wished to see themselves as heirs to the ancient Visigothic kingdom that was destroyed in 711 A.D. by the Moslems.

In many of the repopulated areas, Mozarabic religious communities actively sought out the buildings that had been founded by the fathers of the Hispanic Church and settled there, venerating the sanctuaries and their ruins (San Facundo in Sahagún is a good example). So it is that Mozarabic churches show many Visigothic characteristics: a nave divided by iconostasis (a screen that separates the choir or presbytery from the congregational areas), small sacristies next to the presbytery, and an added apse in the west, a feature that was introduced from north Africa into the Spanish Visigothic Kingdom in the sixth century and may have had funerary significance. Other Visigothic forms are cubic projections that enclose rectangular, semicircular or horseshoe apses; horseshoe arches; domes; barrel vaults with a horseshoe profile, and projecting cornices with brackets decorated with rosettes and trilobes.

Mozarabic buildings were painted on both the exterior and the interior with bright colors that accented the architectural lines and details. Some prominent Mozarabic structures are the monastery of San Miguel de la Escalada, near León (913 A.D.), San Cebrián de Mazote, Santa María de Bamba and Santa María de Lebeña, this last one in Cantabria, San Miguel de Celanova in Orense and Santiago de Peñalba, built by St. Gennadius, restorer of the Visigothic Monastic Rule.

𐤀 Mudéjar. From the Arabic "mudajjan" (permitted to remain), the word designates those Moslems who were trapped behind

Christian lines during the latter's gradual reconquest of Spain. The term came into general use only after the more heavily populated areas under Moslem control passed into Christian hands, beginning c. 1085, when Alfonso VI of León-Castile conquered the city of Toledo. In art and architecture it serves to designate forms produced by these people (as well as by some Christians) for the new Christian masters of the land. Spanning quite a long period (c. 1085-sixteenth century), Mudéjar architecture is outwardly Islamic in appearance, with its eclectic use of brick, stucco and timber. Although Mudéjar buildings are very similar to Islamic buildings in terms of decoration and appearance, their general structure is either Romanesque (in its early phase) or Gothic (in later phases).

As the Christian kingdoms advanced and reconquered territories from the Moslems, their monarchs, churchmen and others came to admire the architecture of the conquered people, so rather than demolish the mosques or other structures, they adopted them to Christian use; even the new constructions were done in the Islamic style. These new churches, palaces and synagogues were decorated in the Islamic style, with stucco rich in arabesques and geometrical patterns, with Latin (or Hebrew) inscriptions just like the Arabic phrases the Moslems had used in their buildings.

Mudéjar churches first sprang up in Toledo after 1085. Although they differ from place to place and there was a definite development in the style, we can say that on most of them you will find brick and stone masonry between brick courses, horseshoe and trefoil arches and elaborate façades.

In Castile-León, the Mudéjar style was introduced by Alfonso VIII (1158-1214), the monarch who defeated the Almohades at the battle of Las Navas de Tolosa (1212). He founded the monastery of Las Huelgas (1187), south of the city of Burgos, and brought master builders from Toledo and Seville to participate in the construction; they decorated it in the purest Almohad style. Its Capilla de Asunción, for example, is a masterwork of the Mudéjar style, with stucco lambrequin arches (decorated in the form of prickly thistle leaves) that support "muqarnas" domes so typical of Islamic architecture. Other Mudéjar features to be found in structures all over Spain are stucco-covered barrel vaults decorated with textile-like patterns, vaults with interlaced ribs like those of the great mosque in Córdoba, and the Mudéjar towers, inspired by the Seville minaret called "La Giralda."

֍   Mullion. A vertical bar or column, of stone or another material, tat divides the panes of a window or the sections of a doorway or portico, usually down the middle.

֍   Narthex. Portico on the western end of a Christian church; vestibule that leads to the nave.

֍   Nave. The main western space in a church, extending in many churches from the choir to the western door. The main area used by the congregation, "nave" means "ship" in Latin and Spanish, and is a word that is applied to this, the main body of the church, as the spiritual vehicle that transports the faithful to a higher realm.

֍   Plateresque. A term derived from "platero," the Spanish for "silversmith," it is used to describe the late Gothic and early Renaissance architecture of sixteenth century Spain. Characteristic of the style is elaborate decorations with florid motifs, so profuse that they tend to overwhelm the structure they are intended to adorn. Essentially, exuberant plateresque designs were built into Gothic structures, but it is also possible to speak of certain buildings where the plateresque is not only a superficial, decorative concept or a type of ornamentation, but also a characteristic style of structure, wall arrangements and volumetry that are derived from ancient or Italian Renaissance architecture. Architects such as Lorenzo Vázquez de Segovia, Enrique Egas, Diego de Riaño, Juan de Álava and Francisco de Colonia designed structures placing particular stress on the possibility of their being richly decorated. Resulting from this line of thought are the Universidad de Salamanca, the Portada de la Pellejería at the Burgos cathedral, and especially the Hospital de Santa Cruz, in Toledo, with a façade by Antón Egas, Enrique Egas and Alonso de Covarrubias.

୬ Pier. A vertical support, like a pillar or column, or the wall between two windows.

୬ Pinnacle. A slender, upright spire at the top of a tower or buttress.

୬ Plinth. An architectural support, such as the base of a column or statue.

୬ Portal. Ornamental doorway, gate or entrance to a building.

୬ Reredos. A screen at the back of an altar, often richly carved or painted. The medieval reredos is often high enough to reach almost the roof of the church.

୬ Respond. An engaged column or pilaster that supports an arch.

୬ Rococo. Artistic and architectural style distinguished by its fanciful and elaborate asymmetric ornamentation.

୬ Romanesque. Romanesque churches derive basically from the Roman basilica, but with entirely new spatial forms and constructional systems, both directly related to the Christian ritual. The transepts which cut the nave and the additional height of the crossing denoting the space for the altar are clear indications of this. Small Romanesque churches with their interiors focusing on the altar are especially relevant.

New Romanesque formulas include the theme of the "portal," which was both religiously significant and novel to the Romanesque architect. The altar at the crossing expressed the idea of a communion table with direct simplicity. Also typical of the Romanesque is the necessity to integrate sculpture and painting with architecture, seen in buildings whose raw concrete walls are marked with finely drawn lines of motifs in relief. Romanesque forms, especially painting, deny naturalism and have a tendency towards abstraction.

The Romanesque presents us with many problems of conservation. In the Middle Ages, relatively new churches were demolished or partially torn down so that newer churches could be built on their sites or new altars incorporated into their structure. These newer constructions rest on the foundations of their predecessors, incorporating varying degrees of the original structures. This prolific and constant expansion has deprived posterity of some of the best expressions of the Romanesque. Also, the dramatic events which constantly shook the destinies of Spain helped thwart any organized attempt to conserve Romanesque buildings in their original purity. The Romanesque was a new and in many ways experimental architecture, evolved in a restless age during which there were fundamental changes in the ways people lived and thought.

Specifically, Romanesque is the name given to Christian architecture in western Europe from the tenth to the thirteenth century. In Spain, this style of architecture had two points of entry in the eleventh century: it first seeped into Catalonia in the east, and later came down the Road to Santiago all along the north, a road that acted like a funnel that brought people and ideas from the rest of Europe into the country.

Before the advent of the Romanesque, Spanish architecture was dominated by the enigmatic "Asturian" style church, with its primitive, vigorous stonework and carved capitals and lintels, most evident in those areas never or briefly conquered by the Moslems. Best examples of the Asturian style are the Naranco palace (c. 850 A.D.), and the churches of Santa María, San Miguel, San Tirso and San Julián (all c. 850 A.D.), all, of course, in Asturias. Mozarabic architecture, produced by Christians fleeing from the Moslem south, became prevalent in the ninth and tenth centuries.

In the Moslem south, the Moorish style was always prevalent over the Romanesque or any other style of architecture; the Moorish style has three main phases being represented by 1) the great Mosque at Córdoba (786-999), with its marvelous array of double-tiered polylobed arches; 2) the Seville Minaret (Giralda), completed in 1198 and in line with the ascetic standards of the Almohades: monumental proportions and subdued decorations, and 3) the lavish decorations of the expiring Moslem courts as represented by the Alhambra palace (1238-1391) in Granada.

In Cataluña, the early Romanesque is best represented by Santa María de Ripoll (1020-1032), and along the Road to Santiago its best example is the Santiago Cathedral itself, begun in 1078.

The one, greatest achievement of Romanesque architects was the development of the stone vault. The stone vault is the direct result of the need to replace the highly flammable wooden roofs of pre-Romanesque structures with masonry vaulting. Thus, barrel shaped, round and pointed vaults (domes) were used to cover the space above, between the walls.

Heavy walls and piers were now needed to hold up the vaults, and the use of massive walls and piers as supports for the heavy stone vaults resulted in the typical Romanesque floor plan, where the building was conceived as a conglomerate of small units, or bays, that are separate, rectangular recesses projecting from the line of the wall, but creating, at the same time, a sense of unity and subordination to the whole.

A term always linked with the concept of the Romanesque in architecture is that of "articulation." This means that Romanesque buildings have a clear sense of geometry: the exterior is a reflection of the interior and each individual element, structural or decorative, is subordinated to the overall logic of the building as a whole. The style thus comes across as severe and simple, with arches that are characteristically semicircular and barrel vaults.

The Romanesque in northern Spain is unique, designed to accommodate large numbers of pilgrims. The Santiago Cathedral, for example, has a triple entrance on the western end, double portals on the transepts and continuous aisles around all four arms; the ambulatory around the apse gives access out to the five radiating chapels and to the Apostle's tomb. Other Romanesque churches in this region are, of course, smaller, with apses at the ends of the aisles and no ambulatory. Yet almost all of them are barrel-vaulted and have a dome on squinches over the crossing, and their piers and responds are "articulated" with half-shafts. Many are also built with ashlar, which allows for much carved decoration on the string courses, capitals and portals.

The Romanesque sculpture that graces buildings in northern Spain is unique as well, specially because of its setting: in Spain, the attention of the sculptors is focused on friezes, wall reliefs and tympana as well as on capitals and corbels. In later Romanesque constructions, column statues line the portals and also act as interior supports. Because of the itinerant nature of Road-related occupations, sculptors and stone masons probably left individual pieces to be set after their departure from each particular site by local masons. This is the best explanation that can be offered for the haphazard way in which some important carvings have been used in constructions along the Road (San Pedro in Estella is a good example).

The theme of Romanesque sculpture is varied: Santiago Cathedral and San Isidoro in León show a dogmatic program of iconographic representation; the Puerta del Cordero, in San Isidoro, adds an element of combative religion as the themes of the "Reconquista" are displayed; the Panteón de los Reyes, also in San Isidoro, gives a posthumous homage to its founder, Fernando I, the monarch who also died there as a penitent. Many other themes are interpreted in

Romanesque sculptures along the Road to Santiago.

        🍖   Squinch. An interior corner support, such as an arch, corbel or lintel that supports weight that rests upon it.

        🍖   Transept. In a cruciform church, the part that crosses the nave at right angles; en effect, the arms of the cross.

        🍖   Trefoil. Architectural ornament in the form of three arcs arranged in a circle, or any ornamental figure resembling a threefold leaf.

        🍖   Triforium. An arcade or shallow passage on the side wall of a church above the nave and below the clerestory. Strictly speaking, the term applies to the three-arched openings that pass through the nave walls into the tribune.

        🍖   Triptych. A painting or carving (especially an altarpiece) on three panels held together by hinges.

        🍖   Tympanum. The triangular space that opens between the cornice and sloping sides of a pediment. The term also applies to the triangle or type of escoinson circumscribed by an archivolt, an entablature and a pilaster. Tympana are usually decorated with bas-reliefs, mosaics or paintings.

        🍖   Vault. A roof or ceiling constructed with stone or concrete, built on the principle of the arch. The vault, thus, has stones or blocks set and arranged concentrically in such a way as to support each other in gravity compression. Vaults are built of non-combustible material and have a deep symbolic meaning as the Vault of Heaven in Christian churches. The *barrel* vault, common in the Spanish Romanesque, is built on the principle of the repeated arch, giving a semicircular or pointed profile and distributing the weight and thrust uniformly throughout its length. Other types of vaults are *annular*, which is actually a circular vaulted passage, usually arranged around an apse, *cellular*, which have no structural ribs and panels but rather multiple folded "cells" that give the impression of a prism of multiple diamond-shaped folds, *cloister* or *trough* vaults, formed by intersecting equal-sized pointed barrel vaults, *curving* vaults, *jumping* vaults, *Lierne* vaults, *net* vaults, *pendant* vaults, *ploughshare, quadripartite, sexpartite, reticulated, star, triradial, sail* vaults, based on the principle of the dome, and *segmental*.

Appendix III

Relative distances on the Road to Santiago, beginning just inside France. Distance given in kilometers.

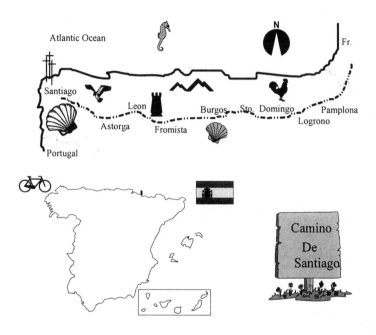

Place	Distance to Previous Place	Distance To Santiago	Distance Covered
St. Jean Pied de Port	0	826	0
Valcarlos	11	815	11

Ibañeta Pass	16	799	27
Roncesvalles	2	797	29
Burguete	3	794	32
Espinal	3	791	35
Pamplona	42	750	76
Puente la Reina	24	726	100
Lorca	12	714	112
Estella	7	707	119
Irache	5	702	124
Los Arcos	16	686	140
Torres del Río	6	680	146
Viana	12	668	158
Logroño	9	659	167
Navarrete	10	649	177
Nájera	16	633	193
Santo Domingo de la Calzada	19	614	212

Belorado	21	593	233
Villafranca Montes de Oca	12	581	245
San Juan de Ortega	16	565	261
Burgos	20	545	281
Villanueva de Argaño	21	524	302
Olmillos de Sasamón	9	515	311
Castellanos de Castro	9	506	320
Castrojeriz	13	493	333
Castrillo de Cabezón	4	490	336
Boadilla del Camino	17	473	353
Frómista	5	468	358
Villalcázar de Sirga	13	455	371
Carrión de los Condes	7	448	378
Terradillo de los Templarios	29	419	407
San Nicolás del Real Camino (Approx. mid-point of journey)	7	412	414
Sahagún	6	406	420

Calzada del Coto	4	402	424
Mansilla de las Mulas	45	357	469
León	18	339	487
Hospital de Órbigo	29	310	516
Astorga	17	293	533
Rabanal del Camino	22	271	555
Foncebadón	8	263	563
Ponferrada	31	232	594
Cacabelos	13	219	607
Villafranca del Bierzo	8	211	615
Trabadelo	10	201	625
Pedrafita do Cebreiro	19	182	644
O Cebreiro	5	177	649
Triacastela	24	153	673
Sarria	23	130	696
Portomarín	24	106	720

Relative Distances on the Road   ✠   250

Palas do Rei	38	68	758
Melide	15	53	773
Castañeda	7	46	780
Arzúa	8	38	788
O Pino	20	18	808
Lavacolla	10	8	818
Monte del Gozo	4	4	822
Santiago de Compostela	4	0	826

Bibliography

Alcolea, S. *La catedral de Santiago.* Madrid, 1948.

Alonso, Juanjo. *El Camino de Santiago en Mountain Bike.* Madrid, Tutor, 1993.

Arrondo, E.G. *Rutas jacobeas. Historia, arte, caminos.* Estella, 1971.

Bevan, Bernard. *Historia de la arquitectura española.* Barcelona, Juventud, 1950.

Bonet Correa, A. *Santiago de Compostela. El camino de los peregrinos.* Madrid-Barcelona, 1985.

Bozal, Valeriano. *Historia del arte en España.* Madrid, Istmo, 1973.

Bravo Lozano, M. *Guía del peregrino medieval.* Sahagún, 1989.

Corpas Mauleón, Juan Ramón. *Curiosidades del Camino de Santiago.* Madrid, El País-Aguilar, 1992.

Davies, H. and M.H. Davies. *Holy Days and Holidays. The Medieval Pilgrimage to Compostela* London-Toronto, 1982.

Fernández Albor, A. "La delincuencia en el Camino de Santiago en la Edad Media," in *Pellegrinaggio Letteratura Jacopea-Perugia,* pp. 127-134.

González-López, Emilio. *Historia de la civilización española.* New York, Las Américas, 1966.

Herwaarden, J van. "The Origins of the Cult of Saint James of Compostela," in *Journal of Medieval History 6* (1980): 1-36.

Huici Urmeneta, Vicente, et. al., *Historia de Navarra*. San Sebastián, Txertoa, n.d.

Huidobro y Serna, J. *Las peregrinaciones jacobeas*. 3 vols. Madrid, 1949-1951.

López Ferreiro, A. *El pórtico de la Gloria, Platerías y el primitivo Altar Mayor*. Santiago de Compostela, 1975; original ed. 1891-1892.

Martín, Paco. *El camino de Santiago*. Madrid, 1990.

Melczer, W. *Pilgrim's Guide to Santiago de Compostela*. New York, 1993.

Moralejo, S., C. Torres and J. Feo. *Liber Sancti Jacobi. Codex Calixtinus*. Santiago de Compostela, 1951.

Pérez-Bustamante, C. *Compendio de historia de España*. Madrid, Atlas, 1966.

Romero de Lacea, C., J. Guerra Campos, and J. Filgueira Valverde. *Libro de la Peregrinación del Códice Calixtino*. Facs. Madrid, 1971.

Ubieto, Antonio, et. al. *Introducción a la historia de España*. Barcelona, Teide, 1969.

Vielliard, J. *Le guide du pèlerin Saint-Jacques de Compostelle*. 5th ed., Paris, 1984.

Williams, J. "Cluny and Spain," in *Gesta* 27 (1988): 93-101.